W9-DIT-930

1000 COMIC BOOKS

BOOKS

You Must Read

TONY ISABELLA

Published by

kp **krause publications**
A subsidiary of F+W Media, Inc.

700 East State Street • Iola, WI 54990-0001
715-445-2214 • 888-457-2873
www.krausebooks.com

Our toll-free number to place an order or obtain
a free catalog is (800) 258-0929.

Identification of the comic-book covers shown in this volume is taken, wherever possible, from the copyright information that appeared on the material as it originally appeared. When it is not possible, copyright information has been culled from reference materials and is indicated by the identification "©*" in the appropriate passage. In many cases, ownership has changed or copyright renewed; in no case does F+W Media claim ownership of the copyright to the material shown.

Library of Congress Control Number: 2008937667

ISBN-13: 978-0-89689-921-6
ISBN-10: 0-89689-921-7

Cover design by Rachael Knier
Interior designed by Shawn Williams and Rachael Knier
Edited by: Maggie Thompson, Brent Frankenhoff, and Mary Sieber

Printed in China

DEDICATIONS

Maggie Thompson and Brent Frankenhoff
great editors and better friends
who kept me going

Harlan Ellison
who's been trying to make me
smarter for decades
and hasn't given up yet

Barry Pearl
the kind of fan and friend
I wrote this book for

Kelly, Eddie, Barb, and Simba
my daughter, son, wife, and cat

Greg Luppino
the neighbor and friend
who's always there for
me and my family

The Grand Comic Book Database
www.comics.org
the most mind-bogglingly useful
research tool for comics fans
in the known universe

ACKNOWLEDGEMENTS

Many fans, friends, and associates assisted with this book, some of them unaware they were doing so. I thank them all, especially any whose names I have inadvertently omitted.

Jack Abromowitz
Mike Ambrose
Henry Andrews
Mark Arnold
Atomic Avenue
Atlas Tales
Jerry Bails
Adam Beechen
Bob Bailey
Daniel Best
Jim Bosomworth
Gary Brown
Bob Buethe
James H. Burns
Kurt Busiek
Nick Caputo
Johanna Draper Carlson
Phillip Carpenter
Michael Catron
Justin Chung
Alan Coil
Peter Croome
Howard Cruse
Al Davison
Dwight Decker
Michael Dewally
Harlan Ellison
Mark Evanier
Terry Fairbanks
Al Feldstein
Paul Fearn
Chuck Fiala
Greg Fischer
William Foster
Brent Frankenhoff
George Freeman
Ralf Haring
Heritage Comic Auctions
Michael Ingrassia
Eddie Isabella
Greg Gatlin
Nat Gertler
Michael T. Gilbert
George Gladir

Tony Gleeson
Mike Gold
Matthew Gore
Victor Gorelick
Grand Comic Book Database
Merlin Haas
Larry Hama
Michael Harbour
Fred Hembeck
Andrew Horn
Horrors of It All
Denys Howard
Richard Howell
Mike Howlett
Bob Ingersoll
Bill Jourdain
Dan Jurgens
Jeff Kapalka
Bob Kennedy
Paul Kennedy
Bill Knapp
Jon Knutson
Rich Koslowski
Joe Kubert
Joe Kurtzman
Brian Saner Lamken
Jerry Lazar
Stan Lee
Steve Leiber
Ken Lemons
James Ludwig
Mitchell Maltenfort
Don Markstein
Dave Massaro
Lou Mazzella
Jeff Mariotte
Tom Michael
Brian Morris
John Morrow
Hoy Murphy
George Nelson
Alex Ness
Jess Nevins
Mike Nielsen
Michelle Nolan

Karen O'Brien
Rik Offenberger
Neil Ottenstein
Pappy's Golden Age Comics Blogzine
Barry Pearl
Andrew Pepoy
John Petty
Jeff Pierce
Richard Pini
Dan Ripoll
Scott Roberts
Trina Robbins
Tony Rose
Steven Rowe
Scott Rowland
Bob Rozakis
Jim Salicrup
Roland Schama
Bill Schelly
Jack Selegue
Dave Serchay
Eric Shanower
Craig Shutt
Alex Simmons
Allen Smith
Andrew Smith
Beau Smith
Bryan Talbot
Adisakdi Tantimedh
Rick Taylor
Bill Thom
Roy Thomas
Maggie Thompson
Anthony Tollin
Jim Vandore
Michael Vassallo
Mark Verheiden
Mike Voiles
Pete Von Sholly
Lawrence Watt-Evans
Len Wein
Craig Wichman
Marv Wolfman
Thom Zahler

CONTENTS

JUST A THOUSAND?

Foreword by Tony Isabella

Did you hear the one about the beloved comics writer/columnist who, when asked to write a book called *1000 Comic Books You Must Read*, immediately responded: "Just a thousand?"

I have loved comic books since I learned to read from them at the age of 4 in my hometown of Cleveland, Ohio — coincidentally, also the hometown of Superman. My mother bought me bargain-priced packages of funny-animal and Western comics from F.W. Woolworth's. When I could buy my own comic books, I bought *Superman* and *Batman* and *Casper the Friendly Ghost*. And I loved them all.

I still love all kinds of comic books. Super-hero comics have always been my favorites, as they have been for many of my fellow comics fans, but I'm also a fan of adventure comics, autobiography, biography, comic kids, crime and detectives, funny animals, glamour girls, graphic novels, historical adventure, horror and monsters, indy and alternative comics, Japanese manga, movie and TV adaptations, parody, political and religious comics, romance, science fiction and fantasy, spies, teen humor, underground comix, war, Westerns, and every other genre or subject you can name.

This book is my journey through seven decades of comic books.

Today, in the true Golden Age of Comics, readers can enjoy both the new groundbreaking material now being published and, thanks to affordable reprints, the classics of the past. There are comics exploring the limits of imagination, as well as the triumphs and the tragedies of our everyday lives. There are comics created by men and women from all over the country, from Europe, from Japan, and more. There are comics for every reader and every taste.

And I love them all.

Decade by decade, this book will introduce you to some of the best comic books ever published and the amazing writers and artists who created them. I won't include every milestone or even the best of the best. I'll most likely omit some of your favorites due to that pesky limit inherent in our title. I will cheat our title at every opportunity, often counting collections, runs of issues, and story arcs as if they were merely single issues. But, by the time you reach the afterword, you will have an impressive list of comic books you must, or, at the very least, *should* read.

We pause for a brief informational note:

Many of the comic books included in the thousand featured here were anthology titles containing more than one story and often with different creative teams for each story. Due to space limitations, I generally focus on just one story in any given issue. Those same limitations are why I also list just one or two writers or artists per issue, even though many more individuals contributed to these issues. And what great issues they are ...

You'll see Superman from his debut as a sarcastic champion of the people, thumbing his nose at authority, to his current standing as a respected citizen of the world. You'll see the tragic moment when Peter Parker and a generation of readers learned that "with great power, there must also come great responsibility" and also the moment when Peter and his Aunt May had a pivotal conversation about his greatest secret.

Beyond the super-heroes, you'll meet such classic characters as Archie and his Riverdale High friends, Uncle Scrooge McDuck, Little Lulu, Sgt. Rock, the kid cowboys of *Boys' Ranch*, Herbie Popnecker, and more. You'll also meet such lesser-known but still beloved characters as the Bone cousins, a human flying saucer, Cutter and Skywise from *Elfquest*, Howard the Duck, Konga, and the Presto Kid.

As your personal Yoda, I'll be instructing you in the artistry and the history of the comics. I'll tell you of the spunky "tween" who became the heroine of the distant planet Smoo ... of a middle-aged writer and his wife and their "cancer year" ... of the World War II officer who hid from the Germans by posing as one of their own soldiers ... and many others.

You'll walk the deserted streets of a neighborhood ruled by an unseen monster. You'll find out why two women cry "We Both Loved Tony!" You'll be right there, when Soviet premier Nikita Khrushchev comes face-to-face with American teenagers. You'll even find out about the only comic book that ever gave me nightmares: an issue of a Catholic-oriented title distributed in parochial schools when I was 10 years old.

Oh, the places we'll go, the remarkable characters we'll meet, the laughs and the thrills we'll share, including my pick for the greatest comic book ever!

Fire up the Batmobile. This is gonna be one sweet ride.

Fire up the Batmobile. This is gonna be one sweet ride.

TONY ISABELLA *has been a comics writer and columnist for more than 35 years. He got his start working for Stan Lee at Marvel Comics as a writer and editor. At DC Comics, he created Black Lightning, the company's first headline African-American hero. He has written hundreds of stories and articles for dozens of publishers. He's a contributing editor and the lead reviewer for* Comics Buyer's *Guide, where he has reviewed more comic books and more different kinds of comic books than anyone else in the magazine's history.*

Just for giggles, he anointed himself "America's most beloved comics writer and columnist." The joke caught on and has continued to this very day. Just remember to keep that lofty title in quotes and no one will get hurt.

HOW TO USE THIS BOOK

It has been suggested I provide an instructional guide to using this book. Now, me, I figure if you're smart enough to buy this book, you're smart enough to use it. However, in case someone smarter than you has given you this book, here are some simple rules for deriving maximum benefit from this book.

1. **Buy this book.**

2. **Read this book.**

3. **Enjoy this book.**

4. **Tell all your friends and relatives to buy this book so they, too, can read and enjoy it.**

5. **Repeat as necessary. Warning: High sales on this book could lead to a sequel.**

There is a chance these instructions are not what my publishers were thinking when they made their request. With your indulgence, I'll add this handy guide to the entries …

We start with a picture of a comic-book cover. That is followed by the title of the comic book. That is followed by writer and artist credits when we know them. When we don't know them, we list them as "uncredited."

We include the name of the publisher of each comic book as well as the indicia date of publication. The indicia is that block of copy found at the bottom of a comic book's inside front cover or opening page. The copy you never read. When available, we then give you the actual copyright information as it appeared in the original comic books. When possible, we also credit the source of the cover images we scanned. Whew!

Finally, you get a few scintillating lines of erudite commentary on each of the one thousand comic books discussed in this book. They will give you hours of reading pleasure, all because you were smart enough to buy this book.

CHAPTER ONE

"This is a Job for Superman!" CHAPTER ONE

8

1000 Comic Books You Must Read

uperman changed the American comic book from a novelty item into an industry. There were comic books before Superman and some of them even looked like *Action Comics* #1 (Jun 38), the issue in which The Man of Steel made his first appearance. And there were comic books way *before* Superman, though most didn't look much like *Action Comics* #1. Yet it remains my firm conviction that it was the son of Jor-L who took what could easily have been a passing fad and made it a permanent part of our national scene.

There are those who will strongly disagree with my assessment of Superman's preeminence in the history of the American comic book. I'm not without sympathy for their viewpoint and their regard for the cave paintings at Lascaux, France, Emperor Trajan's Column in Rome, the Bayeux Tapestry with its rollicking account of the Norman Invasion of England, and other decidedly less cumbersome American publications from the overlapping Pioneer (1500s-1828) and Victorian (1646-1900s) Ages of comic books. However, I suspect my sympathy mostly stems from the hope that tossing around such impressive examples as Trajan's Column will score us some sales with the stuffy academic crowd. Which, as you should be rapidly learning, is not exactly my natural audience.

All kidding aside, there's exciting, remarkable research being done on pre-Superman comic books. The people doing it should write their own books. I'd buy them.

The first comic books that looked like *Action Comics* #1 were composed of reprints of the popular (and even not-so-popular) comic strips found in the newspapers of the era. Those comic books sold so well that their publishers ran out of newspaper comics strips to reprint and began to commission new material that *looked* like comic-strip reprints. But there was something about comic books that demanded an evolution of the art form.

Superman was a bridge between comic strips and the true comic books. The last son of Krypton was created by Cleveland teenagers Jerry Siegel and Joe Shuster in 1933. The high-school buddies, who teamed on their school paper and various science-fiction fanzines, tried for years without success to sell Superman as a newspaper comic strip. But, in 1935, they broke into comic books with sales to Major Malcolm Wheeler-Nicholson's *New Fun Comics* and quickly began to develop exciting storytelling techniques that fit the new medium far better than the usual strip reprints and imitations.

In 1938, when editor Vin Sullivan was looking for features for *Action Comics* #1, editor and cartoonist Sheldon Mayer showed him the Superman strip, which Mayer had rescued from the publisher's rejection pile. Sullivan figured Superman was worth a shot and, after Siegel and Shuster cut and pasted the first several weeks of their strip into comic-book pages, he ran The Man of Steel as the lead feature of that pivotal comic book.

Superman appeared on the cover of that landmark issue, swiftly becoming the first superstar of the fledgling comic-book industry.

The Man of Steel's fame and subsequent fortune led to the creation of hundreds of other costumed champions with powers and abilities far beyond those of ordinary men and women. To a large extent, the super-hero genre Superman launched has driven the American comic-book industry ever since … for better and for worse.

A Superman comic strip began running in newspapers across the country on January 6, 1939. Siegel and Shuster had achieved their original goal of newspaper syndication for their creation.

Superman was and is an American story.

Superman was and is an American story.

His international acclaim notwithstanding, Superman was and is an American story. He is the not-so-strange visitor from another planet, an immigrant come to a land of immigrants from a land only spatially more distant than Europe or Asia. He embraced our ways and became a valued member of our society. His story is the story of our great-grandparents, grandparents, and parents, only with a lot more mad scientists and rampaging robots.

In *The Great Comic Book Heroes,* cartoonist and author Jules Feiffer put forth a theory that Superman's success derived from the wish-fulfillment desires of readers: that, beneath their cheap Clark Kent suits, they, too, might be possessed of amazing strength and the will to accomplish great things. Now, beneath my cheap Clark Kent suit, all you will find is a short, hairy, somewhat overweight Italian-American writer, but I readily buy into Feiffer's concept with an added notion of my own. The Superman of Siegel and Shuster's earliest stories is very much the champion who looks out for the little guy. He challenges authority and power with greater authority and power. He'll even manhandle the mayor of a great metropolitan city, if that's what it takes to get the job done. He stands up to bullies of every kind: common criminals, super-villains, avaricious businessmen, dishonest politicians, and warmongering dictators.

With his assured sense of right and wrong and his great heart, Superman stood up for all us Clark Kents. And, with that frequent, somewhat cocky grin on his face, he made it look like the most fun a man or a superman could have.

You'll see a lot of Superman comic books in this book. Part of that can be attributed to my hometown pride in the character and his creators. Most of it can be attributed to this:

Superman has earned his lofty place in this book. He put the American comic-book industry on overdrive and set the standard for super-heroes around the world.

Here are some of his earliest appearances …

Action Comics #1

Writer: Jerry Siegel
Artist: Joe Shuster
DC (June 1938 © 1938 Detective Comics, Inc.)

Superman saves an innocent woman from execution, slaps around a wife-beater, rescues Lois Lane from hoodlums, and then kidnaps a lobbyist trying to involve the United States in a South American war. Not bad for his first day on the job. (Note: Action Comics was an anthology title; credits here and elsewhere in this chapter are only for the Superman story.)

Action Comics #12

Writer: Jerry Siegel
Artist: Joe Shuster
DC (May 1939 © 1939 Detective Comics, Inc., image courtesy of Heritage Comic Auctions)

Superman teaches hard lessons to traffic violators, to dealers selling shoddy cars, to manufacturers building unsafe new cars, and to the mayor whose police force is lax in enforcing traffic laws. Ralph Nader would be so proud!

Action Comics #13

Writer: Jerry Siegel
Artist: Joe Shuster
DC (June 1939 © 1939 Detective Comics, Inc., image courtesy of Heritage Comic Auctions)

Smashing a protection racket brings Superman face to face with the Ultra-Humanite, his first super-villain. Paralyzed from the waist down, Ultra possesses the most "agile and learned brain on Earth" and is the power behind countless criminal enterprises.

This was my father's Superman and you didn't mess with him.

Superman #1

Writer: Jerry Siegel
Artist: Joe Shuster
DC (Summer 1939 © 1939 Detective Comics, Inc., image courtesy of Heritage Comic Auctions)

*The first American comic book devoted entirely to a single character, it reprinted the Superman stories from **Action Comics** #1-4, with new material explaining his powers, showing how Clark Kent became a reporter, and introducing readers to Siegel and Shuster.*

Action Comics #16

Writer: Jerry Siegel
Artist: Joe Shuster
DC (September 1939 © 1939 Detective
Comics, Inc., image courtesy of Heritage
Comic Auctions)

*Superman goes to war on illegal gambling.
He smashes casinos, forces a corrupt police
commissioner to resign, and even threat-
ens to kill gambling bosses who don't leave
town. This was my father's Superman and
you didn't mess with him.*

Action Comics #18

Writer: Jerry Siegel
Artist: Paul Cassidy (signed as Joe Shuster)
DC (November 1939 © 1939 Detective
Comics, Inc., image courtesy of Heritage
Comic Auctions)

*A sleazy newspaper editor, working with
blackmailers, kidnaps and drugs a senator.
Then they photograph him at a roadhouse
with a lady of dubious morals. Superman
stops the presses — literally — and chases
the blackmailers out of town.*

"This is a Job for Superman!" CHAPTER ONE

11

1000 Comic Books You Must Read

CHAPTER TWO

Superman and his fellow super-heroes were the driving force of the first comics industry boom. Their adventures were loved by the kids and by the older brothers of those kids who, as members of our armed forces, needed cheap and highly portable entertainment that could be stuck in a backpack or a back pocket. Yes, friends, you are allowed to cringe at the thought of such comics treasures being rolled up or folded in half. Don't blame our soldiers and sailors. Back then, they had somewhat more pressing concerns than the future value of their entertainment.

However, from the start, the comics industry diversified. In this pivotal decade, publishers launched titles in multiple genres, just as their pulp-magazine ancestors had done: crime, horror, war, romance, science fiction, jungle thrills, air adventures, Westerns, and more. There were comics featuring cartoon characters and movie stars, precocious kids and swinging teenagers, and every species of funny animal you could imagine. There were even comic books meant to be educational and uplifting for young readers. Even in these early days of the industry, there were critics who saw comic books as a blight upon our youth.

Not all these different kinds of comic books hit their stride until late in the decade. The super-heroes faded when our men came home from war. They had new lives to build and put aside the comic books of their youth. Those who continued reading comics, men and women alike, wanted more sophisticated entertainment. By the end of the 1940s, the colorful super-heroes were barely a blip on the newsstands.

Let's take a walk through that formative decade …

Jumbo Comics #1
Writers: Will Eisner, Audrey Blum, etc.
Artists: Bob Kane, Jack Kirby, etc.
Fiction House (September 1938 © 1938 Real Adventure Publishing Co., image courtesy of Heritage Comic Auctions)
Sheena, the most popular of the jungle queens, made her debut in the first comic book from pulp-magazine publisher Fiction House. The issue also featured early work by comics legends Will Eisner, Jack Kirby, Bob Kane, and Mort Meskin.

Detective Comics #27
Writer: Bill Finger
Artist: Bob Kane
DC (May 1939 © 1939 Detective Comics)
The Batman, created by Kane and Finger, made his debut in a six-page story plagiarized from a pulp adventure of The Shadow. Much of the art consisted of "swipes" from various sources, but the character would quickly become a model of innovation.

Marvel Comics #1

Writers: Carl Burgos, Bill Everett
Artists: Carl Burgos, Bill Everett
Marvel (November 1939 © 1939 Timely Publications, image courtesy of Heritage Comic Auctions)

The android Human Torch and the angry Prince Namor the Sub-Mariner were instant sensations in this, the first comic book from pulp-magazine publisher Martin Goodman. From the start, Marvel's heroes were often feared by the very humans they defended.

Flash Comics #1

Writer: Gardner F. Fox
Artists: Harry Lampert, Dennis Neville
DC (January 1940 © 1939 All-American)

The prolific Fox created such legendary heroes as The Flash (the fastest man alive), and Hawkman (the reincarnation of an Egyptian prince who fought modern-day evil with the weapons of the past and the assistance of his paramour, Hawkgirl).

Pep Comics #1

Writers: Harry Shorten, Jack Cole
Artists: Irv Novick, Jack Cole
MLJ (January 1940 © 1939 MLJ Magazines)

The Shield was the first patriotic super-hero, while second-stringer Comet would become the first super-hero to die in his own strip. But MLJ's quirky heroes would soon be overshadowed and replaced by the teenage Archie Andrews and his pals.

Planet Comics #1

Writers: uncredited
Artists: Dick Briefer, Malcolm Kildale
Fiction House (January 1940 © 1939 Love Romances Publications, image courtesy of Heritage Comic Auctions)

This was the first comic book devoted entirely to science fiction. As with the rest of the Fiction House line, it would be noted for its sturdy heroes, beautiful heroines, solid writing, and some of the finest comics art of the decade.

FEB. 1940

No. 52

Starting this issue: The daring exploits of THE SPECTRE!

MORE FUN COMICS

10¢

More Fun Comics #52

Writer: Jerry Siegel
Artist: Bernard Baily
DC (February 1940 © 1939 Detective Comics, Inc., image courtesy of Heritage Comic Auctions)

Police detective Jim Corrigan is murdered by a gangster but restored to life by the Almighty. As The Spectre, he brings swift retribution to criminals: perhaps the most chilling super-hero of all, if only in his earliest adventures.

...perhaps the most chilling super-hero of all...

Whiz Comics #2

Writer: Bill Parker
Artist: C.C. Beck
Fawcett (February 1940 © 1940 Fawcett Publications, Inc.)

When Billy Batson says "Shazam!" the powers of six legends turn him into Captain Marvel, the only hero to give Superman a run for his money. Also introduced in this issue: Ibis the Invincible, Spy Smasher, and The Golden Arrow.

Shadow Comics Vol. 1 #1

Writers: Walter Gibson, Theodore Sturgeon
Artists: uncredited
Street and Smith (March 1940 © 1940 Street & Smith Publications, Incorporated)

From the pulp magazines that inspired early comic-book writers and artists, The Shadow, Doc Savage, Nick Carter, Bill Barnes, and others made their comics debuts. The prolific Gibson wrote most of the Shadow pulps and comics — and hundred of other stories.

Detective Comics #38

Writer: Bill Finger
Artists: Bob Kane, Jerry Robinson
DC (April 1940 © 1940 Detective Comics Inc., image courtesy of Heritage Comic Auctions)

Orphaned by protection racketeer Anthony Zucco, acrobat Dick Grayson trades his trapeze for a life of crime-fighting alongside his guardian and mentor Bruce Wayne. Robin the Boy Wonder sets the standard for the many costumed kid sidekicks to follow.

Batman #1

Writer: Bill Finger
Artists: Bob Kane, Jerry Robinson
DC (Spring 1940 © 1940 Detective Comics, Inc.)

Three of Batman's greatest foes appear in his first solo comic book: The Joker, Professor Hugo Strange, and Catwoman. The Joker is in two stories and dies in the second. But, as readers and sales prove, you can't keep a great villain down.

All-American Comics #16

Writer: Bill Finger
Artist: Martin Nodell
DC (July 1940 © 1940 All-American Comics, Inc., image courtesy of Heritage Comic Auctions)

Inspired by a subway employee waving a lantern and the legend of Aladdin, Nodell conceived a super-hero whose powers derived from a ring carved from the metal of a magic lantern. Batman co-creator Finger fleshed out the concept.

The Spirit (June 2, 1940)

Writer: Will Eisner
Artist: Will Eisner
Register and Tribune Syndicate (June 2, 1940 © 1940 Everett M. Arnold)

Introduced in a weekly, comic-book-sized newspaper supplement, Will Eisner's masked detective was quickly recognized as a classic work by an undisputed master of the art form. It pioneered storytelling techniques, inspiring comics creators and filmmakers to this day.

Marvel Mystery Comics #9

Writers: Bill Everett, Carl Burgos, John Compton
Artists: Bill Everett, Carl Burgos
Marvel (July 1940 © 1940 Timely Publications, image courtesy of Heritage Comic Auctions)

The title says it: "The Human Torch vs. the Sub-Mariner: The Battle of the Comic Century!" The future pals duke it out for 22 pages and the fight continues next issue. It was a landmark moment in Marvel Universe history.

Writer: Sheldon Mayer
Artist: Sheldon Mayer
DC (November 1940 © 1940 All-American Comics, Inc.)
Tucked between Green Lantern and The Atom, the adventures of cartoonist Scribbly Jibbit were the most personal work of legendary cartoonist/editor Sheldon Mayer. In this story, Scribbly's landlady dons a cooking pot and longjohns to become The Red Tornado!

Wings Comics #1

Writers: uncredited
Artists: Arthur Peddy, George Tuska
Fiction House (September 1940 © 1940 Wings Publishing Co., image courtesy of Heritage Comic Auctions)

Fiction House published several pulp magazines devoted to air adventure/war stories, duplicating that success in this title with such features as The Skull Squad, The Parachute Patrol, Jane Martin, Clipper Kirk, Suicide Smith, Greasemonkey Griffin, and Powder Burns.

All-Star Comics #3

Writer: Gardner F. Fox
Artists: Everett E. Hibbard, Sheldon Moldoff
DC (Winter 1940-1941 © 1940 All-American Comics, Inc.)

"The First Meeting of the Justice Society of America" launches the first ongoing super-hero team. It features the Flash, Hawkman, the Spectre, Hourman, Sandman, Doctor Fate, Atom, and Green Lantern with a comical cameo appearance by The Red Tornado.

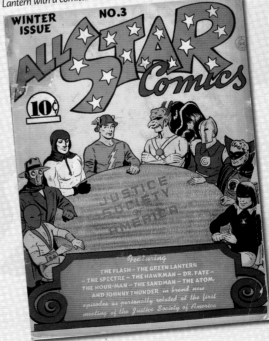

Prize Comics #7

Writers: Dick Briefer, Ken Crossen
Artists: Dick Briefer, Mac Raboy
Prize (December 1940 ©* 1940 Feature Publications, image courtesy of Heritage Comic Auctions)

Two blockbuster debuts: A classic monster is transplanted to modern-day New York in Briefer's "New Adventures of Frankenstein," while the mystically powered Green Lama moves from pulps to comics. Other features include The Black Owl, Power Nelson, and The Great Voodini.

Silver Streak Comics #7

Writer: Jack Cole
Artist: Jack Cole
Lev Gleason (January 1941 © 1940 Your Guide Publications, Inc., image courtesy of Heritage Comic Auctions)

The Claw was one of the great comic-book villains. His origin unknown, he could grow to Godzilla-like proportions and mercilessly wield his long, razor-sharp nails. His first epic battle with the heroic Daredevil begins here and runs for five issues.

The Claw... could grow to Godzilla-like proportions and mercilessly wield his razor-sharp nails.

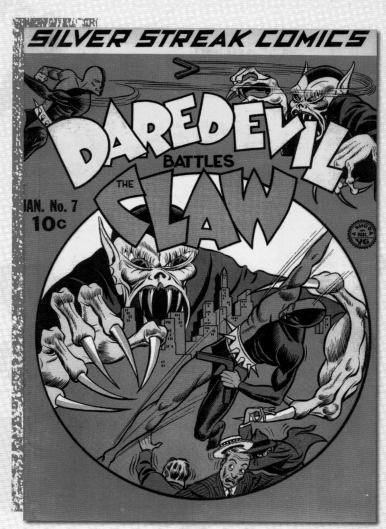

Batman #5

Writer: Bill Finger
Artists: Bob Kane, Jerry Robinson
DC (Spring 1941 © 1941 Detective Comics, Inc.)

"The Case of the Honest Crook" is the best Batman story of the decade, as the hero helps a young convict make a new life. Robin is nearly beaten to death, and Batman takes three bullets to the chest. They don't stop him.

Captain America Comics #1

Writers: Joe Simon, Jack Kirby
Artists: Jack Kirby, Joe Simon
Marvel (March 1941 © 1940 Timely Publications)

Rejected for military service, frail Steve Rogers is given an experimental super-soldier serum and becomes the greatest patriotic super-hero of them all. His four adventures in this issue explode with action so bold they practically leap off the pages.

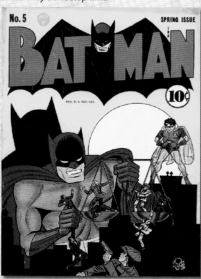

Daredevil Comics #1

Writer: Charles Biro
Artists: Charles Biro, Jack Cole
Lev Gleason (July 1941 © 1941 Your Guide Publications, Inc.)

Daredevil battles Hitler with the help of Silver Streak, Lance Hale, Dickie Dean, Cloud Curtis, and The Pirate Prince. Even the monstrous Claw grabs a slice of this 51-page epic, double-crossing the already-outnumbered Führer.

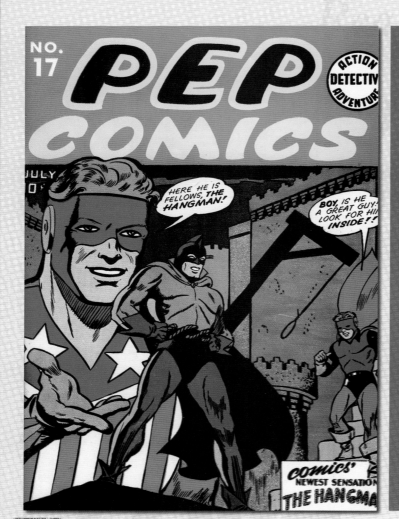

Pep Comics #17

Writer: Joe Blair
Artist: George Storm
MLJ (July 1941 © 1941 M.L.J. Magazines, Inc.)

The Comet (scientist John Dickering) dies saving his brother from gangster "Big Boy" Malone. Bob Dickering takes up the family trade as The Hangman, who visits swift, final justice on criminals luckless enough to catch his attention.

> The Hangman... visits swift, final justice on criminals luckless enough to catch his attention.

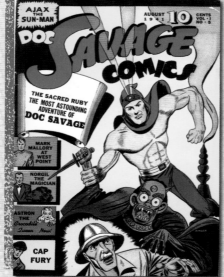

Doc Savage Comics #5

Writer: uncredited
Artist: uncredited
Street & Smith (August 1941 ©* 1941 Street & Smith Publications, image courtesy of Heritage Comic Auctions)

Besides appearing in Shadow Comics, The Man of Bronze starred in his own series. Crashing in Tibet, he found a mystical ruby woven into a hood and became a traditional super-hero. He would remain so until his departure from comics in 1948.

Military Comics #1

Writers: Will Eisner, Jack Cole
Artists: Chuck Cuidera, Jack Cole
Quality Comics (August 1941 © 1941 Comic Magazines, Inc., image courtesy of Heritage Comic Auctions)

Ace pilots from several countries come together to fight Axis powers as The Blackhawks, one of the most popular teams in comics history. Also in this issue: The Death Patrol, who lost a member in every one of their adventures.

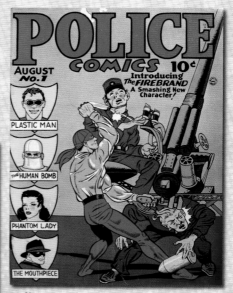

Police Comics #1

Writers: S.M. Iger, Jack Cole
Artists: Reed Crandall, Jack Cole
Quality Comics (August 1941 © 1941 Comic Magazines, Inc.)

Firebrand gets the cover of this first issue, but it was Cole's Plastic Man who quickly became the title's star. Crook Eel O'Brien reforms after he falls into a vat of acid, gaining wild and wacky stretching and shape-changing powers in the process.

Human Torch #5

Writers: Carl Burgos, Bill Everett, Hank Chapman
Artists: Carl Burgos, Bill Everett, Mike Roy
Marvel (Fall 1941 © 1941 Timely Comics, Inc.,
image courtesy of Heritage Comic Auctions)

This legendary 60-page story was written and drawn in a weekend. The Sub-Mariner declares war on the Axis but is swayed by a beautiful, treacherous woman. The Human Torch and sidekick Toro show Namor the error of his lustful ways.

Military Comics #4

Writer: Will Eisner
Artist: Chuck Cuidera
Quality Comics (November 1941 © 1941 Comic Magazines, Inc.,
image courtesy of Heritage Comic Auctions)

Black Tigress, the Gestapo's most dangerous spy, falls hard for Blackhawk. She is the first in a long line of lethal lovelies, on both sides of the war, whose attraction to the team's rugged leader inspires, redeems, and sometimes dooms them.

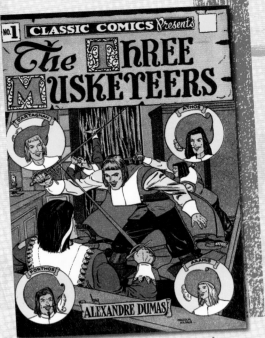

Classic Comics #1: The Three Musketeers

Original Author: Alexandre Dumas
Artist: uncredited
Gilberton (October 1941 ©* 1941 Gilberton Co.,
image courtesy of Heritage Comic Auctions)

Russian-born publisher Albert L. Kanter used the comic book to bring great literature to young readers. His long-running series, best known as **Classics Illustrated**, *began with an adaptation of* **The Three Musketeers**. *Nearly 170 issues would follow.*

More Fun Comics #73

Writer: Mort Weisinger
Artists: Paul Norris, George Papp
DC (November 1941 ©* 1941 Detective Comics, Inc., image courtesy of Heritage Comic Auctions)

On a really good day, editor and writer Mort Weisinger created three new heroes: Green Arrow, Aquaman, and Flash imitator Johnny Quick. The speedster beat the others into print by two issues, but he's long gone and they're still active.

Occupying but six pages beside such heroes as The Shield and The Hangman is a teenager more powerful than either. Before long, the kid would take over the company to such an extent that it would be called "Archie Comics."

All-Star Comics #8

Writers: Gardner F. Fox, William Moulton Marston
Artists: Everett E. Hibbard, Harry G. Peter
DC (December 1941-January 1942 © 1941 All-American Comics, image courtesy of Heritage Comic Auctions)

Dr. Mid-Nite and Starman join the Society, but the real star of this issue is Wonder Woman. Created by psychologist, feminist theorist, and inventor Marston, the Amazon princess comes to man's world to guide us in the ways of peace.

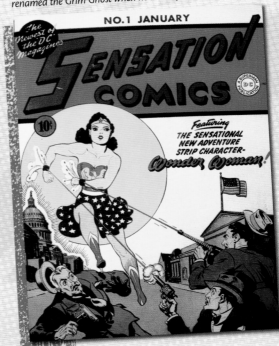

Sensation Comics #1

Writers: William Moulton Marston, Bill Finger
Artists: Harry G. Peter, Irwin Hasen
DC (January 1942 © 1941 J.R. Publishing Co.)

Wonder Woman arrives in man's world and gets top billing. The title also stars Wildcat, Mr. Terrific, Little Boy Blue, the Black Pirate, and the cheerful Gay Ghost, who was, nonetheless, renamed the Grim Ghost when he was reprinted in the 1970s.

Master Comics #22

Writer: William Woolfolk (likely)
Artist: Mac Raboy
Fawcett (January 1942 © 1941 Fawcett Publications, Inc., image courtesy of Heritage Comic Auctions)

Crippled after being attacked by Captain Nazi, Freddy Freeman is given new life and power by Billy Batson and the wizard Shazam. Freddy becomes Captain Marvel Jr. and teams with Bulletman to stop his assailant and other enemies of freedom.

Sheena, Queen of the Jungle #1

Writer: uncredited
Artist: Robert Webb
Fiction House (Spring 1942 ©* 1941 Real Adventures, image courtesy of Heritage Comic Auctions)

It takes a lot to rule the jungle, but Sheena looks the part with her flowing blonde hair and skimpy leopardskin outfit. Her mate Bob Reynolds is a big-game hunter, but he is mostly there to get rescued and look hunky.

Action Comics #47

Writer: Jerry Siegel
Artist: John Sikela
DC (April 1942 © 1942 Detective Comics, Inc.)

An ancient gem from another world — the Powerstone — gives Lex Luthor the super-strength to duke it out with Superman. The evil scientist had now firmly established himself as the Man of Steel's arch-nemesis, an enmity that shows no signs of abating.

Boy Comics #3

Writer: Charles Biro
Artist: Charles Biro
Lev Gleason (April 1942 © 1942 Comic House, Inc., image courtesy of Heritage Comic Auctions)

Teenager Chuck Chandler becomes Crimebuster after his dad is murdered by Nazi agent Iron Jaw. His "costume" is a hockey jersey and his sidekick is a monkey. When he ran out of Nazis to bust, Chuck hunted more common criminals.

Joker Comics #1

Writers: Harry Douglas, Basil Wolverton
Artists: Harry Douglas, Basil Wolverton
Marvel (April 1942 ©* 1942 Complete Photo Story Corp., image courtesy of Heritage Comic Auctions)

Publisher Martin Goodman's first all-humor comic book featured Stuporman, one of the first super-hero parodies, and the debut of Powerhouse Pepper, a dim-witted, good-hearted boxer who possessed super-strength. Pepper's slapstick adventures appeared in several other Goodman titles, as well.

Star Spangled Comics #7

Writers: Joe Simon, Jack Kirby
Artists: Jack Kirby, Joe Simon
DC (April 1942 © 1941 Detective Comics, Inc., image courtesy of Heritage Comic Auctions)

Leaving **Captain America** *after publisher Martin Goodman failed to pay them royalties, Simon and Kirby launched a new feature at DC. The Newsboy Legion consists of smart, tough kids making their way on their own. Policeman Jim Harper is their costumed "Guardian."*

> The Newsboy Legion consists of smart, tough kids making their way on their own.

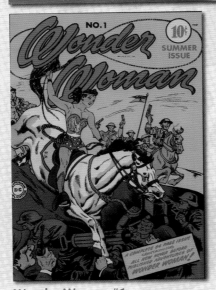

Wonder Woman #1

Writer: William Moulton Marston
Artist: Harry G. Peter
DC (Summer 1942 © 1942 Wonder Woman Publishing Company, Inc.)

Mere months after her debuts in **All-Star** *and* **Sensation Comics***, Wonder Woman received her own book wherein she preached both female empowerment and loving submission to authority while countering the schemes of saboteurs and spies. You go, girl!*

Bill Barnes, America's Air Ace Comics #7

Writer: Walter B. Gibson
Artists: uncredited
Street & Smith (July 1942 ©* 1942 Street & Smith Publications, image courtesy of Heritage Comic Auctions)

Years before Hiroshima, Barnes virtually wipes out Japan with a U-235 bomb. The story is remarkable for its eerie prophecy, its callousness toward the deaths of millions, and the subsequent visit by the FBI to the publisher's offices.

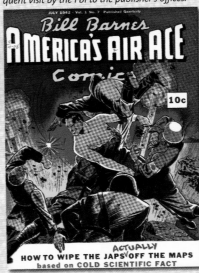

Crime Does Not Pay #22

Writers: Bob Wood, Charles Biro
Artists: Harry Lucey, Alan Mandel
Lev Gleason (July 1942 © 1942 Comic House, Inc.)

The first and greatest of the crime comics: The gangsters of the 1930s were the main draws of this title, but editors Wood and Biro would go as far back as the Middle Ages for their "true" tales of malfeasance and punishment.

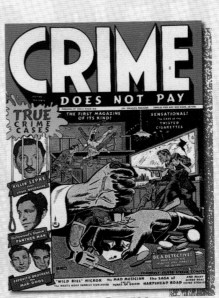

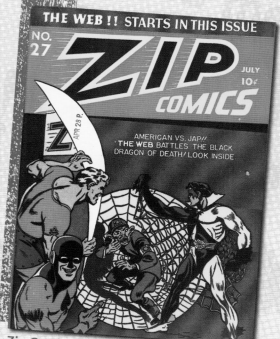

Zip Comics #27

Writer: Uncredited
Artist: John Cassone
MLJ (July 1942 © 1942 M.L.J. Magazines, Inc., image courtesy of Heritage Comic Auctions)

Professor of criminology John Raymond brings swift justice to Nazis and criminals as The Web. Ironically, the gaudily dressed avenger, so grim in the 1940s, would be revived in the 1960s as the henpecked husband of a shrewish wife.

Action Comics #52

Writers: Jerry Siegel, Gardner F. Fox
Artists: Mort Meskin, Fred Ray
DC (September 1942 © 1942 Detective Comics, Inc., image courtesy of Heritage Comic Auctions)

*This one makes the book for its iconic and oft-reprinted Fred Ray cover of Superman and the other **Action** stars: Americommando, the Vigilante, Congo Bill, and Zatara the Magician. The Superman story is an imaginary tale set in post-war America.*

Our Gang Comics #1

Writer: Walt Kelly
Artists: Walt Kelly, Carl Barks
Dell (September 1942 © 1942 Loew's Incorporated)

From Hal Roach's popular short comedy films, Spanky, Froggy, Buckwheat, and the rest of the Little Rascals now starred in comics adventures by Walt Kelly. The title also featured Tom and Jerry and non-Disney funny-animal stories by Carl Barks.

Daredevil Comics #13

Writers: Charles Biro
Artists: Charles Biro
Lev Gleason (October 1942 © 1942 Comic House, Inc.)

Daredevil gets four kid sidekicks, as he battles The Wizard and the German-American Cult. The Little Wise Guys — initially Meatball, Peewee, Scarecrow and Jock — would become more popular than Daredevil and, by 1951, push him out of his own book.

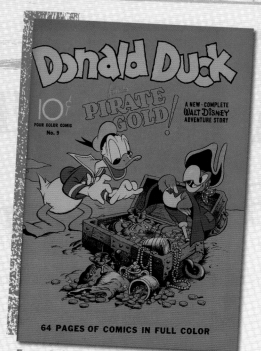

Four Color #9: Donald Duck Finds Pirate Gold

Writer: Bob Karp
Artists: Carl Barks, Jack Hannah
Dell (October 1942 ©* 1942 Walt Disney Productions, image courtesy of Heritage Comic Auctions)

Adapted from an unproduced Mickey Mouse cartoon, this 64-page adventure features Carl Barks' first comic-book work. Barks would soon be recognized as a master of the comics art form, entertaining readers and inspiring comics creators around the world.

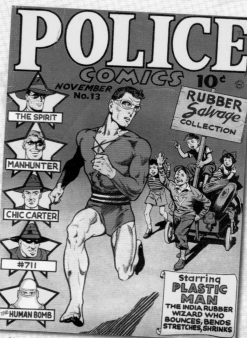

Police Comics #13

Writer: Jack Cole
Artist: Jack Cole
Quality Comics (November 1942 © 1942 Comic Magazines, Inc., image courtesy of Heritage Comic Auctions)

Plastic Man gets a sidekick! Small-time crook Woozy Winks is "the man who can't be harmed," thanks to a gypsy whose life he has saved. Patterned after comedian Lou Costello, his bumbling manner actually makes Plastic Man look serious.

Military Comics #12

Writer: William Woolfolk
Artist: Reed Crandall
Quality Comics (November 1942 © 1942 Comic Magazines, Inc., image courtesy of Heritage Comic Auctions)

In his first Blackhawk script, Woolfolk pits the hero against The Butcher, the brother of the Nazi who murdered his family. His portrayal of Blackhawk's quest for vengeance and the choices a real hero makes leads to an unforgettable conclusion.

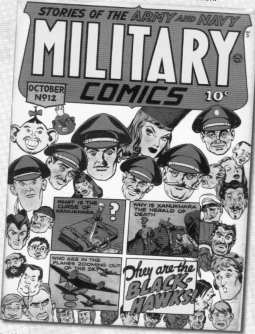

Military Comics #14

Writer: William Woolfolk
Artist: Reed Crandall
Quality Comics (December 1942 © 1942 Comic Magazines, Inc., image courtesy of Heritage Comic Auctions)

Woolfolk follows his Blackhawk debut with this exotic tale of Tondeleyo, a "mysterious girl of the East" who wages psychological warfare on the Blackhawks … and few artists drew femmes fatales who were as enticing as those of the legendary Reed Crandall.

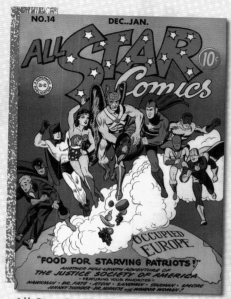

Animal Comics #1

Writer: Walt Kelly
Artist: Walt Kelly
Dell (December 1942 © 1942 Oskar Lebeck)

Pogo Possum and Albert the Alligator were the stars of Kelly's newspaper strip **Pogo** *(1948-1975), but they were created to be humorous sidekicks for Bumbazine, a young boy who lived in the Okeefenokee Swamp in this "funny book" for young readers.*

All-Star Comics #14

Writer: Gardner F. Fox
Artists: Sheldon Moldoff and others
DC (December 1942 ©* 1942 All-American Comics, image courtesy of Heritage Comic Auctions)

Capsules that turn into full meals are the "Food for Starving Patriots" that Hawkman and the Justice Society must deliver to the freedom fighters of Europe. Fox excelled at super-hero adventures with social themes.

Captain Marvel Adventures #18

Writer: Otto Binder
Artists: Marc Swayze, Mac Raboy
Fawcett (December 11, 1942 © 1942 Fawcett Publications, Inc.)

Billy Batson has a twin sister, who was separated from him when their folks died and subsequently raised by a wealthy family. When she says "Shazam!" Mary Bromfield becomes Mary Marvel and gains the same amazing powers as Captain Marvel.

Archie Comics #1

Writers: uncredited
Artists: Bob Montana, Joe Edwards
MLJ (Winter 1942 ©* 1942 M.L.J. Magazines, Inc., image courtesy of Heritage Comic Auctions)

A flashback story reveals how Veronica came to Riverdale and met Archie. In between the issue's several Archie stories, readers meet such animal characters as Cubby the Bear, Bumbie the Bee-Tective, Squoimy the Woim, and Judge Owl.

A flashback story reveals how Veronica came to Riverdale and met Archie.

Boy Commandos #1

Writers: Jack Kirby, Joe Simon
Artists: Jack Kirby, Joe Simon
DC (Winter 1942-1943 © 1942 World's Best Comics Co.)

The ultimate 1940s kid gang: Four orphans from four nations — Brooklyn (United States), André (France), Alfie (England), and Jan (the Netherlands) — form an elite commando squad under the command of Captain Rip Carter. Their comic was a smash hit!

Powerhouse Pepper #1

Writer: Basil Wolverton
Artist: Basil Wolverton
Marvel (January 1943 ©* 1942 20th Century Comics, image courtesy of Heritage Comic Auctions)

Wolverton's dim-witted hero has a heart of gold and the super-strength to knock his opponents cold. He speaks in alliterations and rhymes. His adventures, which appeared in many Marvel titles, were mini-masterpieces of slapstick action.

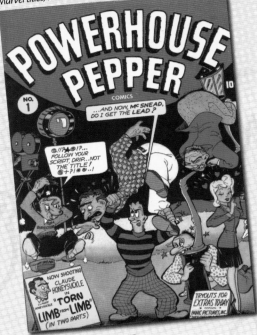

Jumbo Comics #48

Writers: uncredited
Artists: Dan Zolnerowich, Mort Leav
Fiction House (February 1943 ©* 1942 Real Adventure Publications Co.)

Sheena continued to rule over **Jumbo Comics** while Fiction House firmly established its company look: beautifully drawn covers, most often featuring beautiful women. Behind the covers, readers would find solid writing and above-average art.

Daredevil Comics #15

Writer: Charles Biro
Artist: Charles Biro
Lev Gleason (February 1943 © 1942 Comic House, Inc.)

Pee Wee is captured by The Steamrollers. Meatball braves snow and frigid waters to save him. He succeeds but dies of pneumonia. Inspired by Meatball's courage, Curly helps bring his old gang to justice and joins the Little Wise Guys.

Captain Marvel Adventures #22

Writer: Otto Binder
Artist: C. C. Beck
Fawcett (March 26, 1943 © 1943 Fawcett Publications, Inc.)

In "The Monster Society of Evil," a 25-chapter serial, Captain Marvel faces his deadliest foes: Captain Nazi, Sivana, Ibac, and others, all led by the mysterious Mr. Mind. Marvel was so popular his title was now being published twice a month!

Captain Marvel faces his deadliest foes...

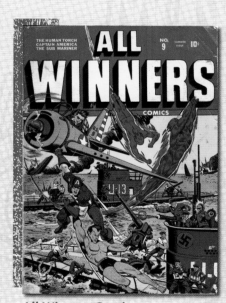

All Winners Comics #9

Writers: uncredited
Artists: Alex Schomburg, Carl Pfeufer
Marvel (Spring 1943 ©* 1943 U.S.A. Publications, image courtesy of Heritage Comic Auctions)

The Human Torch fights gorilla saboteurs. Captain America's sidekick Bucky gets an eerie foreshadowing of his future. A bored Sub-Mariner decides to visit British soldiers on Nazi-held Crete. It ain't a classic comic book, but it sure is fun!

Plastic Man #1

Writer: Jack Cole
Artist: Jack Cole
Quality Comics (Summer 1943 © 1943 Vital Publications, Inc.)

Jack Cole's striking cover launches Plastic Man's own title. Inside the issue are four new Plastic Man stories, five if you count the text page. Nasty villain of the issue: Professor Goodman, who uses a man's disfigurement for his own evil ends.

Detective Comics #76

Writers: Horace L. Gold, Jack Kirby
Artists: Jerry Robinson, Joe Simon
DC (June 1943 © 1943 Detective Comics, Inc.)

Batman's clash with The Joker is by science-fiction writer and editor Horace L. Gold. Even more notable: the Boy Commandoes foil a Nazi invasion of America with the help of The Sandman, Sandy, The Guardian, and The Newsboy Legion.

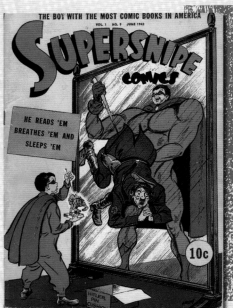

Supersnipe #9

Writer: George Marcoux
Artist: George Marcoux
Street and Smith (June 1943 © 1943 Street & Smith Publications, Inc.)

Koppy McFad is the boy with the most comic books in America. He wants to be a super-hero, patrolling his neighborhood in mask, cape, and red-flannel longjohns. In this issue, he even sort of teams up with Doc Savage.

Jingle Jangle Comics #4

Writer: George Carlson
Artist: George Carlson
Eastern Color (August 1943 ©* Famous Funnies, Inc., image courtesy of Heritage Comic Auctions)

"Comic of the absurd." That's how noted author Harlan Ellison described Carlson's "Jingle Jangle Tales" and "The Pie-Faced Prince of Pretzelburg." Carlson's young readers delighted in the dazzling details and wonderful wordplay they found in the cartoonist's work.

Boy Commandos #4

Writer: Jack Kirby
Artists: Jack Kirby, Joe Simon
DC (Fall 1943 © 1943 World's Best Comics Co., image courtesy of Heritage Comic Auctions)

The Boy Commandos were the ultimate kid gang, and this issue was their finest hour. The multi-chapter "Invasion of Europe" ran an amazing 46 pages. It wouldn't be long before writer-artist Kirby would find himself on those same battlefields.

Miss America Comics #1

Writers: uncredited
Artists: Ken Bald, George Klein
Marvel (January 1944 ©* 1943 20th Century Comics)

Introduced in Marvel Mystery Comics, Madeline Frank gained her super-powers after being struck by lightning. Though she continued to appear in various comics through the 1940s, her own title would undergo a radical change with its next issue.

Archie Comics #7

Writer: Ed Goggin
Artists: Harry Sahle, Janice Valleau
MLJ (March-April 1944 ©* 1944 M.L.J. Magazines, Inc., image courtesy of Heritage Comic Auctions)

Archie tries to take both Betty and Veronica to a show with-out either of them being aware of the other's presence. It's the first of many such "double date" disasters and establishes the "eternal triangle" involving the three teens.

Plastic Man #2

Writer: Jack Cole
Artist: Jack Cole
Quality Comics (August 1944 © 1944 Vital Publications, Inc.)

Another classic cover, as Plastic Man and Woozy Winks visit a town made over to look like the 1890s. Also: a man who can change bodies with anyone, a Lava Man, and a city — other than Washington, D.C. — where everyone has gone crazy!

Four Color #38: Roy Rogers

Writer: Gaylord Du Bois
Artist: Burris Jenkins
Dell (April 1944 ©* 1944 Roy Rogers Enterprises, image courtesy of Heritage Comic Auctions)

It was the first Roy Rogers comic and the first Western comic with a photo cover. More violent than one expects from the "King of the Cowboys," this 49-page thriller is notable for its blazing action, brutal villains, and gritty art.

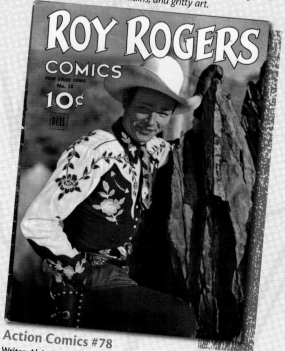

Action Comics #78

Writer: Alvin Schwartz (signed as Jerry Siegel)
Artist: Ira Yarbrough (signed as Joe Shuster)
DC (November 1944 ©* 1944 National Comics Publications, Inc., image courtesy of Heritage Comic Auctions)

"The Chef of Bohemia," one of Schwartz' best Superman tales, is a tribute to his Greenwich Village friend Alex. The Russian owner of the Borsht Bowl restaurant, "Alex was kind of an artist at helping people" and fed many a starving artist.

Miss America Magazine #2

Writers: Stan Lee, Ruth Atkinson
Artists: Ruth Atkinson
Marvel (November 1944 ©* 1944 Miss America Publications,
image courtesy of Heritage Comic Auctions)

Miss America Comics becomes *Miss America Magazine* with
Dolores Conlon portraying the heroine on the cover and a mix
of comics and articles inside. Of more import, it's the debut of
Patsy Walker, soon to be Marvel's biggest teen star.

Detective Comics #98

Writer: Don Cameron
Artist: Dick Sprang
DC (April 1945 ©* 1945 Detective Comics, Inc., image courtesy
of Heritage Comic Auctions)

*A Gotham City banker hits the hobo trail to escape his high-
pressure existence in this romanticized view of hobo life.
When he uses his money to fix up a hobo haven, criminals
recognize him, and Batman and Robin must rescue him.*

Real Screen Funnies #1

Writers: uncredited
Artists: uncredited
DC (Spring 1945 © 1945 Detective Comics, Inc., image courtesy of
Heritage Comic Auctions)

*With rival Dell having licensed the Walt Disney and Warner
Brothers cartoon stars, DC turned to Columbia Pictures. The relatively amiable Fox and the conniving Crow got the cover of most
issues and also starred in their own long-running series.*

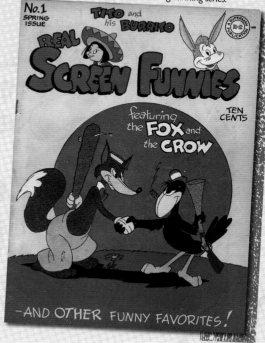

Green Lama #5

Writer: Ken Crossen (signed as Richard Foster)
Artist: Mac Raboy
Spark Publications (May 1945 © 1945 Spark Publications)

*An Army private writes to the Green Lama for advice on
dealing with a bigot in his squad. A trip to Nazi Germany
shows the bigot the wrongness of his prejudice in one of the
few 1940s stories to show African-American servicemen.*

Jungle Comics #66
Writers: uncredited
Artists: Ruben Moreira, Robert Webb
Fiction House (June 1945 ©* 1945 Glen Kel Publications, image courtesy of Heritage Comic Auctions)

One of Fiction House's top titles, it stars Kaanga, seen in the background of a Joe Doolin cover focusing on the jungle lord's mate. Also featured: Wambi the Jungle Boy; Simba, King of Beasts; and Camilla, Queen of the Jungle Empire.

Frankenstein Comics #1
Writer: Dick Briefer
Artist: Dick Briefer
Prize (Summer 1945 ©* 1945 Crestwood Publications, image courtesy of Heritage Comic Auctions)

Briefer went for laughs in his second take on Mary Shelley's classic creation. The Frankenstein Monster moves to a small town, where his neighbors include such other formerly fearful folks as The Wolfman and Dracula. Take that, Herman Munster!

Patsy Walker #1
Writer: uncredited
Artist: Ruth Atkinson
Marvel (Summer 1945 ©* 1945 Bard Publishing Corporation, image courtesy of Heritage Comic Auctions)

Redhead Patsy was Marvel's queen of teen humor, vying for boys and various other prizes with raven-haired Hedy Wolfe, her friend and rival. She remained one of Marvel's most popular stars for two decades and became a super-heroine in the 1970s.

Our Gang Comics #19
Writer: Walt Kelly
Artist: Walt Kelly
Dell (September-October 1945 © 1945 Loew's Incorporated)

The kids of Walt Kelly's "Our Gang" tales were very different from The Little Rascals of MGM's popular comedy shorts. Kelly's kids appeared in exciting, tightly plotted adventures notable for their subtle depictions of racial and gender equality.

Kelly's kids appeared in exciting, tightly plotted adventures...

Classic Comics #26: Frankenstein
Original Author: Mary Shelley
Artists: Ann Brewster, Robert Webb
Gilberton (December 1945 ©* 1945 Gilberton Co.)

Many parents and educators respected and championed publisher Albert Lewis Kanter's comic books as a way to get kids interested in great literature. But it was such scary stories as **Frankenstein** *that were especially compelling to young readers.*

...such scary stories as *Frankenstein*... were especially compelling to young readers.

Mary Marvel #1
Writers: Otto Binder
Artists: Jack Binder (likely)
Fawcett (December 1945 © 1945 Fawcett Publications, Inc.)

Mary Marvel prevents Sivana from committing a crime, defends herself against his daughter, teaches the kids of rural Hog Valley, and deals with unscrupulous businessmen who have tainted the city's water supply. Talk about a full schedule!

Marvel Family #1
Writer: Otto Binder
Artist: C.C. Beck
Fawcett (December 1945 © 1945 Fawcett Publications, Inc.)

The first super-hero family — Captain Marvel, Captain Marvel Jr., Mary Marvel, and even comical Uncle Dudley Marvel — team up to battle Black Adam, an ancient Egyptian villain who was also given incredible powers by their mentor, Shazam.

Rangers Comics #26
Writers: uncredited
Artists: Joe Doolin, Lee Elias
Fiction House (December 1945 © 1945 Flying Stories, Inc.)

Rangers was a war-themed title before expanding its horizons in 1945. The U.S. Rangers kept their top billing for a while but would soon lose their coveted cover spot to Firehair, Queen of the Sagebrush Frontier.

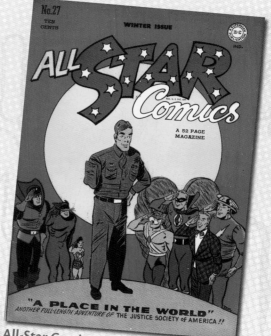

All-Star Comics #27

Writer: Gardner Fox
Artists: Joe Kubert, Paul Reinman
DC (Winter 1945-1946 ©* 1945 All-American Comics, image courtesy of Heritage Comic Auctions)

As our handicapped veterans began to come home, this heartfelt story was requested by the National Institute for the Handicapped. At its conclusion, The Justice Society writes a code of conduct for how their young fans should treat all handicapped people.

Millie the Model #1

Writer: uncredited
Artist: Ruth Atkinson
Marvel (Winter 1945 ©* 1945 Sphere, image courtesy of Heritage Comic Auctions)

Millie made her debut in her own comic, which was rare for the 1940s. Created by Ruth Atkinson, who also co-created Patsy Walker, **Millie** *was one of only three Marvel titles published continuously from the 1940s into the 1960s.*

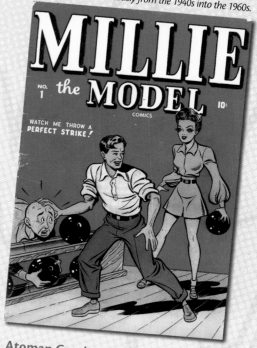

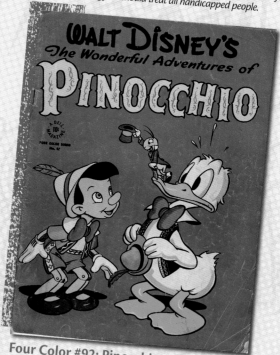

Four Color #92: Pinocchio

Writer: Chase Craig
Artist: Walt Kelly
Dell (January 1946 © 1939, 1945 Walt Disney Productions)

Besides its abridged-but-still-terrific adaptation of the 1940 Disney classic — itself based on the 1883 novel by Carlo Collodi — this issue features "The Wonderful Mis-Adventures of Donocchio," in which Donald Duck wishes he were Pinocchio.

Atoman Comics #1

Writer: Ken Crossen
Artist: Jerry Robinson
Spark Publications (February 1946 © 1945 Ken Crossen, image courtesy of Heritage Comic Auctions)

Though his title ran but two issues, scientist Barry Dale was the first atomic-powered hero in comics. "My body is so geared as a result of working on radium and uranium that it can explode atoms and give me atomic strength."

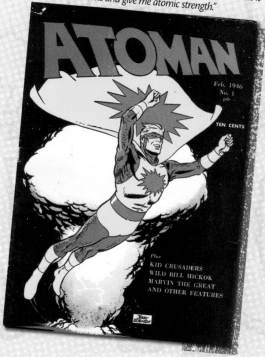

Four Color #97: Little Lulu

Writer: John Stanley
Artist: John Stanley
Dell (February 1946 ©* 1945 Marjorie Henderson Buell,
image courtesy of Heritage Comic Auctions)

Offended by Tubby's lack of respect for girls, Lulu enters a model-plane contest. She forgoes buying a coveted doll to purchase the kit and struggles to build her plane, but this is Lulu. The boys are no match for her.

Treasure Chest of Fun & Fact Vol. 1 #1

Writers: Jay Griffin, Iris Vinton
Artists: Earl Lansbury, Clara Peck
George A. Pflaum (March 12, 1946 © 1946 Geo. A. Pflaum,
Publisher, Inc., image courtesy of Heritage Comic Auctions)

Published biweekly during the school year, this long-running title delivered an entertaining mix of fact and fiction to Catholic students. Its comics included rebellious teen Chuck White, salvage diver Skee Barry, and a "how to" series on building a rumpus room.

Stuntman #1

Writers: Jack Kirby, Joe Simon
Artists: Jack Kirby, Joe Simon
Harvey (April-May 1946 © 1946 Harvey Features Syndicate,
image courtesy of Heritage Comic Auctions)

Aerialist Fred Drake is the secret stunt double for the timid actor Don Daring. Drake is also the costumed crimefighter called — what else? — Stuntman. A short-lived but unforgettable hero from the creators of Captain America and The Boy Commandos.

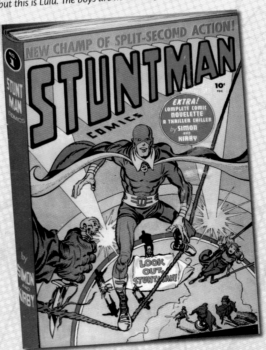

Black Cat #1

Writers: uncredited
Artists: Joe Kubert, Bob Powell
Harvey (June-July 1946 © 1946 Harvey Features Syndicate, image courtesy of Heritage Comic Auctions)

Another Hollywood hero from Harvey. Movie star and former stuntwoman Linda Turner dons her sexy costume to battle Nazis and more homegrown criminals, often while simultaneously pursuing her acting career. Multi-tasking is a must for super-heroines.

Four Color #114: Fairy Tale Parade

Writer: "The Great Unknown"
Artist: "The Great Unknown"
Dell (July 1946 © 1946 Oskar Lebeck)

No one has yet identified the creator of this issue's non-Disney version of "The Sorcerer's Apprentice," but the beautifully drawn, brilliantly written story is easily among the best "young readers" comic books of the decade.

Action Comics #100

Writer: Alvin Schwartz
Artist: Ira Yarbrough
DC (September 1946 © 1946 Detective Comics, Inc., image courtesy of Heritage Comic Auctions)

Scotland Yard's Inspector Hawkins is determined to prove Clark Kent is Superman, the first of many attempts he will make over the years, thus establishing the template for the countless "Lois tries to prove Clark is Superman" stories of later decades.

The Challenger #3

Writers: uncredited
Artist: Joe Kubert
Interfaith Publications/T.C. Comics (September 1946 © 1946 Interfaith Committee of Protestant Digest, Inc., image courtesy of Heritage Comic Auctions)

Published by the Interfaith Committee of Protestant Digest, this comic featured stories about race prejudice, discrimination, and fascism. "The Golem," an 18-page story drawn by comics legend Kubert, is the highlight of the title's four issues.

All Select Comics #11

Writer: Stan Lee
Artists: Syd Shores, Charles Nicholas
Marvel (Fall 1946 ©* 1946 Daring Comics, image courtesy of Heritage Comic Auctions)

Louise Grant is private detective Mark Mason's secretary and secretly assists him as The Blonde Phantom. She fights crime in a mask, evening gown, and high heels. The sheer absurdity of this is why she's my favorite 1940s super-heroine.

Fight Comics #46

Writers: uncredited
Artists: Bob Lubbers, Matt Baker
Fiction House (October 1946 © 1946 Fight Stories, Inc.,
image courtesy of Heritage Comic Auctions)

This anthology title starred Senorita Rio, that being the code name of actress Rita Farrar, a U.S. Intelligence agent operating in South America. Other Fight stars include prizefighter Kayo Kirby, soldier of fortune Captain Fight, and Tiger Girl.

> This anthology title starred Senorita Rio, code name of actress Rita Farrar...

The Spirit (October 6, 1946)

Writer: Will Eisner
Artist: Will Eisner
Register and Tribune Syndicate (October 6, 1946 © 1946
Everett M. Arnold)

"I am P'Gell ... and this is not a story for little boys!" One of the great femmes fatales, P'Gell never succeeds in seducing The Spirit into crime. She is more successful with an alarmingly high number of deceased husbands.

Four Color #128: Santa Claus Funnies

Writer: Oskar Lebeck
Artist: Morris Gollub
Dell (December 1946 © Oskar Lebeck)

A young angel falls asleep while polishing stars for Heaven's Christmas party, drifting to the snow-covered forest below. Kind-hearted woodland creatures and Santa himself come to the cherub's rescue in this charming holiday tale.

Eerie #1

Writers: Edward Bellin, uncredited
Artists: Joe Kubert, Fred Kida
Avon (January 1947 © 1947 Avon Comics, Inc., image courtesy of Heritage Comic Auctions)

There wouldn't be a second issue until 1951, but Eerie #1 was the first horror comic book not based on existing pulp magazines, radio shows, movies, or literature. It had an adult, occasional sexual vibe but didn't go in for heavy gore or violence.

Marvel Family #10

Writer: Otto Binder
Artists: Pete Costanza, Jack Binder
Fawcett (April 1947 © 1947 Fawcett Publications, Inc.)

It's a family feud that stretches across the centuries, as The Marvel Family does battle with The Sivana Family in past, present, and future Atlantis. Have the villains really found a way to block our heroes from their Shazam powers?

My Date Comics #1

Writers: Joe Simon, Jack Kirby
Artists: Jack Kirby, Joe Simon
Hillman (July 1947 ©* 1947 Hillman Periodicals, Inc., image courtesy of Heritage Comic Auctions)

This title kicks off with "My Date with Swifty Chase," a 14-page tale that features a parody of Humphrey Bogart. The short-lived series was a bridge between teen humor comics and true "love" books such as the duo's own groundbreaking *Young Romance*.

Animal Comics #28

Writer: Walt Kelly
Artist: Walt Kelly
Dell (August 1947 © 1947 Oskar Lebeck)

In a funny six-page story, **Pogo** creator Kelly requests letters from **Animal Comics** readers of all ages. More hilarious is his "Nibble and Nubble" about a conniving mouse and a naive kitten who hasn't learned the natural order of things.

Young Romance #1

Writers: Joe Simon, Jack Kirby
Artists: Jack Kirby, Bill Draut
Prize (September-October 1947 ©* 1947 Feature Publications, image courtesy of Heritage Comic Auctions)

The first true romance comic. "Designed for the more adult readers of comics," this debut issue presented such provocative-sounding tales as "Misguided Heart," "The Plight of the Suspicious Bridegroom," and "I Was a Pick-Up!"

All-Star Comics #37

Writer: Robert Kanigher
Artists: Irwin Hasen, Joe Kubert
DC (October-November 1947 ©* 1947 All-American Comics,
image courtesy of Heritage Comic Auctions)

In the first great battle between teams of super-heroes and su-
per-villains, The Injustice Society of the World plots to destroy
The Justice Society. The villains: The Gambler, Brain Wave,
Vandal Savage, The Wizard, Per Degaton, and The Thinker.

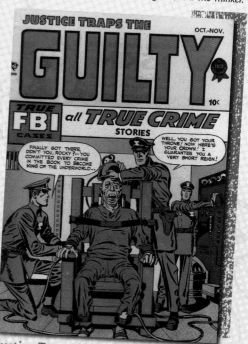

Justice Traps the Guilty #1

Writers: Joe Simon, Jack Kirby
Artists: Jack Kirby, Bill Draut
Prize (October-November 1947 ©* 1947 Headline
Publications, image courtesy of Heritage Comic Auctions)

The Simon-Kirby team never met a genre they couldn't
master. Their entry into crime comics includes such
grim stories as "I Was a Come-On Girl for Broken
Bones, Inc.," "The Head in the Window," and "The Case
against Scarface!"

Four Color #169: Woody Woodpecker

Writer: John Stanley
Artist: John Stanley, Dick Hall
Dell (October 1947 © 1947 Walter Lantz Productions,
image courtesy of Heritage Comic Auctions)

Woody is on both sides of the law in this comic book.
In "Man Hunter of the North," he's an Alaskan ranger
hunting down an arch-criminal. In "The Evil Genius," a
drug turns him into the greatest evil mastermind of all!

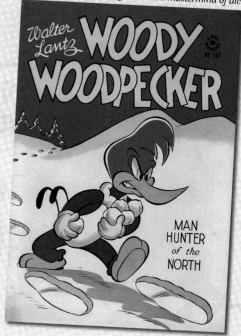

Our Gang with Tom & Jerry #40

Writers: uncredited
Artists: uncredited
Dell (December 1947 © 1947 Loew's Incorporated)

MGM's "Tom and Jerry," who were beating both Warner
Brothers and Walt Disney for animation Oscars, took over
the cover spot of this comic and, within a couple of years,
pushed the Our Gang kids right out of the long-running title.

Detective Comics #130

Writer: Bill Finger
Artists: Bob Kane, Charles Paris
DC (December 1947 © 1947 National Comics Publications, Inc., image courtesy of Heritage Comic Auctions)

One of the grimmest of all Batman stories, as "The Box" passes from one criminal to another and always brings them sudden death. The tale ends with Batman knowing the perpetrator of these murders will never pay for his crime.

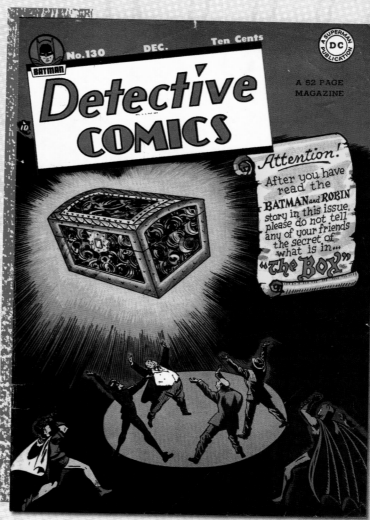

...the perpetrator of these murders will never pay for his crime.

Four Color #178: Donald Duck

Writer: Carl Barks
Artist: Carl Barks
Dell (December 1947 © 1947 Walt Disney Productions)

The first appearance of Uncle Scrooge McDuck. In this story, he's more reclusive and less dynamic than the tough tycoon of later adventures, but we can still see why he is unquestionably the best character ever created by the legendary Barks.

Funnyman #1

Writer: Jerry Siegel
Artist: Joe Shuster
Magazine Enterprises (January 1948 © uncredited)

TV comedian Larry Davis nabs a genuine crook during what is supposed to be a publicity stunt and decides to continue fighting crime as the outlandish Funnyman. This was the final collaboration of Superman creators Siegel and Shuster.

Captain Marvel Adventures #82

Writer: Otto Binder
Artist: C.C. Beck
Fawcett (March 1948 © 1947 Fawcett Publications, Inc.)

Tawky Tawny, a civilized tiger who chose to live among humans, was the most charming member of Captain Marvel's supporting cast. In this, his second appearance, his deductive ability allows him to clear an old friend framed for murder.

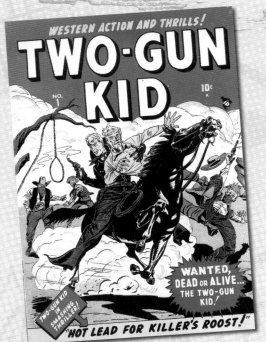

Two-Gun Kid #1

Writer: uncredited
Artist: Syd Shores
Marvel (March 1948 ©* 1947 Marvel Comics, image courtesy of Heritage Comic Auctions)

Marvel's first Western had a theme that would become familiar among its cowboy characters: a hero unjustly accused of crimes, roaming the West and helping others. A new, entirely different Two-Gun Kid would be introduced in 1962.

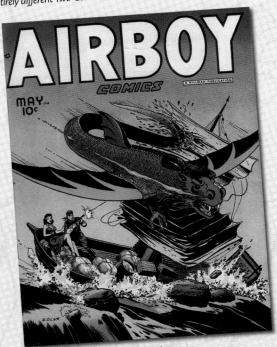

Airboy Comics Vol. 5 #4

Writer: uncredited
Artist: Fred Kida
Hillman (May 1948 © 1948 Hillman Periodicals, Inc.)

Visiting a buddy in Shanghai, Airboy is scammed into helping a vicious businessman solidify his power over his workers. Exotic settings, harrowing perils, and a gorgeous **femme fatale** make this one of the young pilot's most exciting post-war adventures.

Wonder Woman #28

Writer: William Moulton Marston
Artist: Harry G. Peter
DC (March-April 1948 ©* 1948 National Comics Publications, Inc., image courtesy of Heritage Comic Auctions)

Transformation Island is where Wonder Woman takes her foes in hope of reforming them. A prison break led by the Saturnian leader Evilness pits the Amazon against an army of villains in a thriller so big it took 36 pages to tell.

Planet Comics #55

Writers: uncredited
Artists: George Evans, Matt Baker
Fiction House (July 1948 © 1948 Love Romances Pub. Co., Inc., image courtesy of Heritage Comic Auctions)

The anthology's 1948 line-up included The Lost World (in which humans battle the alien Voltamen who have conquered Earth) as well as Futura, Space Rangers, Star Pirate, Mysta of the Moon, and Auro, Lord of Jupiter. The title ended in 1953.

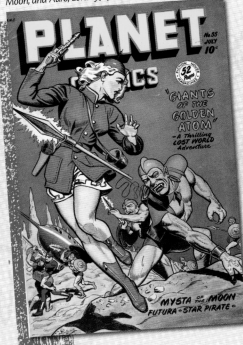

True Crime Comics Vol. 1 #3

Writer: Jack Cole
Artist: Jack Cole
Magazine Village (July 1948 ©* 1948 Magazine Village Inc., image courtesy of Heritage Comic Auctions)

The cover is shocking, but it pales next to "Murder, Morphine, and Me," the "true" confessions of drug smuggler Mary Kennedy. The panel of a crazed addict threatening to plunge a needle into Mary's fear-widened eye still gives me the creeps.

All-American Comics #100

Writer: Robert Kanigher
Artist: Alex Toth
DC (August 1948 © 1948 National Comics Publications, Inc., image courtesy of Heritage Comic Auctions)

Having promised his late mother that he would avoid violence, schoolteacher John Taine becomes Johnny Thunder to aid his sheriff father secretly. Green Lantern is bumped from the cover, a sure sign the first age of super-heroes is ending.

Scribbly #1

Writer: Sheldon Mayer
Artist: Sheldon Mayer
DC (August-September 1948 © 1948 National Comics Publications, Inc., image courtesy of Heritage Comic Auctions)

Mayer retired from editing in 1948 to devote himself to full-time cartooning, returning to this semi-autobiographical character. In this first issue, Scribbly seeks a job at Rational Comics, only to end up working at a rodeo.

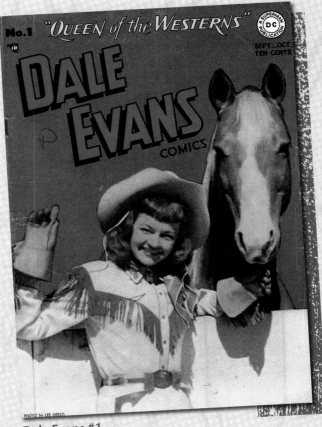

Dale Evans #1

Writers: uncredited, Joe Millard
Artists: Maxwell Elkan, Alex Toth
DC (September-October 1948 © National Comics Publications, Inc., image courtesy of Heritage Comic Auctions)

DC obtained the license to publish comics starring The Queen of the West, even though Dell had her husband, Roy Rogers. Back-up feature "Sierra Smith" is a Western detective, the first DC private eye to appear in a title other than **Detective Comics***.*

THE SPIRIT

ACTION Mystery ADVENTURE

THE SPIRIT

BY Will Eisner

BEFORE WE BEGIN THIS STORY WE WANT TO MAKE ONE POINT VERY CLEAR..

THIS IS NOT A FUNNY STORY!!

...AND WHILE THE AUTHOR DOES NOT EXPECT YOU TO BELIEVE ALL OF THIS..HE FEELS BOUND TO ASSURE YOU THAT HE CANNOT GUARANTEE A COMPLETE ABSENCE OF RESEMBLANCE BETWEEN PERSONS LIVING OR DEAD AND THE CHARACTERS HERE PORTRAYED.

WE MEAN TO GIVE YOU A SIMPLE ACCOUNT OF GERHARD SHNOBBLE... BEGINNING AT THE POINT WHEN HE FIRST DISCOVERED HE COULD FLY.

PLEASE....NO LAUGHTER....

The Spirit (September 5, 1948)

Writer: Will Eisner
Artist: Will Eisner
Register and Tribune Syndicate (September 5, 1948 © 1948 News Syndicate Co., Inc.)

Some of the best Spirit tales had the hero playing a secondary role to a one-shot character. Such is the case with this sad fable of an ordinary little man with a secret he keeps from a world that never learns how extraordinary he is.

...sad fable of an ordinary little man with a secret...

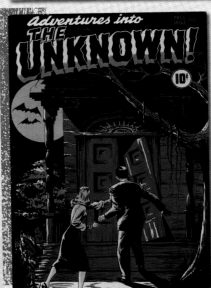

Adventures into the Unknown #1

Writers: uncredited
Artists: Edvard Moritz, Fred Guardineer
American Comics Group (Fall 1948 © 1948 B.&I. Publishing Co., Inc., image courtesy of Heritage Comic Auctions)

The first ongoing horror anthology. More restrained than the horror comics that would follow it, this title featured everything from traditional ghost stories to fanciful science fiction. This issue adapts an 18th century Gothic novel in just seven pages.

Candy #6

Writer: Harry Sahle
Artist: Harry Sahle
Quality Comics (October 1948 © 1948 Comic Magazines, Inc., image courtesy of Heritage Comic Auctions)

Candy is my favorite comics teen queen. She had a long run in Police Comics alongside the likes of Plastic Man and The Spirit. Her funniest adventures were by Sahle, who was also a top "Archie" artist in the 1940s and 1950s.

Four Color #199: Donald Duck

Writer: Carl Barks
Artist: Carl Barks
Dell (October 1948 © 1948 Walt Disney Productions)

Guided by his knowledge of old Western movies, Donald becomes the sheriff of Bullet Valley. In his typical bumbling-but-fearless manner, he seeks to bring high-tech rustler Blacksnake McSquirt to justice. A masterful mix of action and comedy.

The Spirit (October 10, 1948)

Writer: Will Eisner
Artist: Will Eisner
Register and Tribune Syndicate (October 10, 1948 © 1948 News Syndicate Co. Inc.)

A notorious outlaw descends from the hills decades after he should have been dust and bones, leading The Spirit into a weird Western tale that highlights how much sheer story, atmosphere, and action Eisner could get into an eight-page adventure.

The Spirit (November 7, 1948)

Writer: Will Eisner
Artist: Will Eisner
Register and Tribune Syndicate (November 7, 1948 © 1948 News Syndicate Co, Inc.)

*She is Plaster of Paris, the toast of Montmartre, and a woman so consumed with dark passion she would kill for her man. This was her only appearance, but she remains one of the most unforgettable **femmes fatales** in comics history.*

Archie Comics #35

Writers: uncredited
Artists: Ray Gill, Bill Vigoda
Archie (November-December 1948 ©* 1948 M.L.J. Magazines, Inc., image courtesy of Heritage Comic Auctions)

Fed up with teenage angst, inconsiderate neighbors, and even his job, Archie's dad prepares to move the family to a new city. Which is when the Andrews clan learns how special their small town of Riverdale really is.

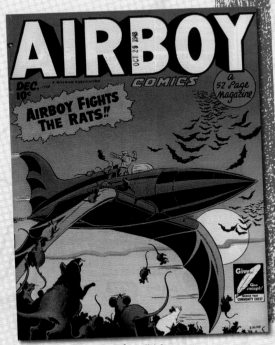

Airboy Comics Vol. 5 #11

Writer: uncredited
Artist: Ernest Schroeder
Hillman (December 1948 © 1948 Hillman Periodicals, Inc.)

In the first of two chilling adventures, Airboy learns that rats are far more intelligent than he's ever dreamed and that they've declared war on mankind. In their initial strike, the rats reduce the population of a small town to skeletons.

Kid Colt, Outlaw #3

Writer: uncredited
Artist: Russ Heath
Marvel (December 1948 © 1948 Leading Comic, image courtesy of Heritage Comic Auctions)

Kid Colt was the most prominent of Marvel's "unjustly branded an outlaw" cowboys. His title started out as **Kid Colt, Hero of the West**, changed its name to **Kid Colt Outlaw** with this issue, and ran 229 issues until its cancellation in 1979.

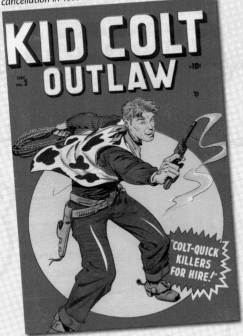

Action Comics #127

Writers: uncredited, Otto Binder
Artists: Al Plastino, Curt Swan
DC (December 1948 © 1948 National Comics Publications, Inc.)

Superman goes on **Truth or Consequences**, the popular radio show hosted by Ralph Edwards. Such real-life celebrity guest stars were not unusual. Also in this issue: Tommy Tomorrow, an intergalactic policeman, makes his series debut.

Airboy Comics Vol. 5 #12

Writer: uncredited
Artist: Ernest Schroeder
Hillman (January 1949 © 1948 Hillman Periodicals, Inc.)

The rats have targeted Airboy for death; their fanatical army is massing in uncountable numbers to attack the United States. In a finale both thrilling and unsettling, the young aviator is man's last chance to defeat this seemingly unstoppable enemy.

Firehair Comics #1

Writer: uncredited
Artist: Bob Lubbers
Fiction House (Winter 1948-1949 © 1948 Flying Stories, Inc., image courtesy of Heritage Comic Auctions)

Firehair is a Boston socialite taken in by the Dakota tribe after her father is murdered. She excels at the skills she was taught and becomes a respected protector of her tribe and any others who wish to live in peace.

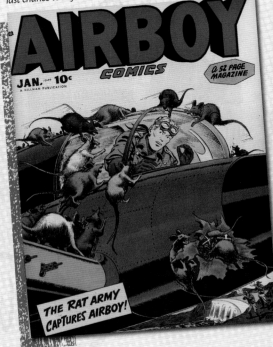

Walt Disney's Comics and Stories #100

Writer: Carl Barks
Artist: Carl Barks
Dell (January 1949 © 1944, 1945, 1946, 1948 Walt Disney Productions)

"Donald vs. nephews" was a frequent theme in the 10-page Barks tales that ran in this title. This issue has one of my favorites: master truant officer Donald matching wits and tricks with Huey, Dewey, and Louie.

Donald vs. nephews

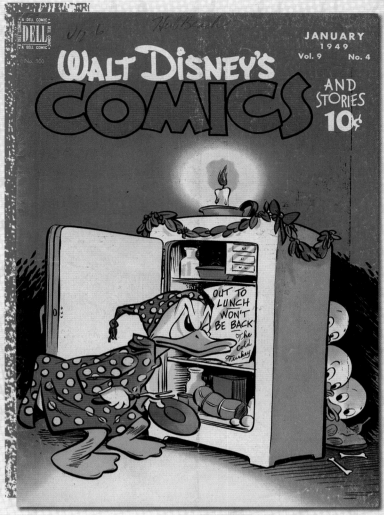

Tessie the Typist #20

Writer: uncredited
Artist: uncredited
Marvel (February 1949 ©* Timely Publications, image courtesy of Heritage Comic Auctions)

*No one did alliterative career girls the way Marvel did. In addition to **Tessie** — and isn't that a wonderfully busy office scene on this cover? — it published **Millie the Model** and **Nellie the Nurse**. Who knows? Maybe some day we'll get **Patty the President**!*

Wings Comics #101

Writers: uncredited
Artists: Bob Lubbers, George Evans
Fiction House (January 1949 ©* 1948 Wings Publication Co., image courtesy of Heritage Comic Auctions)

*It took a few years for the **Wings** aces to switch from fighting the Axis to fighting communists. Captain Wings had the lead spot, while The Ghost Squadron added eerie fantasy to the post-war mix. **Wings** took its last flight in 1954.*

War Against Crime #5

Writers: Johnny Craig, Al Feldstein
Artists: Johnny Craig, Graham Ingels
EC (February-March 1949 © 1948 L.L. Publishing Co, Inc.)

In the first title launched by Bill Gaines following his father's death, Craig gives readers one of his trademark shady ladies, Ingels shows a flair for horror even in a non-horror story, and Feldstein offers a tale narrated by an electric chair.

Ka'a'nga #1

Writers: uncredited
Artists: Tom Cataldo, Ruben Moreira
Fiction House (Spring 1949 ©* 1949 Glen-Kel Publications)

Ka'a'nga made his debut in **Jungle Comics** *#1 (1940) and was in all 163 issues of that title. Perhaps the most successful of the Tarzan imitators, his own title ran 20 issues, ending in 1954, when Fiction House got out of comics.*

Four Color #223: Donald Duck

Writer: Carl Barks
Artist: Carl Barks
Dell (April 1949 © 1949 Walt Disney Productions)

In search of square chickens that lay square eggs, Donald and his nephews find a lost land whose squat inhabitants have Southern accents. Wonder and absurdity blend in an adventure many consider the best Donald Duck tale of all.

Millie the Model #18

Writer: Stan Lee
Artist: Dan DeCarlo
Marvel (June 1949 ©* Sphere, image courtesy of Heritage Comic Auctions)

This issue starts DeCarlo's decade-long run on **Millie** *and his equally long collaboration with Lee, who genuinely enjoyed writing this book. A master at drawing both comedy and sexy women, DeCarlo was the primary* **Betty & Veronica** *artist in later years.*

Raggedy Ann and Andy #38

Writers: John Stanley, Walt Kelly
Artists: John Stanley, Walt Kelly
Dell (July 1949 © 1949 Western Printing & Lithographing Company. All Raggedy Ann material © 1949 The Johnny Gruelle Co.)

Based on the popular children's books by Johnny Gruelle, Ann and Andy enjoyed a healthy run in comics aimed at pre-teen readers. However, in the title's later issues, Stanley added a distinctly darker tone to the duo's adventures.

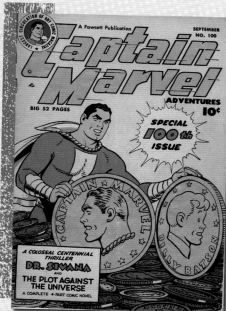

Captain Marvel Adventures #100

Writer: Otto Binder
Artist: C.C. Beck
Fawcett (September 1949) © 1949 Fawcett Publications, Inc.

Captain Marvel knew how to celebrate an anniversary. "The Plot against the Universe" has a retelling of Cap's origin, Talky Tawny, the wizard Shazam in deadly jeopardy, and Sivana's most diabolical scheme ever. It's 33 pages of action-packed fun!

Headline Comics #37

Writers: uncredited
Artists: Vic Donahue, John Severin
Prize (September-October 1949 ©* 1949 American Boys Comics, image courtesy of Heritage Comic Auctions)

When Joe Simon and Jack Kirby assumed the editorship of this title, they switched its format to true-crime stories. The burglar on the cover is Kirby himself, who was guilty only of fudging that "true" part in the name of exciting stories.

The Spirit (September 11, 1949)

Writer: Will Eisner
Artist: Will Eisner
Register and Tribune Syndicate (September 11, 1949 © 1949 News Syndicate Co., Inc.)

Eisner follows the previous week's mildly whimsical tale with the deadly serious "Ten Minutes," a tight depiction of the last 10 minutes of a man's life. It's not just one of the best Spirit stories; it's one of the best comics stories of all time.

Walt Disney's Christmas Parade #1

Writers: Carl Barks, uncredited
Artists: Carl Barks, Bill Wright
Dell (November 1949 © 1949 Walt Disney Productions, image courtesy of Heritage Comic Auctions)

Donald and Scrooge do battle over a gift for Huey, Dewey, and Louie in the hilarious "Letter to Santa." This 132-page seasonal spectacular also stars Mickey Mouse, the Seven Dwarfs, Cinderella, Dumbo, Bambi, and other Disney favorites.

Man Comics #1

Writers: uncredited
Artists: George Tuska, Syd Shores
Marvel (December 1949 ©* 1949 Newstand Publications, image courtesy of Heritage Comic Auctions)

*Did the readers of **Boy Comics** grow up to read **Man Comics**? If they did, they found two longer-than-usual adventures purporting to be "torn from real life" plus a clever "Are You a Detective?" short by Golden Age veteran Allen Bellman.*

War Against Crime #10

Writers: Al Feldstein, Johnny Craig
Artists: Al Feldstein, Johnny Craig
EC (December 1949-January 1950 © 1949 L.L. Publishing Co, Inc.)

*This otherwise-nondescript crime comic is noteworthy because it introduces The Vault-Keeper, narrator of the first in a series of outright horror stories. With issue #12, the title of the comic book would be changed to **The Vault of Horror**.*

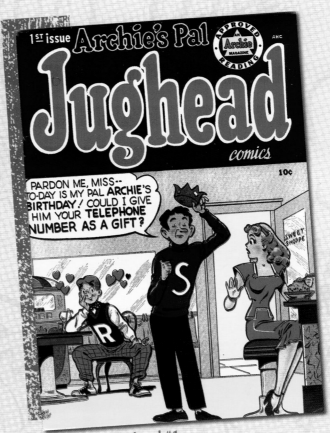

Archie's Pal Jughead #1

Writers: uncredited
Artists: uncredited
Archie (1949 ©* 1949 M.L.J. Magazines, Inc., image courtesy of Heritage Comic Auctions)

Jughead is the first of Archie's friends to get his own title. His character is still being formed here — he's on the football team in one story, not on it in another — but his aversion to girls has already been firmly established.

CHAPTER THREE

World War II was over. The boys who went to war had come back as men, ready to pursue careers and start families. Most of them put aside the comic books that had gone to war with them.

The comics writers and artists who had gone to war were also back, their ranks augmented by newcomers to the industry. Some of those new artists learned the basics of their craft via the G.I. Bill of 1944, which provided college and vocational training for returning veterans.

The end of the war likewise brought an end to wartime restrictions of resources. There was paper for plenty of comics, magazines, and paperbacks — maybe *too many* comics, magazines, and paperbacks, all competing for space on the nation's newsstands. The decade started out strong for the comic-book industry, but it was soon assailed by difficulties beyond overproduction.

Critics of comic books had emerged almost simultaneously with the industry's initial success. The critics got a whole lot louder in the 1950s, blaming the comics for juvenile delinquency and all manner of societal ills. Churches and schools held comic-book burnings.

Laws restricting the sale of comics were passed on local and state levels. There were even congressional hearings, hearings horribly biased in favor of the critics. In effect, the industry was put on trial before a succession of hanging judges.

The distribution end of the industry had its problems, as well. The distributors couldn't handle so many comics effectively, so issues sometimes never left the warehouses. Magazines and paperbacks were more profitable, anyway.

During the decade, several distributors went out of business or merged with other outfits. Many comics publishers could not survive the mercurial nature of their distribution systems. Publishers who had been major players in the industry in the 1940s were gone by the middle of the 1950s.

Adding to industry woes was the emergence of television as the major source of entertainment for most Americans. Those early sets weren't cheap, but, once they were purchased, they provided families with hours of free entertainment.

Bad business decisions, distribution snags, overproduction, public vilification, and now television. The comics industry didn't know what hit it. It would survive, but much diminished from its great prosperity of the previous decade.

Still, as is the case in every one of the industry's seven decades, there were lots of great comics published during the 1950s. Carl Barks, whom fans of the era knew only as "The Good Duck Artist," was doing some of the best work of his career on *Donald Duck* and *Uncle Scrooge* during this decade.

Bill Gaines, son of the late Max Gaines, had revitalized his father's company. He and editors Al Feldstein and Harvey Kurtzman produced exceptional comics in multiple genres: horror, war, crime, science fiction, and humor — the last category represented by the downright revolutionary *Mad*. With mixed results, some comics publishers tried to duplicate E.C.'s success in those genres, some tried to blaze new trails, and others turned to cartoons, movies, and television to license properties and personalities for their comic books.

Innovation and imitation were the watchwords of the comics of the 1950s. As we shall see …

Young Romance #17

Writers: uncredited
Artists: Jack Kirby, Joe Simon
Prize (January 1950 ©* 1949 Feature Publications, image courtesy of Heritage Comic Auctions)

"The Girl Who Tempted Me" has been called a true masterpiece in its unflinching depiction of the romantic triangle between a righteous farmer, his wayward brother, and the brazen beauty they both love. This is not a gentle love story.

Captain America's Weird Tales #75

Writers: uncredited
Artists: Gene Colan, uncredited
Marvel (February 1950 ©* 1949 Canam Publishers Sales Corp.,
image courtesy of Heritage Comic Auctions)

*The star-spangled hero didn't even appear in the final issue of his own title, which, instead, featured three non-series horror tales. Cover artist Colan would gain renown for his later Marvel work on **Iron Man**, **Tomb of Dracula**, and **Howard the Duck**.*

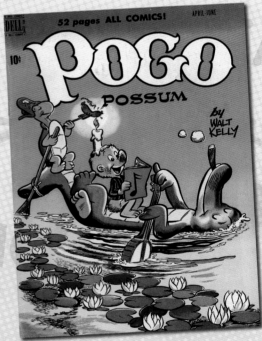

Pogo Possum #2

Writer: Walt Kelly
Artist: Walt Kelly
Dell (April-June 1950 © 1950 Western Printing & Lithographing Co.)

Pogo, Albert, and the rest of the Okefenokee Swamp characters had been appearing in a nationally syndicated newspaper strip for close to a year, but Kelly continued to create new stories for this comic book through its next-to-last issue in 1954.

Black Rider #8

Writer: uncredited
Artists: Syd Shores, Joe Maneely
Marvel (March 1950 ©* 1949 Current Detective Stories)

Once feared as The Cactus Kid, Doc Masters renounced violence but regularly broke that vow to visit brutal justice on outlaws as The Black Rider. It is believed Marvel Editor Stan Lee himself donned the mask for this photo cover.

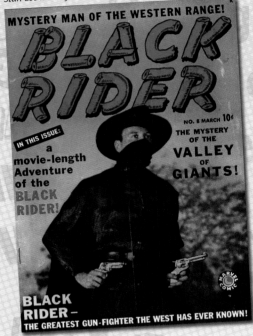

Jon Juan #1

Writer: Jerry Siegel
Artist: Alex Schomburg
Toby (Spring 1950 © Toby Press, Inc., image courtesy of Heritage Comic Auctions)

Stealing his first hearts in ancient Atlantis, Jon was beaten by a jealous husband and frozen in an iceberg. Thawed and now immortal, he seduces women throughout history. This one-issue wonder is the only comic book drawn entirely by legendary cover artist Schomburg.

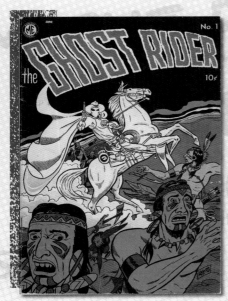

Ghost Rider #1

Writer: uncredited
Artist: Dick Ayers
Magazine Enterprises (May 1950 © 1950 Magazine Enterprises, Inc.)

Federal marshal Rex Fury uses a spectral costume and various tricks to make outlaws believe they are being pursued by an actual ghost. His foes can be just as scary. Some — the odd vampire or were-wolf — turn out to be the real deal.

Walt Disney's Vacation Parade #1

Writers: Carl Barks, Carl Fallberg
Artists: Carl Barks, Paul Murry
Dell (July 1950 © 1950 Walt Disney Productions)

It's 132 pages of fun, as Donald and the boys go camping and visit Grandma Duck's farm. The issue also features Murry's first Mickey Mouse art and short stories of Chip 'n' Dale, Little Hiawatha, Li'l Bad Wolf, and Bucky Bug.

Young Romance #23

Writers: uncredited
Artists: Jack Kirby, Joe Simon
Prize (July 1950 ©* 1950 Feature Publications)

"Gang Sweetheart" is an uncommonly grim romance set in the slums of New York amid the violence of teen gangs. Young lovers Jimmy and Meg are unjustly marked by their "poor background" and struggle to make a better life for themselves.

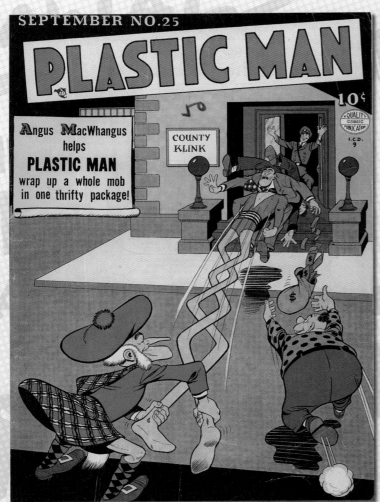

Plastic Man #25

Writers: Bill Woolfolk, uncredited
Artist: Jack Cole
Quality Comics (September 1950 © 1950 Comic Magazines)

"The Menace of Mr. Aqua" ends abruptly when the villain, who can turn into water, is drunk by thirsty sidekick Woozy Winks. When this story was reprinted — after the introduction of the censorious Comics Code — Woozy merely spilled the criminal.

"The Menace of Mr. Aqua" ends abruptly...

Tomahawk #1

Writers: uncredited

Artists: Bruno Premiani, Fred Ray

DC (September-October 1950 © 1950 National Comics Publications, Inc., image courtesy of Heritage Comic Auctions)

Three years after making his debut in Star Spangled Comics, *Revolutionary War freedom fighter Tom Hawk got his own book. Artist Fred Ray, an authority on the era's military uniforms, was a consultant to the Smithsonian Institution and wrote books on American history.*

Freedom fighter Tom Hawk got his own book

Crime Can't Win #41

Writers: uncredited

Artists: Gene Colan, uncredited

Marvel (September 1950 ©* 1950 Comic Combine Corp., image courtesy of Heritage Comic Auctions)

Its numbering continued from teen humor comic Cindy Smith, *this is actually the first issue of Marvel's first crime title. No one did busier crime covers than Marvel, filling nearly every available inch with characters, props, and lurid come-on copy.*

Crime Must Lose! #4

Writers: uncredited

Artists: Allen Bellman, uncredited

Marvel (October 1950 ©* 1950 Sports Action)

Just in case readers didn't get the message about the futility of crime with its previous comic, Marvel followed up with this just a month later. I'm amazed they never got around to publishing a comic called Crime Is Bad, Bad, Bad!

Crime and Punishment #31

Writers: uncredited

Artist: Bill Everett

Lev Gleason (October 1950 © 1950 Lev Gleason Publications, Inc., image courtesy of Heritage Comic Auctions)

The "True Criminal Case History" cover blurb has to be taken with a grain of salt, but Sub-Mariner creator Bill Everett's depiction of a street thug's obsession with getting away with his crime makes "The Button" a memorable short story.

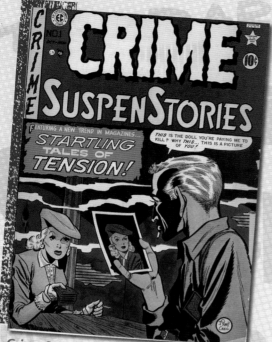

Crime SuspenStories #1

Writers: Johnny Craig, Al Feldstein
Artists: Johnny Craig, Wally Wood
E.C. (October-November 1950 © L.L. Publishing Co., Inc.)

With its tales of unfaithful spouses, white-collar criminals, and ordinary people whose lives take extraordinary turns for the worse, E.C. crafted a different and more mature crime comic while retaining the twist endings so beloved by its readers.

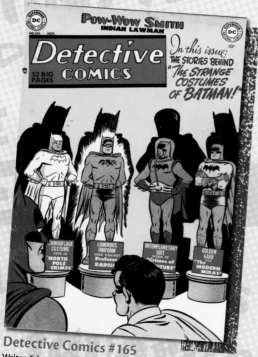

Detective Comics #165

Writer: Edmond Hamilton
Artists: Dick Sprang, Charles Paris
DC (November 1950 © 1950 National Comics Publications, Inc., image courtesy of Heritage Comic Auctions)

Batman always had the best toys, and, in this issue, we learned that he had special costumes for every occasion, including a "gold-cloth costume" used to impersonate a gold statue. Talk about planning for every contingency!

Girl Comics #5

Writers: uncredited
Artists: Russ Heath, uncredited
Marvel (October 1950 © 1950 Cornell Publications, image courtesy of Heritage Comic Auctions)

After four issues as a traditional romance comic, this title added adventure, mystery, and suspense to its stories. This new direction lasted for two years, but the book was cancelled with issue #12 and its numbering continued as *Girl Confessions*.

Real Clue Crime Stories #57

Writers: uncredited
Artists: Bernard Krigstein, uncredited
Hillman (November 1950 ©* 1950 Hillman Periodicals, Inc.)

This was a standard crime comic with the usual contemporary thugs and gangsters. But this issue's "Lily-White Joe" is notable for its superb portrait of a "respectable businessman" who secretly invests in criminal enterprises that escalate beyond his control.

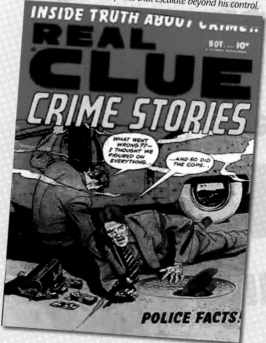

Skypilot #10

Writers: uncredited
Artists: Norman Saunders, Frank Borth
Ziff-Davis (November 1950 © 1950 Ziff-Davis Publishing
Company, image courtesy of Heritage Comic Auctions)

John Hawks is known for his fists and his scripture. Ministering to a bullying lumberjack with the former, he opines, "The meek shall inherit the Earth, as it is written, but sometimes they need a little help."

It Rhymes with Lust

Writers: Arnold Drake and Leslie Waller
Artists: Matt Baker and Ray Osrin
St. John Publications (1950 © 1950 St. John Publishing Company)

Passion and political corruption inflame a steel town in an adult-oriented "picture novel" now recognized as one of the first graphic novels. St. John published a second picture novel — **The Case of the Winking Buddha** — but neither book sold well.

Two-Fisted Tales #19

Writers: Harvey Kurtzman, Johnny Craig
Artists: John Severin, Harvey Kurtzman
E.C. (January-February 1951 © 1950 Fables Publishing Co., Inc.)

More than just a war comic, this anthology took its readers around the world and throughout history in search of adventure. Editor Kurtzman's "Jivaro Death" is a dark tale of a con man who, even in death, manages to cheat his enemies.

Archie's Girls Betty and Veronica #1

Writers: uncredited
Artists: uncredited
Archie (1950 ©* 1950 Archie Publications)

The girls compete for Archie's affections, drive around in a clown car, and have a sleepover in poor little rich girl Veronica's big, lonely mansion. But the funniest story in this key issue has Betty strolling through town with a shotgun.

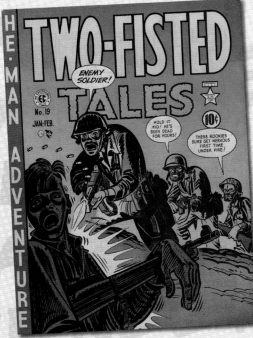

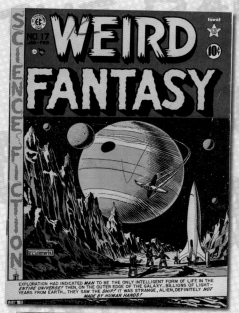

Weird Fantasy #17 (actually, #5)

Writers: Al Feldstein, Harvey Kurtzman
Artists: Al Feldstein, Harvey Kurtzman
E.C. (January-February 1951 © 1950 I.C. Publishing Co., Inc.)

E.C. was always proudest of its science-fiction titles and with good reason. This issue's gems were Feldstein's "Child of Tomorrow," a chilling tale set in the aftermath of an atomic war, and Kurtzman's satirical "The Time Machine and the Shmoe."

Man Comics #6

Writers: Hank Chapman, uncredited
Artists: Sol Brodsky, Mike Sekowsky
Marvel (February 1951 © 1950 Newsstand Publications, Inc., image courtesy of Heritage Comic Auctions)

An insanely jealous stuntman, crooked boxing promoters, a selfless doctor, and his ruthless brother (a hardened criminal looking for an easy score). The brilliant "Black Hate" and three other manly tales make this one of the best comics of the 1950s.

Young Romance #30

Writers: uncredited
Artists: Jack Kirby, Joe Simon
Prize (February 1951 ©* Feature Publications, Inc.)

"Different" is a powerful story about prejudice and, specifically, anti-Semitism. Comics artist-historian Richard Howell writes, "This was obviously a deeply felt effort ... so favored by Jack Kirby (born Jacob Kurtzberg) that he kept most of the original art."

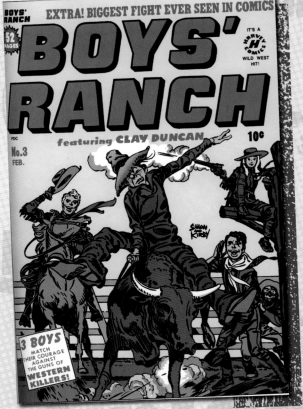

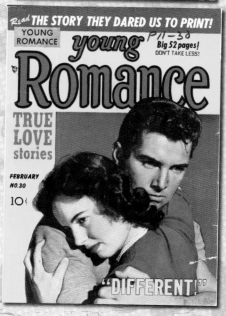

Boys' Ranch #3

Writers: uncredited
Artists: Jack Kirby, Joe Simon
Harvey (February 1951 © 1950 Harvey Features Syndicate)

The greatest Western comic ever. Spurned saloon owner Delilah seeks revenge on rancher Clay Duncan through one of the orphans under his care. But, in the story's heartrending finale, her unexpected love for the boy redeems her.

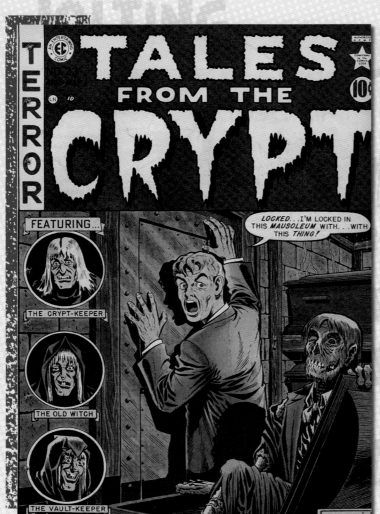

Tales from the Crypt #23

Writer: Al Feldstein
Artists: Al Feldstein, Graham Ingels
E.C. (April-May 1951 © 1951 I.C. Publishing Co., Inc.)

E.C.'s horror comics were its moneymakers, and readers could count on four tales of good ghoulish fun per issue. Feldstein's "Reflection of Death" builds masterfully to its shocking conclusion. Ingels, Jack Davis, and Johnny Craig all shine, as well.

...four tales of
ghoulish fun
per issue.

Lars of Mars #10

Writer: Jerry Siegel
Artist: Murphy Anderson
Ziff-Davis (May 1951 © 1951 Approved Comics, Inc., image courtesy of Heritage Comic Auctions)

Lars is a concerned visitor from a nearby planet, come to Earth to guard against mankind's blowing up the solar system with our nukes. It is super-heroics mixed with satire but, despite clever writing and terrific art, it ran but two issues.

Haunt of Fear #7

Writer: Al Feldstein
Artist: Jack Davis
E.C. (May-June 1951 © 1951 Fables Publishing Co., Inc.)

Simply put, "The Basket" is an unforgettable story. I first read it in a 1965 paperback that reprinted eight EC classics. To this day, the dialogue, "Hey! The basket! He had it on his left shoulder!" still makes me shudder.

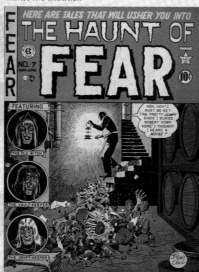

Lone Ranger #38

Writers: Paul S. Newman
Artists: Ernest Nordli, Tom Gill
Dell (August 1951 © 1951 The Lone Ranger, Inc., image courtesy of Heritage Comic Auctions)

The Lone Ranger was a star of radio, comic strips, movie serials, television, and comic books. His Dell series began with comic-strip reprints, switching to original stories with this issue. Sidekicks Tonto and Silver would each headline their own comic-book series, as well.

Roy Rogers' Trigger #2

Writer: Gaylord Du Bois
Artists: uncredited
Dell (September-November 1951 © 1951 Roy Rogers Enterprises)

Trigger's famous owner didn't appear in this comic book, but the golden palomino and "Trigger, Junior" took care of outlaws, rattlesnakes, and cougars on their own. Other equine stars with their own comics: Lone Ranger's Silver, Black Fury, and Mister Ed.

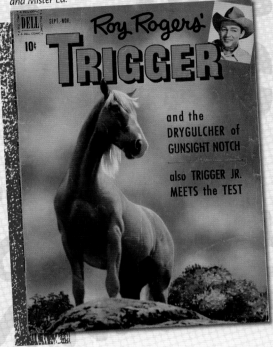

Tarzan #25

Writer: Gaylord Du Bois
Artist: Jesse Marsh
Dell (October 1951 © 1951 Edgar Rice Burroughs, Inc.)

Taking nothing away from Tarzan, but what makes this issue special is the debut of "Brothers of the Spear," the long-running back-up series about two young kings, one black, one white, who join forces to reclaim their thrones and protect their people.

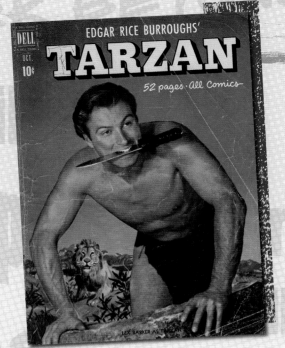

Combat Kelly #1

Writers: Hank Chapman, uncredited
Artists: Russ Heath, uncredited
Marvel (November 1951 ©* 1951 Sphere Publications, image courtesy of Heritage Comic Auctions)

Marvel's first war comic devoted to a single hero. Inspired by John Wayne movies, Kelly was a two-fisted infantryman whose tour of duty outlasted the Korean War and who may well have influenced the later Sgt. *Fury and His Howling Commandos*.

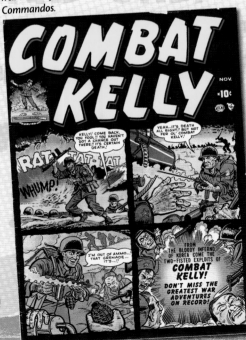

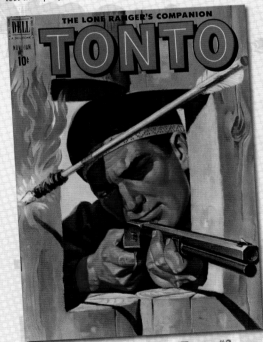

Lone Ranger's Companion Tonto #3

Writers: uncredited
Artists: uncredited
Dell (November 1951 ©* 1951 The Lone Ranger, Inc., image courtesy of Heritage Comic Auctions)

Though there are some who found the character degrading, Tonto has always been portrayed as a heroic, intelligent friend and partner to the Lone Ranger. In this series, he was quite capable of foiling bad guys and helping people on his own.

Venus #17

Writer: Bill Everett
Artist: Bill Everett
Marvel (December 1951 © 1951 Leading Magazine Corp., image courtesy of Heritage Comic Auctions)

She began her career as a super-hero, but Venus adapted to changing times, shifting her title to romance, horror, and science fiction. But no one brought more gusto and sensuality to her adventures than Sub-Mariner creator Bill Everett.

Four Color #367: Donald Duck

Writer: Carl Barks
Artist: Carl Barks
Dell (January 1952 © 1951 Walt Disney Productions)

The best Christmas tale ever created for comics. Donald's nephews want to make a memorable holiday for poor kids, while Uncle Scrooge faces the loss of the fortune he's spent his life building. It's a clever, funny, and heartwarming tale.

House of Mystery #1

Writers: uncredited
Artists: Curt Swan, Bob Brown
DC (December 1951-January 1952 © 1951 National Comics Publications, Inc., image courtesy of Heritage Comic Auctions)

Never as horrific as its contemporary rivals, this anthology title shifted from the supernatural to science fiction after the outcry against those rivals. After playing host to super-heroes in the 1960s, it found its way back to horror in the 1970s.

Thun'da #1

Writer: Gardner Fox
Artist: Frank Frazetta
Magazine Enterprises (January 1952 © 1952 Sussex Publishing Company, Inc., image courtesy of Heritage Comic Auctions)

Created by legendary fantasy painter Frank Frazetta, Thun'da is an American who crashes in a lost valley of dinosaurs ruled by the requisite beautiful princess. It's one of the few comic books with Frazetta art from cover to cover.

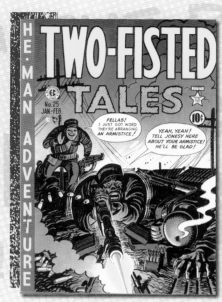

Two-Fisted Tales #25

Writer: Harvey Kurtzman
Artists: Harvey Kurtzman
E.C. (January-February 1952 © 1951 Fables Publishing
Co., Inc.)

Kurtzman's "Corpse on the Imjin" — one of only eight stories he'd draw for this series and Front-line Combat — is a true masterpiece, an eloquent statement of the personal and impersonal nature of war and of war's inevitable consequences.

Chamber of Chills Magazine #6

Writers: uncredited
Artists: Bob Powell, Vic Donahue
Harvey (March 1952 ©* 1951 Witches Tales, Inc.,
image courtesy of Heritage Comic Auctions)

*Best known for **Casper the Friendly Ghost** and **Richie Rich**, Harvey also published gruesome horror comics. In this issue, monsters in the subway tunnels beneath New York City plan to destroy mankind. Not recommended for readers allergic to melting flesh.*

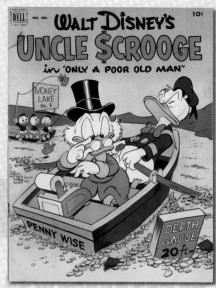

Four Color #386: Uncle Scrooge

Writer: Carl Barks
Artist: Carl Barks
Dell (March 1952 © 1952 Walt Disney Productions)

The essence of Scrooge. He likes to swim in his money, dive in it like a porpoise, burrow through it like a gopher, toss it up and let it hit him on the head. Because no man is poor who can do what he wants once in a while.

Frankenstein Comics #18

Writer: Dick Briefer
Artist: Dick Briefer
Prize (March 1952 © 1951 Feature Publications, Inc., image courtesy of Heritage Comic Auctions)

With horror proving to be a gold mine for comics publishers, Briefer returned to basics for his third and final version of the classic monster. Gone is the Addams Family-style humor, replaced by mad scientists, zombies, werewolves, and killer plants.

...mad scientists, zombies, werewolves, and killer plants.

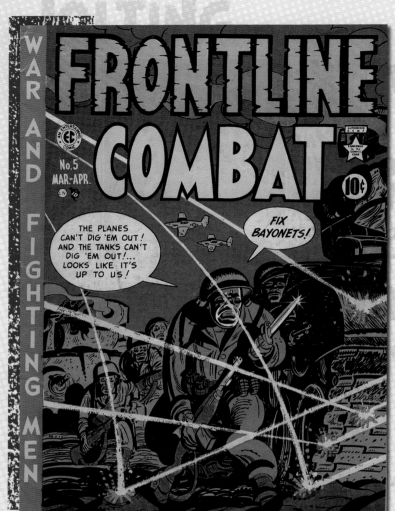

Frontline Combat #5

Writer: Harvey Kurtzman
Artists: Harvey Kurtzman, Jack Davis
E.C. (March-April 1952 © 1951 Tiny Tot Comics, Inc.)

Kurtzman's "Big 'If'" is another of his masterpieces, an intensely human story of the randomness of war. I also have a fondness for his "Stonewall Jackson," a sharp little tale that proves Jack Davis was born to draw Civil War stories.

...an instensely human story of the randomness of war.

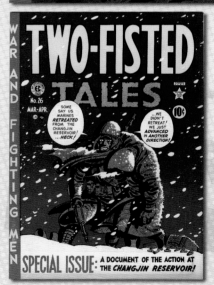

Two-Fisted Tales #26

Writer: Harvey Kurtzman
Artists: John Severin, Jack Davis
E.C. (March-April 1952 © 1951 Fables Publishing Co., Inc., image courtesy of Heritage Comic Auctions)

1950: the Changjin Reservoir was the site of a battle in which the Chinese halted the northward advance of the United Nations forces. It was a gutsy move for Editor Kurtzman to devote an entire issue to that action.

Haunt of Fear #12

Writer: Al Feldstein
Artists: Graham Ingels, Jack Davis
E.C. (March-April 1952 © 1951 Fables Publishing Co., Inc.)

The Ingels-drawn "Poetic Justice" is the best story in this issue, but, when we talk unforgettable, the nod goes to "What's Cookin'?" in which one murderous villain is barbecued and his fat-drippings used to deep-fry his equally murderous partner. Yummy!

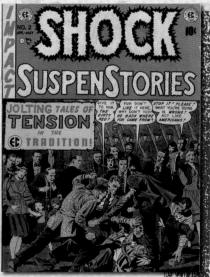

Shock SuspenStories #2

Writer: Al Feldstein
Artists: Jack Kamen, Jack Davis
E.C. (April-May 1952 © 1952 Tiny Tot Comics, Inc.)

My favorite E.C. title. It started out as a sampler of E.C.'s horror, war, crime, and science-fiction stories but found its true voice with "The Patriots," a chilling cautionary tale of patriotic zeal taken to extremes.

Superman #76

Writer: Edmond Hamilton
Artists: Curt Swan, Stan Kaye
DC (May-June 1952 © 1952 National Comics Publications, Inc., image courtesy of Heritage Comic Auctions)

Superman and Batman had palled around on **World's Finest** covers, but this was their first real team-up. They went on a cruise, learned each other's secret identities, caught a smuggler, and outwitted Lois Lane. It was a dream vacation.

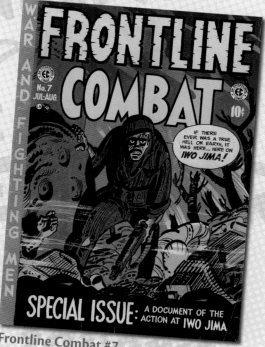

Frontline Combat #7

Writer: Harvey Kurtzman
Artists: Wally Wood, John Severin
E.C. (July-August 1952 © 1952 Tiny Tot Comics, Inc.)

These special issues were a treat for comics readers and military history buffs as well, and Kurtzman's "document" of the battles for Iwo Jima is no exception, blessed as it is with outstanding art by some of E.C.'s finest artists.

Battlefield #2

Writers: Hank Chapman
Artists: Paul Reinman
Marvel (June 1952 ©* 1952 Postal Publications, image courtesy of Heritage Comic Auctions)

E.C. led 1950s comics in quality, but there were many other gems from the decade, as well. Chapman's "Atrocity Story," a topical look at then-current inhumanities, is one of the most powerful war stories ever. Reinman's visuals are equally commanding.

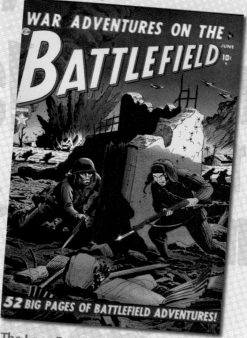

The Lone Ranger's Famous Horse Hi-Yo Silver #3

Writer: uncredited
Artist: uncredited
Dell (July 1952 © 1952 The Lone Ranger, Inc., image courtesy of Heritage Comic Auctions)

How popular were the Western stars of the 1950s? Their **horses** got their own comics! After two issues with Dell's **Four Color** series, Silver's series would run another 34 issues before the last "Hi-yo, Silver, away!" into a setting sun.

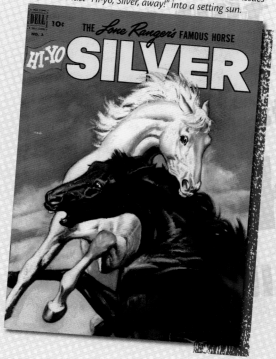

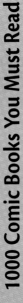

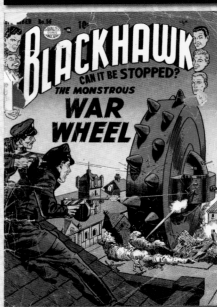

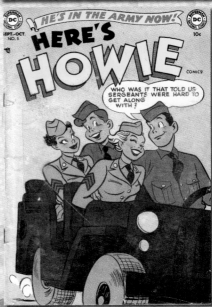

Strange World of Your Dreams #1

Writers: uncredited
Artists: Jack Kirby, Mort Meskin
Prize (August 1952 © 1952 Headline Publications, Inc., image courtesy of Heritage Comic Auctions)

Said to have been "dreamed up" by Meskin, this is one of the oddest horror anthologies of the decade. Stories were allegedly based on actual dreams with the editors offering to buy dreams sent to them by readers.

Blackhawk #56

Writer: uncredited
Artist: Reed Crandall
Quality Comics (September 1952 © 1952 Comic Magazines, image courtesy of Heritage Comic Auctions)

I get a little crazy about this, but "The War Wheel" is the coolest weapon of destruction in comics. The Blackhawks enjoyed a few more good years before their publisher closed shop and sold them to DC, where they were never quite the same.

Here's Howie #5

Writer: uncredited
Artist: Owen Fitzgerald
DC (September-October 1952 © 1952 National Comics Publications, Inc.)

This started as typical teen humor but shifted to military humor, when Howie and best friend Melvin were drafted. This issue has five fast-paced, funny stories starring the new recruits and the comely-but-not-too-bright Winnie the WAC.

Journey into Mystery #3

Writers: uncredited
Artists: Mike Sekowsky, Carmine Infantino
Marvel (October 1952 ©* 1952 Atlas Magazines, Inc., image courtesy of Heritage Comic Auctions)

This is a fine issue with delightfully creepy stories. But, I must confess, it's here because I love its wacky cover, which has nada to do with the cover-listed story and which was likely drawn by the woefully underrated Sol Brodsky.

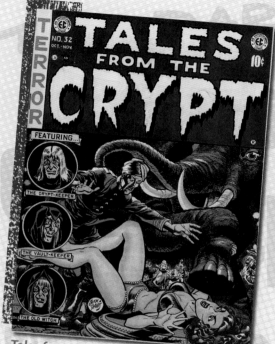

Tales from the Crypt #32

Writer: Al Feldstein
Artist: Jack Davis
E.C. (October-November 1952 © 1952 I.C. Publishing Co., Inc.)

E.C. justice makes me giggle. During World War II, a butcher sells good stuff to rich customers and bad stuff to everyone else. He ends up in his own butcher case. The story is titled " 'Tain't the Meat … It's the Humanity!" I am so very twisted.

Teen-Age Temptations #1

Writer: Dana Dutch
Artist: Matt Baker
St. John (October 1952 ©* 1952 St. John Publishing Co., image courtesy of Heritage Comic Auctions)

Dutch wrote stories of surprisingly liberated — for the era — young women determined to find love on their own terms and, if they made mistakes, learn from them and move on. This issue's "Tourist Cabin Escapade" is one such mistake.

Frontline Combat #9

Writer: Harvey Kurtzman
Artists: John Severin, Jack Davis
E.C. (November-December 1952 © 1952 Tiny Tot Comics, Inc.)

The first of seven planned issues covering the Civil War. Lincoln is profiled, the first shot is fired, men chose sides, and Bull Run makes it clear the war will not end quickly. Sadly, only two more issues of this ambitious effort would be published.

Journey into Fear #10

Writers: uncredited
Artists: uncredited
Superior Publishers Limited (November 1952 ©* 1952 Superior Publications, image courtesy of Heritage Comic Auctions)

The first Canadian horror series earns its place here for the seriously weird "Crawling Evil," wherein a woman who hates men finds a spells book, turns men into worms, and squishes them. Naturally, the worms eventually turn on her.

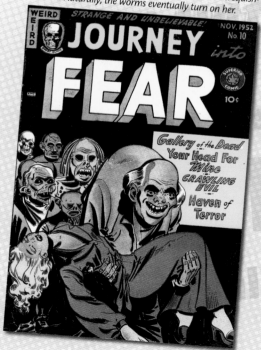

Horrific #3

Writers: uncredited
Artists: uncredited
Comic Media (January 1953 ©* 1952 Harwell Publications, Inc., image courtesy of Heritage Comic Auctions)

*Don Heck did 11 "head shot" covers for this horror anthology title, but this is my favorite and the most literal. In the 1960s, Heck would draw the first Iron Man adventures for Marvel Comics and many early issues of **The Avengers**.*

Weird Science #17

Writers: Al Feldstein, Ray Bradbury
Artists: Wally Wood, Joe Orlando
E.C. (January-February 1953 © 1952 Fables Publishing Co., Inc.)

Two classics in this issue. "Plucked" is a darkly humorous tale of scientific speculation and alien incursions, while "The Long Years" is one of Bradbury's most poignant stories. In the latter, artist Orlando matches the author's craft beat for beat.

Weird Fantasy #17

Writers: Ray Bradbury, Al Feldstein
Artists: Wally Wood
E.C. (January-February 1953 © 1952 I.C. Publishing Co., Inc.)

After Bradbury caught E.C. "borrowing" plots of his stories, he cut a deal allowing them to do credited adaptations. "There Will Come Soft Rains …" is a magnificently illustrated tale of a "smart house" in the aftermath of a nuclear war.

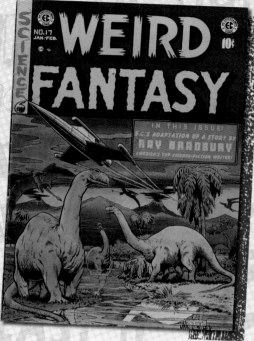

Shock SuspenStories #7

Writers: Ray Bradbury, Al Feldstein
Artists: George Evans, Jack Kamen
E.C. (February-March 1953 © 1952 Tiny Tot Comics, Inc.)

Bradbury's "The Small Assassin" is another unforgettable story with Evans creating haunting visuals throughout the tale. Also in the issue, "Beauty and the Beach" allows Kamen to show his considerable skill in portraying troubled marriages.

Four Color #456: Uncle Scrooge

Writer: Carl Barks
Artist: Carl Barks
Dell (March 1953 © 1953 Walt Disney Productions)

Scrooge returns to the Klondike, the rough-and-tumble land where he made his fortune, and reunites with former flame Glittering Goldie. Five pages were cut from the story's appearance here, including a barroom brawl I once described as "Jack Kirby with ducks!"

Scrooge returns to the Klondike... and reunites with Glittering Goldie.

Weird Fantasy #18

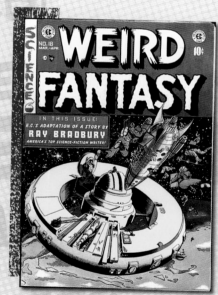

Writer: Al Feldstein
Artist: Joe Orlando
E.C. (March-April 1953 © 1953 I.C. Publishing Co., Inc.)

Comics have often addressed racial injustice, but no story ever hit me as hard as Feldstein's "Judgment Day." Orlando's closing panel conveys the pain that lingers even centuries after such prejudice has been overcome. Arguably E.C.'s finest hour.

Mad #4

Writer: Harvey Kurtzman
Artists: Wally Wood, Bill Elder
E.C. (April-May 1953 © 1953 Educational Comics, Inc.)

Before Mad the magazine became an American institution, it was the funniest comic book on the planet. In this issue, Kurtzman sends up two pop-culture icons with his hilarious "Superduperman!" and the inspired "Shadow!"

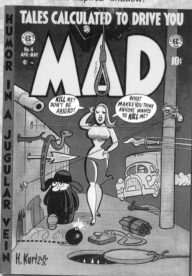

Frontline Combat #12

Writer: Harvey Kurtzman
Artists: George Evans, Alex Toth
E.C. (May-June 1953 © 1953 Tiny Tot Comics, Inc.)

This special issue is a positive portrayal of the Air Force at home and in Korea. The lead story stresses the importance of the Ground Observer Corps, and the inside back cover invites readers to sign up for that civilian organization.

Pictorial Romances #19

Writer: Dana Dutch
Artist: Matt Baker
St. John (May 53 © 1953 St. John Publishing Co.)

In "Elopement Hid Our Sins," Jen, weary of her reputation as a pick-up, agrees to become a bride in name only to Eddie, who's hiding his own sins. It's a compelling drama in which both characters grow in surprising and satisfying ways.

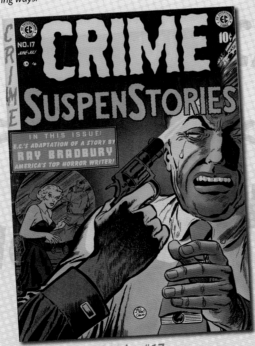

Crime SuspenStories #17

Writers: Ray Bradbury, Al Feldstein
Artists: Johnny Craig, Jack Kamen
E.C. (June-July 1953 © 1952 L.L. Publishing Co., Inc.)

Craig's adaptation of Bradbury's "Touch and Go" has been called "a technical masterpiece" and it is. But readers shouldn't overlook Feldstein's cleverly connected "One for the Money ..." and "... Two for the Show" with art by Jack Kamen and Bill Elder.

Casper, the Friendly Ghost #10

Writers: uncredited
Artists: uncredited
Harvey (June 1953 © 1953 Paramount Pictures Corporation, image courtesy of Heritage Comic Auctions)

Casper's stories are basic: He tries to avoid scaring people while other ghosts try to scare them. This issue introduces his city-bred cousin Spooky — "The Tuff Little Ghost" — who finds the country far more frightening than any urban apparitions.

Menace #5

Writer: Stan Lee
Artists: Bill Everett, Joe Maneely
Marvel (July 1953 ©* 1953 Hercules Publishing Corp., image courtesy of Heritage Comic Auctions)

This horror anthology seems to have been a favorite of Lee's, as he often wrote entire issues. The Everett-drawn "Zombie" would be "revived" in the 1970s as the star of Marvel's black-and-white horror magazine *Tales of the Zombie*.

1000 Comic Books You Must Read

Weird Science #20

Writers: Al Feldstein, Ray Bradbury
Artists: Wally Wood, Al Williamson
E.C. (July-August 1953 © 1953 Fables Publishing Co., Inc.)

Future lust is the driving force of Bradbury's "Surprise Package" and the Williamson-drawn "50 Girls 50" — but it's "The Loathsome" that will break your heart and stay with you forever: "To whoever finds this note … I love you."

Black Cat Mystery #45

Writers: Bob Powell, uncredited
Artists: Bob Powell, Howard Nostrand
Harvey (August 1953 ©* 1953 Harvey Features Syndicate, image courtesy of Heritage Comic Auctions)

The Black Cat's crime-fighting exploits had been replaced by horror stories two years earlier. This issue has one of the better ones. Powell's "Colorama" is a downright psychedelic tale of a man whose life is suddenly overwhelmed by blobs of color.

Strange Fantasy #7

Writers: uncredited
Artists: uncredited
Ajax/Farrell (August 1953 ©* 1953, image courtesy of Heritage Comic Auctions)

Dozens of publishers launched horror comics to cash in on the trend and some added kink to the mix. In "Grave Rehearsal," a whip-wielding health-resort operator covers her rich clients in soothing mud and then not-so-soothing cement.

Little Dot #1

Writers: uncredited
Artists: uncredited
Harvey (September 1953 ©* 1953 Harvey Publications, image courtesy of Heritage Comic Auctions)

Little Dot has three claims to fame: her nigh-psychotic obsession with dots, an impossibly huge family of uncles and aunts with their own obsessions, and, in one of this issue's back-up stories, she gave Richie Rich his start in comics.

Three Stooges #1

Writer: uncredited
Artist: Norman Maurer
St. John (September 1953 © 1953 St. John Publishing Co., image courtesy of Heritage Comic Auctions)

Moe Howard got more than a son-in-law, when his daughter Joan married Norman Maurer in 1947. Two years later, Maurer produced the first Three Stooges comic book, and his association with The Stooges continued for decades in comics, movies, and cartoons.

Moe Howard got more than a son-in-law...

1,000,000 Years Ago #1

Writer: Joe Kubert
Artist: Joe Kubert
St. John (September 1953 © 1953 St. John Publishing Co., image courtesy of Heritage Comic Auctions)

His conscience and decency set Tor apart from the other men of his prehistoric era. His perilous encounters with dinosaurs, tyrants, and volcanoes thrilled readers, but his stories doubled as subtle psychological inquiries into the nature of man.

Pogo Parade #1

Writer: Walt Kelly
Artist: Walt Kelly
Dell (September 1953 © 1944, 1945. 1946, 1947, 1953 Walt Kelly)

There would only be a few more new Pogo comics after this special issue reprinting nearly 100 pages of classics from the 1940s Animal Comics. But Pogo had a good run in comic books and an even better one in newspapers.

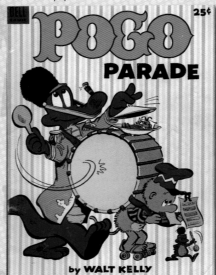

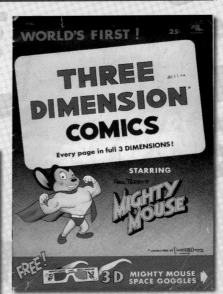

Three Dimension Comics #1

Writers: uncredited
Artists: uncredited
St. John (September 1953 © 1953 Terrytoons, Inc.)

Joe Kubert saw 3-D magazines while stationed in Germany and came up with the idea of 3-D comics. With partner Norm Maurer, he converted an issue of Mighty Mouse into the format. It was a huge, instant, and short-lived success.

Weird Fantasy #21

Writers: Ray Bradbury, Al Feldstein
Artists: John Severin, Will Elder
E.C. (September-October 1953 © 1953 I.C. Publishing Co., Inc., image courtesy of Heritage Comic Auctions)

E.C.'s Ray Bradbury adaptations were among the finest comics stories ever. The restrictive Comics Code would end that partnership but, thankfully, not before this issue's "The Million Year Picnic," one of the author's best Martian tales.

Daring Love #1

Writer: uncredited
Artist: Steve Ditko
Key Publications (September-October 1953 © Gilmor Magazines, Inc., image courtesy of Heritage Comic Auctions)

This issue's "Paper Romance" is the first published work of the co-creator of Spider-Man. According to comics historian Blake Bell, "So buried was this title in the dustbin of history that Ditko's contributions went undiscovered until the late 1980s."

Haunt of Fear #21

Writers: Al Feldstein
Artists: Reed Crandall
E.C. (September-October 1953 © 1953 Fables Publishing Co., Inc.)

To the end, E.C. brought its readers the best in horror. Set in 1867 Paris, "The High Cost of Dying" is a tale of a grieving husband who seeks the means to bury his wife before a corrupt official sells her body to medical students.

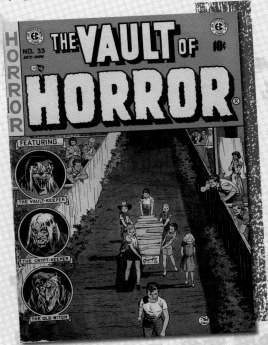

Vault of Horror #33

Writers: Al Feldstein, Bill Gaines
Artists: Johnny Craig, Jack Davis
E.C. (October-November 1953 © 1953 L.L. Publishing Co., Inc.)

A group of solemn kids hold a funeral procession past their amused, baffled parents. But why have they asked adults about such things as kidnapping, jury trials, and penalties? "Let the Punishment Fit the Crime" is yet another unforgettable E.C. shocker.

Walt Disney's Comics & Stories #158

Writer: Carl Barks
Artist: Carl Barks
Dell (November 1953 © 1950, 1953 Walt Disney Productions, image courtesy of Heritage Comic Auctions)

My favorite Donald Duck story. His nephews raise bees for a Junior Woodchucks contest and he ends up hospitalized. Offered bread with their prize-winning honey, he painfully, proudly proclaims, "Ah! We parents! What rich rewards we reap!"

Weird Science #22

Writers: Al Feldstein, Ray Bradbury
Artists: Wally Wood, Joe Orlando
E.C. (November-December 1953 © 1953 Fables Publishing Co., Inc.)

The last issue before merging with Weird Fantasy. "My World" is a spectacularly drawn love letter to science fiction, while Bradbury's "Outcast of the Stars" — about a poor man determined to give his children the stars — still brings tears to my eyes.

Shock SuspenStories #12

Writer: Al Feldstein
Artists: Joe Orlando, Reed Crandall
E.C. (December 1953-January 1954 © 1953 Tiny Tot Comics, Inc.)

Two punch-to-the-gut Feldstein classics. "The Monkey" grimly traces the descent of a teenager into drug addiction. "The Kidnapper" has a man trying to save his wife from the madness that took her with the kidnapping of their baby.

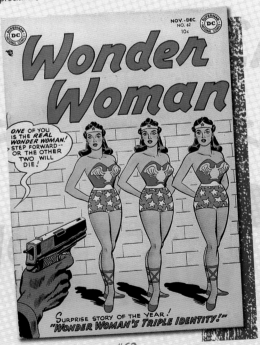

Wonder Woman #62

Writer: Robert Kanigher
Artist: Harry G. Peter
DC (November-December 1953 © 1953 National Comics Publications, Inc., image courtesy of Heritage Comic Auctions)

Covers and stories with multiple Wonder Women were a frequent bit in this comic. This issue also features the Amazon relighting the magical "Lamp of the Leprechauns" with fire from Halley's Comet and the "origin" of her earrings. Really.

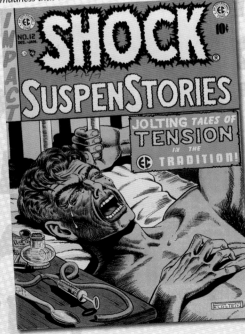

Young Men #24

Writers: uncredited, Bill Everett
Artists: Russ Heath, John Romita
Marvel (December 1953 © Interstate Publishing Corp., image courtesy of Heritage Comic Auctions)

The Human Torch, Captain America, and Sub-Mariner are back! Sadly, despite outstanding art, especially by Sub-Mariner creator Everett, the time wasn't right for the return of the heroes. They would all be back in retirement within two years.

> ...the time wasn't right for the return of the heroes.

Weird Science-Fantasy #23

Writers: Al Feldstein, Ray Bradbury
Artists: Wally Wood, Bernard Krigstein
E.C. (Spring 1954 © 1953 Fables Publishing Co., Inc.)

Feldstein launches E.C.'s now-solitary science-fiction anthology with "The Children," in which creeping fear gives way to a heartwarming display of parental love. In the issue's other gem, Krigstein gives an elegant look to Bradbury's "The Flying Machine."

Fantastic Fears #5

Writer: Bruce Hamilton
Artist: Steve Ditko
Ajax/Farrell (January-February 1954 © 1953 [no holder listed; published by Four Star Publications, Inc.], image courtesy of Heritage Comic Auctions)

"Stretching Things," Ditko's first professional comics assignment, reveals his already-evident talent. Hamilton would become a renowned comics historian and, in the 1980s, publish a 30-volume hardcover set reprinting all 500-plus Disney Duck stories of Carl Barks.

Panic #1

Writer: Al Feldstein
Artists: Bill Elder, Jack Davis
E.C. (February-March 1954 © 1953 Tiny Tot Comics, Inc.)

This comic was literally banned in Boston for Feldstein and Elder's hilariously irreverent take on "The Night before Christmas." The other highlight of the issue is "My Gun Is the Jury," a Davis-drawn parody of Mickey Spillane's I, the Jury.

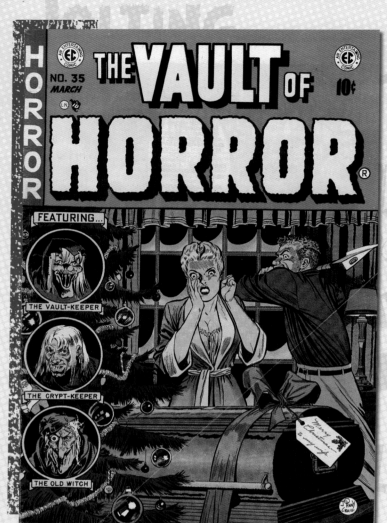

Vault of Horror #35

Writer: Johnny Craig
Artists: Johnny Craig, Graham Ingels
E.C. (February-March 1954 © 1954 L.L. Publishing Co., Inc.)

"And All through the House ..." is a chilling **noir** tale of spousal murder and a maniac dressed as Santa. The issue also has *"Shoe-Button Eyes,"* in which a teddy bear administers vengeance on an abusive stepfather.

> ...a chilling noir tale of spousal murder and a maniac dressed as Santa.

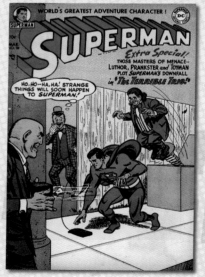

Superman #88

Writers: William Woolfolk
Artists: Wayne Boring, Stan Kaye
DC (March 1954 © 1954 National Comics Publications, Inc., image courtesy of Heritage Comic Auctions)

Luthor teams up with the Prankster and the Toyman in "The Terrible Trio." Did he lose a bet? Also in this issue, Clark Kent works in construction and as a truck driver for a *Daily Planet* story on "The Toughest Job in the World!"

Crime SuspenStories #22

Writer: Al Feldstein
Artists: Reed Crandall, Bernard Krigstein
E.C. (April-May 1954 © 1954 L.L. Publishing Co., Inc.)

Publisher Bill Gaines defended this cover before Congress as being in good taste because it didn't show blood dripping from the severed head. However, before being cropped — with new art added to the top — the original art showed just that.

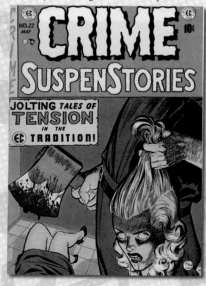

Queen of the West Dale Evans #3

Writer: uncredited
Artist: uncredited
Dell (April-June 1954 © 1954 Dale Evans Enterprises, image courtesy of Heritage Comic Auctions)

After two years of DC's *Dale Evans Comics*, Dell licensed the rights to publish new adventures of The Queen of the West. Artists on the series included Alex Toth, Russ Manning, and Warren Tufts, and the last issue was published in 1959.

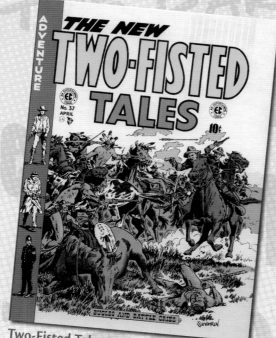

Two-Fisted Tales #37

Writer: Colin Dawkins
Artists: John Severin
E.C. (April 1954 © 1954 Fables Publishing Co., Inc.)

With **Frontline Combat**, E.C.'s other war series, canceled, **Two-Fisted** switched to general adventure tales, got a new editor (Severin), and added such recurring characters as Black Jack Slaughter, Cheyenne Hawk, and Ruby Ed Coffee.

Black Magic Vol. 4 #6

Writer: uncredited
Artists: Jack Kirby, Bruno Premiani
Prize (May-June 1954 ©* 1954 Crestwood Publishing Co., Inc., image courtesy of Heritage Comic Auctions)

Joe Simon and Jack Kirby never went in for blood and gore in their "horror" comics but they knew how to bring the scary to the party. In "The Head of the Family," a woman in love discovers her future in-laws are unlike any family she's ever seen.

Ghost Comics #11

Writers: uncredited
Artists: George Evans, Jerry Grandenetti
Fiction House (Summer 1954 © 1954 Fiction House, Inc., image courtesy of Heritage Comic Auctions)

This horror anthology mixed new material with reprints of various series from earlier Fiction House titles, such as "Werewolf Hunter" and "The Secret Files of Dr. Drew" from the 1940s **Rangers Comics**. This was the final issue of the title.

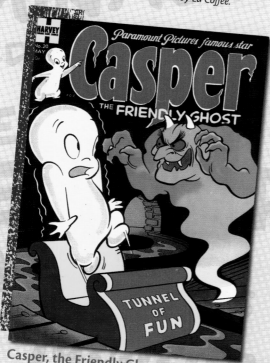

Casper, the Friendly Ghost #20

Writer: uncredited
Artist: uncredited
Harvey (May 1954 © 1954 Paramount Pictures Corporation, image courtesy of Heritage Comic Auctions)

This issue introduced Wendy the Good Little Witch as a friend for Casper and a back-up strip. Wendy could relate to Casper; he lived with The Ghostly Trio and she with her traditionally witchy aunts. She received her own title in 1960.

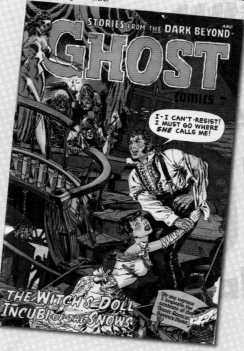

Writers: Harvey Kurtzman
Artists: Will Elder, Wally Wood
E.C. (June 1954 © 1954 Educational Comics, Inc., image courtesy of Heritage Comic Auctions)

My favorite issue, due in no small part to "Starchie," Kurtzman's delightfully vicious parody of Archie. The satirical master also sliced-and-diced the movie **From Here to Eternity,** *the comic strip* **Mark Trail,** *and 3-D comics.*

Batman #84

Writers: David Vern
Artists: Sheldon Moldoff, Stan Kaye
DC (June 1954 © 1954 National Comics Publications, Inc., image courtesy of Heritage Comic Auctions)

Catwoman enters a beauty contest, succumbs with other contestants to a strange sleeping sickness, wakes up, wins the prize, and it's all part of a diamond-smuggling scheme. Does crime really have to be **this** *complicated?*

Teen-Age Temptations #8

Writer: Dana Dutch
Artist: Matt Baker
St. John (June 1954 © 1954 St. John Publishing Co.)

In the shocking "Masquerade Marriage," predators trick two women into sex via a **faux** *minister and sham marriages. The sex happens between scenes, but it clearly does happen. It still packs a wallop 55 years after it was written.*

Marvel Family #89

Writer: uncredited
Artist: Kurt Schaffenberger
Fawcett (June 1954 © 1953 Fawcett Publications, Inc., image courtesy of Heritage Comic Auctions)

This cover is particularly apt. Captain Marvel, the only competitor to give Superman a run for his money, reaches the end of his Golden Age adventures. He and his family would not be seen again until DC published **Shazam!** *#1 in 1973.*

Walt Disney's Uncle Scrooge #6

Writer: Carl Barks
Artist: Carl Barks
Dell (June-August 1954 © 1954 Walt Disney Productions)

When Scrooge suffers a money-related nervous breakdown, Donald and the boys take him to Tralla La, a valley in the Himalayas with no monetary system — until Scrooge inadvertently creates one. A classic tale of avarice and humanity.

Strange Suspense Stories #19

Writers: uncredited
Artists: Steve Ditko, Joe Shuster
Charlton (July 1954 © 1954 Charlton Comics Group, image courtesy of Heritage Comic Auctions)

Charlton was the lord of low-budget comics, but it did publish many good issues and gave work to many down-on-their-luck artists. Ditko excelled there — check out this cover — and Superman co-creator Shuster drew his final stories for the company.

The Thing #15

Writers: uncredited
Artist: Steve Ditko
Charlton (July-August 1954 © 1954 Charlton Comics Group, image courtesy of Heritage Comic Auctions)

*This issue has Ditko art from cover to cover. "The Worm Turns" is a terrifying **tour de force** of mad scientist and monster mayhem in which laws of nature are violated, civilization is destroyed, and mankind's destruction is inevitable. Or is it?*

Action Comics #195

Writer: William Woolfolk
Artists: Wayne Boring, Stan Kaye
DC (August 1954, image courtesy of Heritage Comic Auctions)

When she witnesses Tiger Woman knock Clark Kent into molten steel, Lois Lane goes into shock and assumes the criminal's identity. I find it disturbing that Lois is so incredibly hot as a villainess. Maybe she missed her true calling.

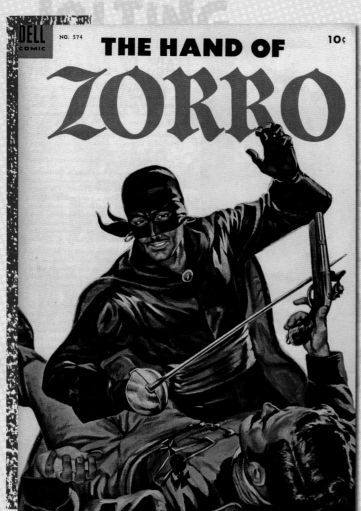

Four Color #574: Hand of Zorro

Writer: Paul S. Newman
Artist: Everett Raymond Kinstler
Dell (August 1954 © 1954 Johnston McCulley, image courtesy of Heritage Comic Auctions)

The fourth of seven adaptations of the original Johnston McCulley novels. Kinstler would become a revered portrait painter. His work hangs in the National Portrait Gallery; his subjects include John Wayne, Ronald Reagan, and the first President Bush.

Kinstler would become a revered portrait painter.

Shock SuspenStories #16

Writer: Carl Wessler
Artist: Reed Crandall
E.C. (August-September 1954 © 1954 Tiny Tot Comics, Inc.)

Veteran writer Wessler produced thousands of stories for all kinds of comics and all four stories in this issue. "A Kind of Justice" is bold even by E.C. standards: a chilling tale of rape, mob fury, and the abuse of power.

Casper, The Friendly Ghost #24

Writers: uncredited
Artists: uncredited
Harvey (September 1954 © 1954 Paramount Pictures Corporation)

*I love "comics in the comics" stories. Casper befriends an artist and, with him, creates a hit comic book starring … Casper! But making up stories about helping people isn't as satisfying to the friendly ghost as **actually** helping people.*

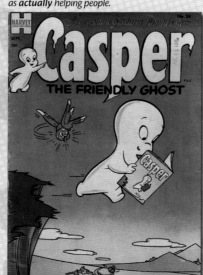

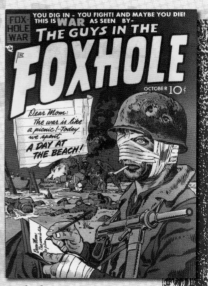

Foxhole #1

Writers: uncredited
Artist: Jack Kirby
Mainline (September 1954 © 1954 Mainline Publications, Inc., image courtesy of Heritage Comic Auctions)

He didn't go for blood in spooky comics, but Kirby wasn't reticent about showing the horrors of war. He'd learned war close up, and his battlefield experience shows on what could be the most powerful war-comic cover of all.

World's Greatest Songs Illustrated #1

Writers: uncredited
Artists: Russ Heath, Joe Maneely
Marvel (September 1954 ©* 1954 Male Publications, image
courtesy of Heritage Comic Auctions)

A one-hit wonder. This odd title took lyrics to songs performed by such contemporary stars as Eddie Fisher and Frank Sinatra and turned them into comics. This one and only issue also featured Fisher's life story ... in four pages!

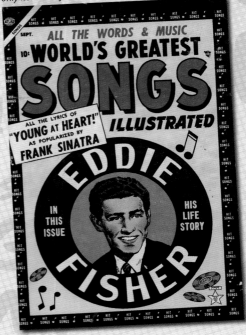

Adventures of Dean Martin and Jerry Lewis #16

Writers: uncredited
Artists: uncredited
DC (October 1954 © 1954 York Pictures Corporation, image courtesy of Heritage Comic Auctions)

Dean Martin and Jerry Lewis were superstars of radio, movies, and TV. DC figured they would be equally successful in their own comic. They headlined 40 issues until their real-life breakup necessitated a change in the comic book's format.

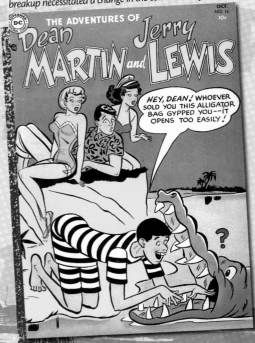

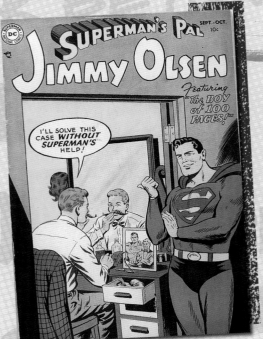

Superman's Pal, Jimmy Olsen #1

Writer: Otto Binder
Artists: Curt Swan, Ray Burnley
DC (September-October 1954 © 1954 National Comics Publications, Inc., image courtesy of Heritage Comic Auctions)

Jack Larson's portrayal of Jimmy on TV's **Adventures of Superman** was so popular the cub reporter got his own comic within two years of the series' launch. The Jimmy of these early issues was less of a goof than he became in the 1960s.

Piracy #1

Writers: uncredited
Artists: Wally Wood, Reed Crandall
E.C. (October-November 1954 © 1954 I.C. Publishing Co., Inc.)

The loss of its profitable horror titles led E.C. to new directions. This anthology of sea stories was meticulously researched to be as true to life as possible but it never found an audience and ended after only six issues.

Black Magic Vol. 5 #3

Writer: uncredited
Artists: Jack Kirby, Joe Simon
Prize (November-December 1954 ©* 1954 Crestwood
Publications, image courtesy of Heritage Comic Auctions)

Before Jaws, *there was "Lone Shark!" A shark is mutated by undersea atomic testing and grows a tumor-like second brain, giving him human intelligence. He's so smart that he's actually the narrator of this scary and simultaneously sad story.*

Weird Science-Fantasy #26

Writer: Al Feldstein
Artists: Wally Wood, Reed Crandall
E.C. (December 1954 © 1954 Fables Publishing Co., Inc.)

Publisher Gaines and Editor Feldstein devoted this entire issue to supposedly factual illustrated accounts of flying saucers. The documentary-style presentation ended with E.C. challenging the Air Force "to tell us the truth about the flying saucers."

Classics Illustrated #124: The War of the Worlds

Writers: H.G. Wells, Henry Miller
Artist: Lou Cameron
Gilberton (January 1955 ©* 1954 Gilberton Co.)

One of the few Classics I bought myself ... because War of the Worlds *is my favorite Wells novel and because the art captured the story so well. Cameron also painted paperback covers and wrote several novels and more than 300 short stories.*

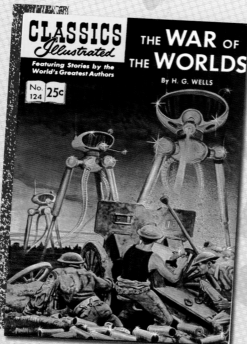

Tales from the Crypt #46

Writer: Al Feldstein
Artists: Jack Davis, George Evans
E.C. (February-March 1955 © 1954 I.C. Publishing Co., Inc., image courtesy of Heritage Comic Auctions)

The last issue of the E.C. horror comics goes out with stories drawn by Davis, Joe Orlando, Graham Ingles, and one more classic: "Blind Alleys" by Feldstein and George Evans. "And then some idiot turned out the lights!"

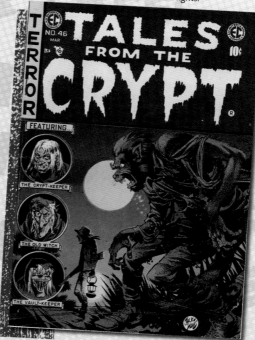

Adventure Comics #210

Writer: Otto Binder
Artist: Curt Swan, Sy Barry
DC (March 1955 ©* 1954 National Comics Publications, Inc., image courtesy of Heritage Comic Auctions)

Krypto lands in Smallville. He was Superboy's dog on Krypton until Jor-El used him as a test animal and shot him into space. Most of us would have serious issues with a father who did that to our pet. The Kents raised Kal-El right.

Impact #1

Writers: Al Feldstein, Carl Wessler
Artists: Reed Crandall, Bernard Krigstein
E.C. (March-April 1955 © 1954 I.C. Publishing Company, Inc.)

Every story in this issue is a gem, but Krigstein's groundbreaking storytelling for Feldstein's "Master Race" elevated the tale of a concentration camp commander's final moments to masterpiece status. One of the greatest stories in comics history.

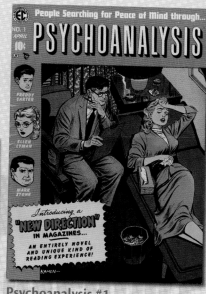

Psychoanalysis #1

Writer: uncredited
Artist: Jack Kamen
E.C. (March-April 1955 © 1955 Tiny Tot Comics, Inc.)

The oddest of E.C.'s "New Direction" titles featured tales of three "people searching for peace of mind" through sessions with a never-named psychiatrist. One patient was "cured" in the third issue and the remaining two in the fourth and final issue.

Extra! #1

Writers: Johnny Craig, unknown
Artists: Johnny Craig, John Severin
E.C. (March-April 1955 © 1955 L.L. Publishing Co., Inc.)

My favorite of E.C.'s "New Direction" books. Reporter Keith Michaels, photographer Rick Rampant, and "roving newspaperman" MacDuff chased stories around the world. Pretty Geri Hamilton took MacDuff's spot with the third of the title's five issues.

They chased stories around the world

1000 Comic Books You Must Read

80

My Girl Pearl #1

Writer: Stan Lee
Artist: Dan DeCarlo
Marvel (April 1955 ©* 1955 Atlas)

*Who knows what modern readers would make of "America's Darling Dim-Wit?" Lee loved writing humor comics with gorgeous girls, and no one drew those girls better than DeCarlo, who would set the style for **Betty & Veronica** in the 1960s.*

> Lee loved writing humor comics with gorgeous girls.

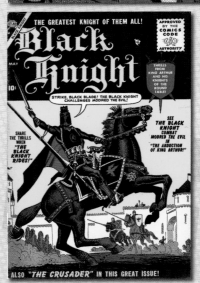

Black Knight #1

Writer: Stan Lee
Artist: Joe Maneely
Marvel (May 1955 © 1955 Margood Publishing Corp., image courtesy of Heritage Comic Auctions)

Sir Percy seemed no more than a foppish fool but he was secretly The Black Knight, King Arthur's bravest and most powerful warrior. Armed with a mystic sword forged by Merlin, he fought for Camelot through five exquisitely drawn issues.

My Greatest Adventure #3

Writers: uncredited
Artists: John Prentice, uncredited
DC (May-June 1955 ©* 1955 National Comics Publications, Inc., image courtesy of Heritage Comic Auctions)

This anthology title specialized in such first-person adventure stories as "I Found Captain Kidd's Treasure!" It soon switched to more fantastic thrillers: "I Was a Cop from Outer Space!" and "We Fought the Giant of Island X!"

Valor #2

Writers: Carl Wessler, uncredited
Artists: Al Williamson, Bernard Krigstein
E.C. (May-June 1955 © 1955 L.L. Publishing Co., Inc.)

Historical adventure — heavy on knights and gladiators — was the theme of this "New Direction" title. Yet valor could come from the most unlikely individuals, as was the case with poet Chou Po in the Krigstein-drawn "Poetic Justice."

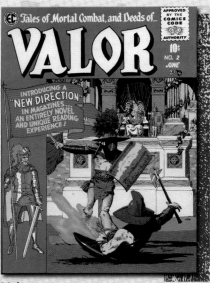

Annie Oakley #5
Writers: uncredited
Artists: Ross Andru, Mike Esposito
Marvel (June 1955 © 1955 Annie Oakley Enterprises)

Historical figures are fair game for any publisher, but only Marvel and Dell gave sharpshooter Annie her own title. Dell's was based on a TV show; Marvel's featured the first in a long line of beauties drawn by the Andru-Esposito team.

M.D. #2
Writers: Carl Wessler, uncredited
Artists: Joe Orlando, Graham Ingels
E.C. (June-July 1955; © 1955 Fables Publishing Co., Inc.)

Dedicated doctors were the heroes of this "New Direction" title, and the "villains" they battled were leukemia, cerebral palsy, optical hypertension, and a brain tumor. Compelling human-interest stories make this another favorite of mine.

Boy Comics #112
Writers: Charles Biro, Virginia Hubbell
Artists: Joe Kubert, Carl Hubbell
Lev Gleason (June 1955 © 1955 Lev Gleason Enterprises Corp.)

The new Comics Code Authority was not enamored of the word "crime," so teen hero Crimebuster became known as just plain Chuck Chandler, and his adventures took on more of a human interest vibe. Gleason would cease publishing by year's end.

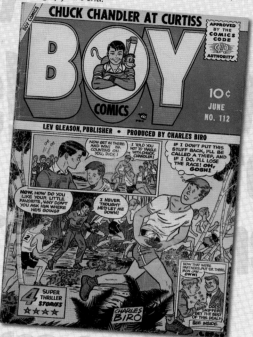

Mad #24
Writers: Harvey Kurtzman, Ernie Kovacs
Artists: Will Elder, Wally Wood
EC (July 1955 © 1955 Educational Comics, Inc., image courtesy of Heritage Comic Auctions)

With the Comics Code stacked against them, Publisher Bill Gaines and Editor Kurtzman turned their most successful comic into an even more successful magazine, recruiting such celebrity writers as Kovacs, Stan Freberg, Bob and Ray, and even Eli Wallach.

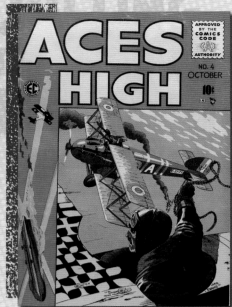

Aces High #4

Writers: Carl Wessler, uncredited
Artists: Wally Wood, Jack Davis
E.C. (September-October 1955 © 1955 L.L. Publishing Co., Inc.)

Devoted to tales of World War I aerial combat, though World War II stories ran in its fifth and final issue. This issue's "The Novice and the Ace" is a cautionary yarn about fear and perception with a cunning twist ending.

Little Dot #13

Writers: uncredited
Artists: uncredited
Harvey (September 1955 © 1955 Harvey Features Syndicate)

No disrespect to Dot, but the "From Richie to Rags" backup is what makes this issue special. When Richie's poor pals think his family is broke, they help him earn money. Like him, they know friendship is more important than wealth.

Incredible Science Fiction #31

Writer: Jack Oleck
Artists: Roy G. Krenkel, Wally Wood
E.C. (September-October 1955 © 1955 Fables Publishing Co., Inc.)

Under a new name, E.C.'s science-fiction tradition was drawing to a close. In this issue appear fantasy artist Roy G. Krenkel's only solo E.C. work, two stories drawn by Wood, and one by Bernard Krigstein. The title would end with #33.

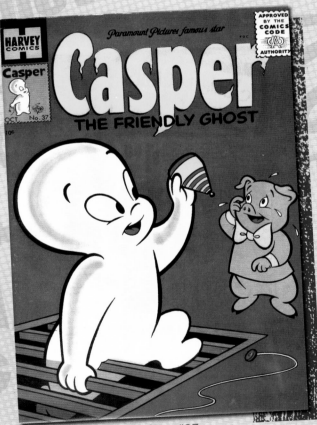

Casper, the Friendly Ghost #37

Writers: uncredited
Artists: uncredited
Harvey (October 1955 ©* 1955 Paramount Pictures Corporation, image courtesy of Heritage Comic Auctions)

When Wendy struggles to clean her aunts' rundown house, Casper asks "The Witch Widow" for a magical home makeover. The sexy widow flies on a vacuum cleaner and could be a dark-haired ringer for Elizabeth Montgomery in TV's Bewitched, which made its debut in 1964.

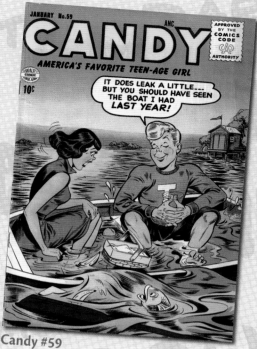

Candy #59

Writers: uncredited
Artists: uncredited
Quality Comics (January 1956 © 1955 Comic Magazines)

Sassy Candy was like Archie's Betty in that she came from a typical middle-class family and like Veronica in her determination to get what she wants without regard for her long-suffering boyfriend, Ted. Her title would end with #64.

Sugar and Spike #1

Writer: Sheldon Mayer
Artist: Sheldon Mayer
DC (April-May 1956 © 1956 National Comics Publications, Inc.)

Toddlers Sugar Plumm and Cecil "Spike" Wilson can talk with each other and to other infants. Their attempts to figure out the adult world around them are unfailingly hilarious, making this comic book Mayer's greatest masterpiece.

Uncle Scrooge #13

Writer: Carl Barks
Artist: Carl Barks
Dell (March-May 1956 © 1956 Walt Disney Productions)

When earthquakes threaten Scrooge's money bin, Donald, the boys, and he investigate and learn the quakes are the result of a sporting competition between underground dwellers known as Terries and Fermies. "Land Beneath the Ground" is a Barks classic.

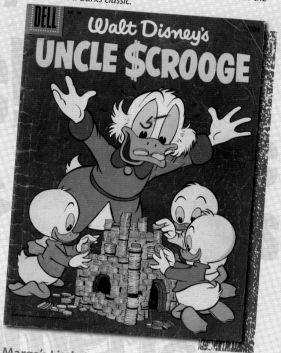

Marge's Little Lulu and Her Friends #4

Writer: John Stanley
Artist: John Stanley, Irving Tripp
Dell (1956 © 1956 Marjorie Henderson Buell)

This 100-page spectacular is filled with Lulu getting the better of Tubby and the boys, Lulu telling stories to Alvin as she baby-sits him, and master detective Tubby proving, once again, that the **crime du jour** was committed by Lulu's father!

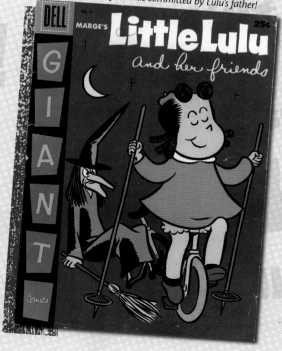

Superboy #49

Writers: Jerry Coleman, Otto Binder
Artists: John Sikela
DC (June 1956 ©* 1956 National Comics Publications, Inc., image courtesy of Heritage Comic Auctions)

Superboy is stranded on an asteroid surrounded by kryptonite dust; an ancient robot from Krypton is "Friday" to his "Robinson Crusoe." Plus: "The Loneliest Boy in Town" finds new respect for his doorman father after Dad helps Superboy on a case.

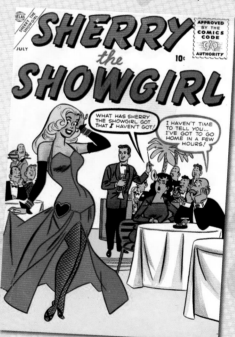

Sherry the Showgirl #1

Writer: uncredited
Artist: Dan DeCarlo
Marvel (August 1956 ©* 1956 Atlas)

Besides that she appeared in about a dozen comics in 1956 and 1957, all I know about Sherry is that she is a showgirl, she looks like a cuter Marilyn Monroe, and she is drawn by the brilliant DeCarlo. I think I could love her.

Detective Comics #233

Writer: Edmond Hamilton
Artists: Sheldon Moldoff, Stan Kaye
DC (July 1956 © 1956 National Comics Publications, Inc., image courtesy of Heritage Comic Auctions)

Ex-circus performer and heiress Kathy Kane has it bad for Batman, so she decides to fight crime as "The Bat-Woman." Her utility belt holds weapons disguised as such feminine products as lipstick and hairnets, an unfortunate sign of the times.

Sugar & Spike #3

Writer: Sheldon Mayer
Artist: Sheldon Mayer
DC (August-September 1956 © 1956 National Comics Publications, Inc., image courtesy of Heritage Comic Auctions)

In Sugar and Spike's world, all babies speak the same "baby talk" language. In this issue, when a restaurant lobster asks the kids to return him to the sea, we learn all baby animals speak the same language, as well.

Showcase #4: The Flash

Writers: Robert Kanigher, John Broome
Artists: Carmine Infantino, Joe Kubert
DC (September-October 1956 © 1956 National Comics Publications, Inc.)

The second age of super-heroes began in this issue of DC's "try-out" title, when police scientist Barry Allen is doused by chemicals and struck by lightning. Like his favorite comics hero from the 1940s, he uses his super-speed to fight crime as The Flash!

...police scientist Barry Allen is doused by chemicals and struck by lightning.

Superman #107

Writer: Bill Finger
Artist: Wayne Boring
DC (August 1956 ©* 1956 National Comics Publications, Inc., image courtesy of Heritage Comic Auctions)

I was fascinated by this cover as a kid. But the story never made sense to me. Example: When the future people use a time machine to send Superman back to 1956, does his body still remain in that giant tube for 1,000 years?

Mad #29

Writers: Ernie Kovacs, uncredited
Artists: Bill Elder, Wally Wood
E.C. (September 1956 © 1956 E.C. Publications, Inc., image courtesy of Heritage Comic Auctions)

*Al Feldstein succeeds Harvey Kurtzman as editor, though it's safe to assume some material was prepared before Kurtzman's departure. Feldstein would make **Mad** the most successful humor magazine in the history of American publishing.*

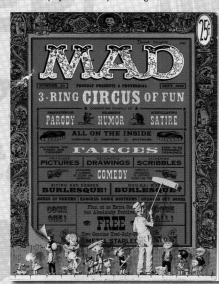

Yellow Claw #1

Writer: Al Feldstein
Artist: Joe Maneely
Marvel (October 1956 ©* 1956 Marjean Magazine Corp., image courtesy of Heritage Comic Auctions)

*This title was the "Yellow Peril" genre from pulp fiction with side orders of scary Chinese communism and science fiction. Feldstein wrote this before becoming editor of **Mad**. Jack Kirby wrote and drew the remainder of the series' four-issue run.*

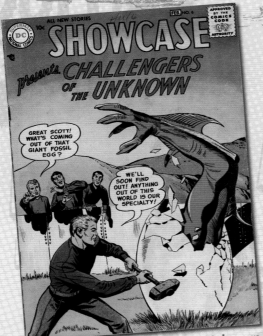

Showcase #6: Challengers of the Unknown

Writers: Jack Kirby, Dave Wood
Artist: Jack Kirby
DC (January-February 1957 © 1956 National Comics
Publications, Inc.)

Four heroes survive what should have been a fatal plane crash and vow to spend their "borrowed time" challenging the unknown. DC's "tryout" title was a hit-making machine; the Challengers' own title ran for 16 years.

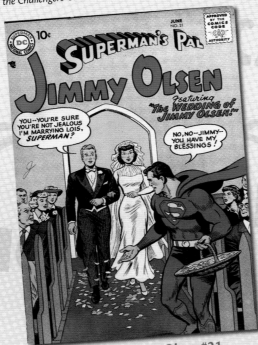

Superman's Pal, Jimmy Olsen #21

Writer: Otto Binder
Artists: Curt Swan, Ray Burnley
DC (June 1957 ©* 1957 National Comics Publications, Inc.,
image courtesy of Heritage Comic Auctions)

When Lois researches an article on him, Jimmy thinks she's in love with him. Naturally, he proposes, and, naturally, she accepts until she can let him down easy. Like … at the church. Some women are just plain bad for men.

Caught #5

Writers: uncredited
Artists: John Severin, Don Heck
Marvel (April 1957 ©* 1957 Vista Publications, image
courtesy of Heritage Comic Auctions)

Using "crime" in the title of a comic book was prohibited by the Comics Code, but publishers still tried to extend the genre into the late 1950s. This issue boasts art by Reed Crandall, Frank Bolle, Bernard Krigstein, and Bernard Baily.

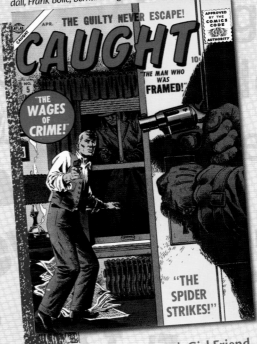

Showcase #9: Superman's Girl Friend, Lois Lane

Writers: Jerry Coleman, Otto Binder
Artists: Al Plastino, Ruben Moreira
DC (July-August 1957 © 1957 National Comics Publications, Inc.)

Lois meets Superboy sweetheart Lana Lang for the first time; then she stops trying to prove Superman is Clark Kent for all of eight pages; then she dreams she's Superman's wife; then she gets her own series, which runs for 137 issues.

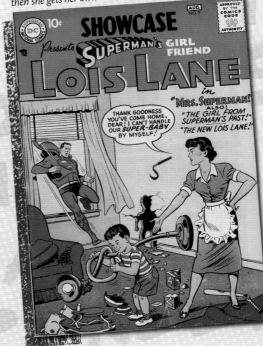

Adventure Comics #240

Writers: Edmond Hamilton, uncredited
Artists: John Sikela, George Papp
DC (September 1957 ©* 1957 National Comics Publications, Inc., image courtesy of Heritage Comic Auctions)

"The Super-Teacher from Krypton" was constructed to test Superboy's worthiness. Jor-El is like the insane stage mother from beyond the grave. In a prophetic back-up story, Green Arrow struggles to pay the mortgage on his Arrow Cave.

Black Rider #1

Writers: uncredited
Artists: John Severin, Jack Kirby
Marvel (September 1957 ©* 1957 Canam Publishers Sales Corp., image courtesy of Heritage Comic Auctions)

With the collapse of its distribution system, Marvel canceled 80% of its line, including 14 Western titles. Despite exceptional art by Jack Kirby, this revival of the 1940s hero turned out to be the only issue published.

Detective Comics #247

Writers: Bill Finger, Jack Miller
Artists: Sheldon Moldoff, Ruben Moreira
DC (September 1957 © 1957 National Comics Publications, Inc., image courtesy of Heritage Comic Auctions)

Professor Milo attempts to end Batman's career by giving the hero a fear of bats. The Caped Crusader adopts a new identity: Starman! This issue's back-up features: "J'onn J'onzz, Manhunter from Mars" and "Roy Raymond, TV Detective."

House of Mystery #66

Writers: uncredited
Artists: Mort Meskin, Jack Kirby
DC (September 1957 © 1957 National Comics Publications, Inc.)

A fairly typical issue of the long-running science-fiction and supernatural anthology title. As a kid, having already read a great many comic books and mythology books, I figured out the secret of "The Girl in the Iron Mask!" from the cover.

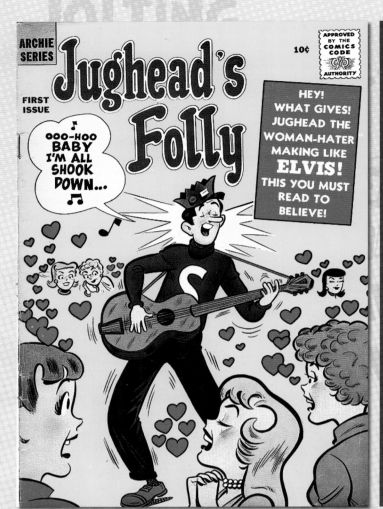

Jughead's Folly #1

Writer: Joe Edwards
Artist: Joe Edwards
Archie (1957 ©* 1957 Close-up Publications, image courtesy of Heritage Comic Auctions)

Jughead becomes an Elvis Presley-style singing sensation in a rare-for-the-times book-length tale. The extended spoof makes this issue a favorite of Elvis collectors, and, as a result, it's become one of the rarest Archie comics.

One of the rarest Archie comics.

Adventure Comics #247

Writer: Otto Binder
Artist: Al Plastino
DC (April 1958 ©* 1958 Superman, Inc., image courtesy of Heritage Comic Auctions)

"The Legion of Super-Heroes" came from the future to haze and then recruit Superboy. The Legion eventually matured beyond their bitchy frat-boys origin to become one of the most popular super-hero teams in comics.

Action Comics #241

Writer: Jerry Coleman
Artists: Wayne Boring, Stan Kaye
DC (June 1958 ©* Superman, Inc., image courtesy of Heritage Comic Auctions)

Someone has broken into the Fortress of Solitude and Superman must solve the mystery. Coleman played fair with his clues, but I still didn't guess the identity of the intruder. I literally read this comic book to pieces as a kid.

Showcase #15: Space Ranger

Writers: Gardner Fox, Edmond Hamilton
Artist: Bob Brown
DC (July-August 1958 © 1958 National Comics Publications, Inc.)

Wealthy CEO Rick Starr secretly fights intergalactic evil as Space Ranger, assisted by shapely gal pal Myra and shape-changing alien sidekick Cryll. He appeared in Tales of the Unexpected and Mystery in Space until mid-1965.

Superboy #68

Writer: Otto Binder
Artist: George Papp
DC (October 1958 © 1958 Superman, Inc., image courtesy of
Heritage Comic Auctions)

Alvin Schwartz created Bizarro for the Superman newspaper strip, but this teen version of the character got into
print first. Binder's poignant tale portrays Bizarro as a con-
fused innocent in a world that fears him.

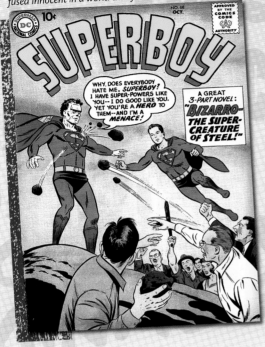

The Friendly Ghost Casper #3

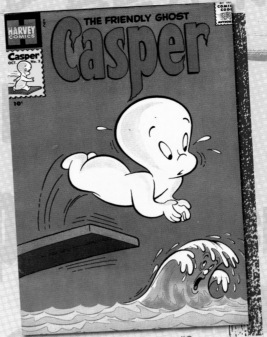

Writers: uncredited
Artists: uncredited
Harvey (October 1958 ©* 1958 Harvey Famous Cartoons,
image courtesy of Heritage Comic Auctions)

Harvey relaunched Casper with his descriptive phrase over
his name, possibly to better attract fans of his cartoons.
In the funny "How to Be Nice," Casper tries to teach The
Ghostly Trio to be good for a visit from their Aunt Softy.

Superman's Pal, Jimmy Olsen #32

Writers: Alvin Schwartz, Otto Binder
Artists: Curt Swan, Ray Burnley
DC (October 1958 © 1958 Superman, Inc., image courtesy of
Heritage Comic Auctions)

Strange transformations were common for Jimmy Olsen.
This time, friendly scientists from Jupiter turn him into one
of their kind to help him with an experiment. Far from his
oddest transformation, but still a memorable one.

Showcase #17: Adventures on Other Worlds

Writer: Gardner Fox
Artists: Mike Sekowsky, Bernard Sachs
DC (November-December 1958 © 1958 National Comics
Publications, Inc.)

Archaeologist Adam Strange is Zeta-beamed to the planet
Rann, falls in love with beautiful Alanna and becomes Rann's
champion. He must catch a new beam every few weeks to return. From his tryouts here, he moved to *Mystery in Space*.

Red Mask #1

Writers: Gardner Fox, Carl Memling
Artists: Frank Bolle, Dick Ayers
I. W. Publishing, Super Comics (1958 ©* Magazine Enterprises)

I enjoyed Red Mask, but it was Ayers' Presto Kid who fascinated me. A hero who caught outlaws with magic instead of guns, the Kid only appeared in a few stories. But I read them over and over and even tried to learn his tricks. Israel Waldman bought original art and printing plates from defunct companies and republished the material with new covers. The comics, sold in 3-for-25¢ packs in department stores, were the first comics my mother bought for me.

Tales of the Mysterious Traveler #10

Writers: uncredited
Artist: Steve Ditko
Charlton (November 1958 © 1958 Charlton Comics Group)

My allowance didn't stretch far enough for me to buy Ditko's early comics when they were originally published, but his artfully weird designs always caught my eye. Once I **could** buy them, he became one of my favorite artists.

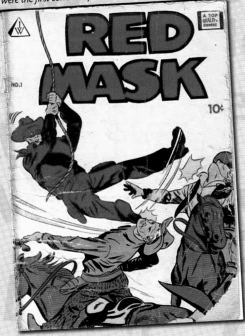

Archie #99

Writers: uncredited
Artists: uncredited
Archie (March 1959 © 1958 Archie Comics Publications, Inc.)

One of my favorite aspects of reading old Archie comics is comparing what things were like then to what they're like now. A dollar's worth of gas today would be half a gallon tops. It wouldn't even bring my car up to "empty."

House of Mystery #85

Writers: uncredited
Artist: Jack Kirby
DC (April 1959 ©* 1959 National Comics Publications, Inc.)

Science-fiction monsters were big business at the movies and as shown on TV by Cleveland's Ghoulardi and other local hosts. It's not surprising they also came to dominate comic books that had previously offered more supernatural terrors.

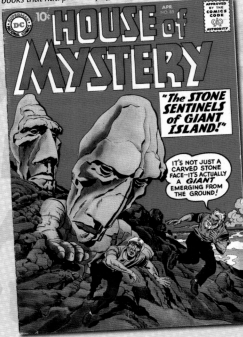

Showcase #20: Rip Hunter ... Time Master

Writer: Jack Miller
Artist: Ruben Moreira
DC (May-June 1959 © 1959 National Comics Publications, Inc.)

Hunter invented a Time-Sphere and went adventuring through the ages with his friends. If you ignored the frequent aliens and monsters, his stories were historically accurate. His own title was a modest success, running from 1961 to 1965.

> Hunter invented a Time-Sphere and went adventuring through the ages...

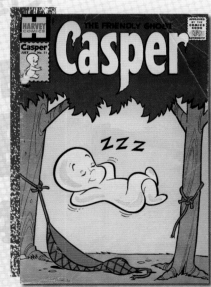

The Friendly Ghost Casper #11

Writers: uncredited
Artists: uncredited
Harvey (July 1959 © 1959 Harvey Famous Cartoons)

The artist who creates Casper's comics is on vacation. An ambitious cartoonist breaks into his studio and, without regard for Casper, starts doing the comic book his way. Sadly, there are guys just like him working on many of today's comic books.

Action Comics #252

Writer: Otto Binder, Robert Bernstein
Artist: Al Plastino
DC (May 1959 ©* 1959 Superman, Inc., image courtesy of Heritage Comic Auctions)

What a classic issue! The origin of Supergirl, secret passion of my youth! Superman's first battle with Metallo, cyborg criminal with a heart of kryptonite! Congorilla, the golden ape with the mind of a man! All in color for a dime!

Sugar & Spike #24

Writer: Sheldon Mayer
Artist: Sheldon Mayer
DC (August-September 1959 © 1959 National Comics Publications, Inc.)

*Mayer was a genius. Remember how the babies in this comic all speak the same language? Well, "Sugar's Great-Great-Great Grampa Plumm" can also speak with and understand them. **Because he's going through his second childhood!** I love that!*

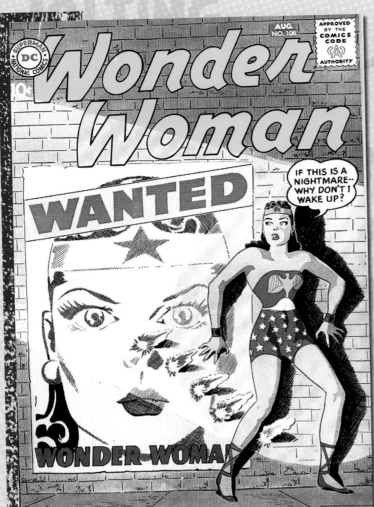

Wonder Woman #108

Writer: Robert Kanigher
Artists: Ross Andru, Mike Esposito
DC (August 1959 © 1959 National Comics Publications, Inc., image courtesy of Heritage Comic Auctions)

*Aliens mind-control the Amazon into committing crimes. She makes them regret it. It wasn't cool for boys to buy this book, no matter **how** gorgeous Wonder Woman was drawn, but this cover grabbed me. I bought the issue when no one was looking.*

> It wasn't cool for boys to buy this book.

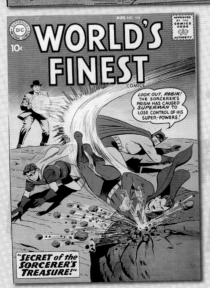

World's Finest Comics #103

Writer: Bill Finger
Artists: Dick Sprang, Sheldon Moldoff
DC (August 1959 © 1959 Superman, Inc., image courtesy of Heritage Comic Auctions)

One of my favorite Superman-Batman thrillers. It's action all the way, as curio-shop owners Atkins and Bork locate four magical items of immense power. Our guys use their brains and their brawn to stop them for using the treasures for evil.

Showcase #22: Green Lantern

Writer: John Broome
Artists: Gil Kane, Joe Giella
DC (September-October 1959 © 1959 National Comics Publications, Inc.)

Editor Julius Schwartz remade another 1940s hero, as test pilot Hal Jordan gets a power ring from a dying alien policeman. A canny mix of science fiction and human interest made this series a hit, and GL is still a super-star today.

Superboy #75

Writer: Otto Binder
Artists: John Sikela, George Papp
DC (September 1959 ©* 1959 Superman, Inc., image courtesy of Heritage Comic Auctions)

This is an unforgettable but disturbing tale of the Kents playing cruel tricks on their invulnerable son to discipline him. The issue also flashes back to Superboy's first day in school and has Krypto chasing a dinosaur bone through history.

World's Finest Comics #104

Writer: Bill Finger
Artists: Dick Sprang, Sheldon Moldoff
DC (September 1959 © 1959 Superman, Inc., image courtesy
of Heritage Comic Auctions)

*Set at a science exposition filled with incredible inventions,
this story had me on the edge of my seat from the chilling
cover image to its finale. Finger was a master at conceiv-
ing exciting visuals, and Sprang drew them with gusto!*

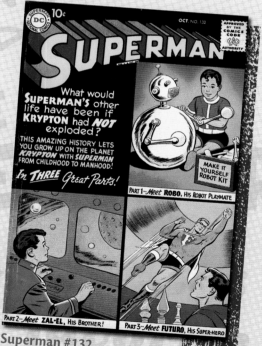

Superman #132

Writer: Otto Binder
Artists: Wayne Boring, Stan Kaye
DC (October 1959 ©* 1959 Superman, Inc., image courtesy of
Heritage Comic Auctions)

*Superman uses a super-computer to imagine what his life
on Krypton would have been like if the planet hadn't exploded. Is it possible Binder invented virtual reality years
before the most rudimentary attempts at creating it?*

Battle #66

Writers: uncredited
Artists: Jack Kirby, Joe Sinnott
Marvel (October 1959 © 1959 Male Publishing Corporation)

*This issue had an all-star line-up of artists: Kirby, Sinnott,
Jack Davis, Don Heck, and John Severin, but what makes
it an uncommonly collectible comic is "The Man with the
Beard," a pro-Castro story from before he went all com-
mie on us.*

Detective Comics #273

Writer: uncredited
Artists: Sheldon Moldoff, Charles Paris
DC (November 1959 © 1959 National Comics Publications,
Inc., image courtesy of Heritage Comic Auctions)

*Commissioner Gordon tells police academy graduates
how Batman never gave up, even though he faced a gang
so cunning he began to doubt he could stop them. This
inspirational tale is one of my favorite Batman stories
of all time.*

Love Romances #84

Writers: uncredited
Artists: Matt Baker, Vince Colletta
Marvel (November 1959 ©* 1959 Atlas Magazines, Inc.)

My namesake is a painter. Rich Susan dumps Tony because she knows it's Kathy who will inspire him to become a great painter. I paid $20 for this issue in 2004 … because I'd never seen my name in a story title before.

Dennis the Menace #7: Dennis the Menace in Hollywood

Writer: Fred Toole
Artist: Al Wiseman
Hallden, Fawcett (Winter 1959 © The Hall Syndicate Inc.)

The TV show premiered about the same time I bought this issue, but I knew Dennis from his newspaper comics. This 100-page special made Hollywood seem like a wonderful, magical place. Of course, this was before reality shows.

Superman #133

Writer: Jerry Siegel
Artists: Al Plastino, Wayne Boring
DC (November 1959 © 1959 Superman, Inc.)

This issue marked the return of Siegel to his greatest creation. He wrote two stories: "How Perry White Hired Clark Kent," a flashback tale, and "Superman Joins the Army," wherein an overzealous officer gets his comeuppance.

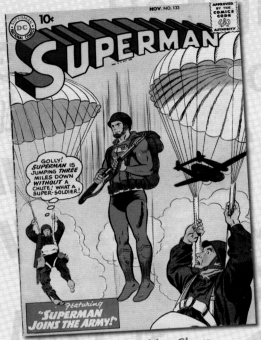

The Crab with the Golden Claws

Writer: Hergé, Danielle Gorlin (translator)
Artist: Hergé
Golden Press (1959 © 1947 Editions Casterman, Paris and Tournai, text © 1959 Golden Press, Inc.)

Young reporter Tintin is one of the most popular comics characters in the world. His adventures began in the children's supplement of a Belgian newspaper on January 10, 1929, and have delighted readers of all ages in many countries.

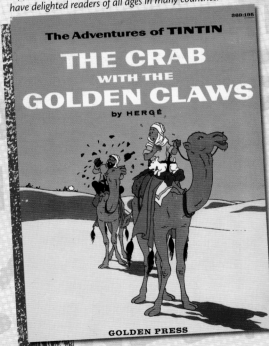

The Adventures of TINTIN

370:195

THE SECRET OF THE UNICORN

by HERGÉ

GOLDEN PRESS

The Secret of the Unicorn

Writer: Hergé, Danielle Gorlin (translator)
Artist: Hergé
Golden Press (1959 © 1947 Editions Casterman, Paris and Tournai, text © 1959 Golden Press, Inc.)

The "Tintin" tales of Hergé (Georges Remi) span 24 albums of exciting adventures, exotic locales, dastardly villains, and such wonderful supporting characters as the oft-volatile Captain Haddock. Hergé's art in these albums is breathtakingly beautiful.

...exciting
adventures,
exotic locales,
dastardly
villains...

CHAPTER FOUR

The golden age of comics is 12.

I don't know who first coined that adage, but it fit me like a glove. I was born in December 1951, and it was in the summer of 1963 that my interest in comic books became a passion. I was still an avid baseball fan, had developed a liking for monster movies and science-fiction novels, and was starting to notice that the girls who went to school with me were getting cuter by the day, but the comic books were my special thing.

Let me tell you what the comic-book world of the 1960s looked like to me.

National Periodical Publications, better known as DC Comics, was the biggest star in my comic-book universe. It had Superman, Batman, and a wide range of other titles. When I had a few extra coins in my pocket, or could swing a trade, I'd get its science-fiction, war, and Western comics — and even such licensed comics as *The Many Loves of Dobie Gillis* and *The Adventures of Jerry Lewis.* DC got more of my allowance than any other publisher.

Marvel Comics wasn't on my radar at the start of the decade, but the comics created by Stan Lee, Jack Kirby, Steve Ditko, Dick Ayers, Don Heck, and others would be the ones that cemented my love of the art form.

The golden age of comics is 12.

Dell was easily as big as DC, but, aside from the occasional movie adaptation, I rarely read its comic books. When Western Publishing, which actually held Dell's most valuable movie and TV licenses, split from Dell to form Gold Key Comics, I started buying some of its adventure titles. However, it wouldn't be until the 1970s that I would begin to appreciate the genius of such creators as Carl Barks and John Stanley.

Funny animals? Those were for kids. Just like comics *about* kids, though I read and enjoyed the Dennis the Menace comic books published by Fawcett and, when no one was looking, the Casper the Friendly Ghost titles from Harvey Comics.

Archie Comics had a couple of super-hero titles I read whenever they fell into my hands, as well as the offbeat *Madhouse* and *Tales Calculated to Drive You Bats,* but my interest in Archie, Jughead, Betty, Veronica, and the rest of the Riverdale High kids was a good decade away.

Every two weeks during the school year, I'd get a new issue of *Treasure Chest,* a Catholic comic book published by George A. Pflaum of Dayton, Ohio, and sold through such Catholic grade schools as my own Sts. Philip and James. It was in *Treasure Chest* that I first saw the work of such terrific comic-book artists as Frank Borth, Joe Sinnott, and Reed Crandall.

Various relatives occasionally gave me various issues of *Classics Illustrated.* The only one I ever *bought* was an adaptation of *The War of the Worlds* by H.G. Wells, the purchase inspired by my seeing the 1953 movie at one of my school's weekly movie showings. The showings were also where I first viewed such lifelong favorites as *Gorgo, Konga,* and *Invaders from Mars.*

American Comics Group published a handful of titles that featured non-series science-fiction and supernatural thrillers. As clever as those stories were, I didn't buy any ACG comics until I discovered the remarkable *Herbie.*

Charlton Comics were somewhat more prevalent, but I didn't buy its comics, either — not until it began publishing ongoing *Gorgo* and *Konga* titles. The best of those monstrously entertaining comic books were drawn by Steve Ditko, soon to be known as the co-creator of The Amazing Spider-Man.

The comics world of the 1960s was a relatively tame place at the decade's start, but it wouldn't stay that way long. Stan Lee and Jack Kirby's *Fantastic Four* would change the industry forever.

Classic E.C. horror and science-fiction comics of the previous decade would be reprinted in mass-market paperbacks and introduce the new generation of readers to wonders that originally saw print in *Tales from the Crypt* and *Weird Science.* Indeed, the artistry of E.C. would inspire publisher Jim Warren's *Creepy,* a black-and-white magazine featuring many of E.C.'s finest artists.

With the success of DC's *Justice League of America* and such 1940s revivals as *The Flash* and *Green Lantern,* with the greater success of Marvel's *Fantastic Four* and *Amazing Spider-Man,* an exciting new age of super-heroes was upon us. And, by the end of the 1960s, our comics world would grow to include new publishers, new writers, new artists, and bold new concepts.

If the 1940s had been the Golden Age of Comics, the 1960s were the Silver Age. Here are some of the comics that made the decade so groundbreaking and so much fun …

Challengers of the Unknown #11

Writer: Ed Herron (tentative)
Artist: Bob Brown
DC (January 1960 © 1959 National Periodical Publications,
Inc., image courtesy of Heritage Comic Auctions)

The Challengers boldly go to another dimension to liberate a world from creatures who plan to conquer Earth. The cover, with its Jack Adler wash tones and color, is eye-catching, and the story finale is one of the most thrilling in comics history.

Love Romances #86

Writers: uncredited
Artist: Vince Colletta
Marvel (March 1960 ©* 1959 Atlas Magazines, Inc.)

Working gal Carol meets playboy Glenn and serious doctor Alan on a cruise. Who will win her? But the special meaning "The Night of June 16th" holds for me is that June 16 — in 1984 — is when I married my own beautiful Barb.

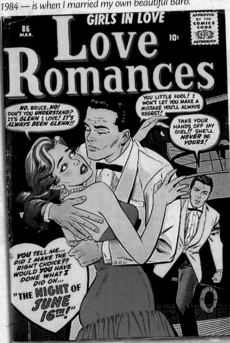

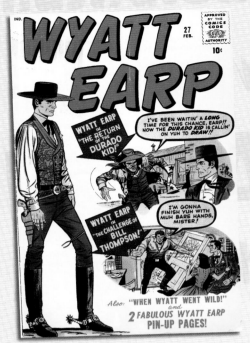

Wyatt Earp #27

Writer: Stan Lee
Artist: Dick Ayers
Marvel (February 1960 © 1959 Interstate Publishing Corp.)

Several companies published comics starring historical figure Wyatt Earp, but this is my favorite. Lee and Ayers delivered an entertaining mix of grim gunfights, profound object lessons, and even comedy, all in stories of just five or six pages.

Space Adventures #33

Writer: Joe Gill
Artist: Steve Ditko
Charlton (March 1960 ©* 1959 Charlton Comics, image courtesy of Heritage Comic Auctions)

Introducing Captain Atom, the first nuclear-powered super-hero of the 1960s. Air Force Captain Adam goes from being blown up in an atomic rocket to battling "enemy agents" with his newly acquired abilities. The Cold War meets science fantasy.

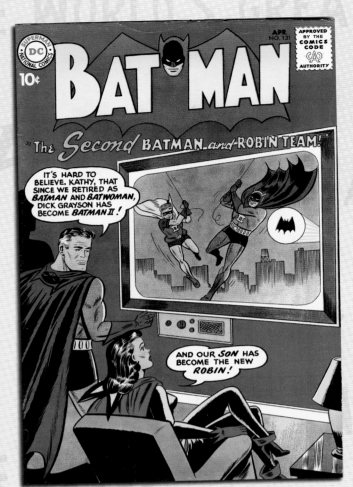

Batman #131

Writer: Bill Finger
Artist: Sheldon Moldoff
DC (April 1960 © 1960 National Comics Publications, Inc., image courtesy of Heritage Comic Auctions)

This is the first of a series of stories "written" by Alfred wherein Batman's butler imagines a future in which Dick Grayson has assumed the mantle of Batman, and the son of the retired Bruce Wayne and Kathy (Batwoman) Kane is Robin.

> This is the first of a series of stories "written" by Alfred.

Star Spangled War Stories #90

Writer: Robert Kanigher
Artists: Ross Andru, Mike Esposito
DC (April-May 1960 ©* National Comics Publications, Inc., image courtesy of Heritage Comic Auctions)

"Island of Armored Giants" launched one of the oddest and yet most compelling concepts of the 1960s, action-packed tales in which American G.I.s battled dinosaurs in a misty war that time forgot. The series continued for an amazing eight years.

The Brave and the Bold #29: Justice League of America

Writer: Gardner Fox
Artists: Mike Sekowsky, Bernard Sachs
DC (April-May 1960 © 1960 National Comics Publications, Inc.)

The Justice League of America had its first meeting two issues earlier, but this adventure has a villain from 10,000 years in the future seeking to defeat the super-heroes … just as he read in a history book of his time!

World's Finest Comics #110

Writer: Jerry Coleman
Artists: Dick Sprang, Sheldon Moldoff
DC (June 1960 © 1960 National Periodical Publications, Inc., image courtesy of Heritage Comic Auctions)

An alien commits crimes with impunity because he has captured Robin's life force, and any harm he suffers is felt more severely by The Boy Wonder. For 10-year-old me, it was heartrending to watch the young hero get weaker by the page.

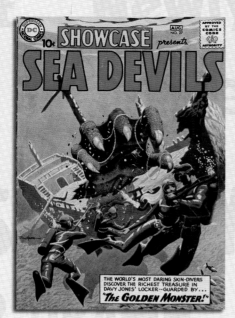

Showcase #27: The Sea Devils

Writer: Robert Kanigher
Artist: Russ Heath
DC (July-August 1960 © 1960 National Comics Publications, Inc.)

The Sea Devils — handsome leader Dane, romantic interest Judy, their younger brother Nicky, and tough guy Biff — were notable for the breathtaking art of Russ Heath and their fantastic adventures. They even fought a giant underwater gorilla. Honest.

Jughead's Fantasy #1

Writer: uncredited
Artist: uncredited
Archie (August 1960 ©* 1960 Archie Publications)

*The Jughead-as-dreamer theme from **Jughead's Folly** is revisited in this first of three issues. In "Sir Jugalot and the Dragon," he dons armor to save a fair princess. Subsequent stories would show him as a private eye and the son of Hercules.*

Rawhide Kid #17

Writer: Stan Lee
Artists: Jack Kirby, Dick Ayers
Marvel (August 1960 © 1960 Atlas Magazines, Inc., image courtesy of Heritage Comic Auctions)

Same name, different cowboy. This new Rawhide Kid is Johnny Clay, short of stature but fast on the draw and the toughest little guy in the West. After avenging the murder of the uncle who raised him, he is unjustly branded an outlaw.

Four Color #1120: Dinosaurus

Writers: Eric Freiwald, Robert Schaefer
Artist: Jesse Marsh
Dell (August 1960 © 1960 Jack H. Harris)

A secluded tropical island, frozen dinosaurs dredged up from a harbor project, and lightning. We're talking "B" movie heaven in comic-book form, adapted from the 1960 film by producer and writer Jack H. Harris and starring Ward Ramsey.

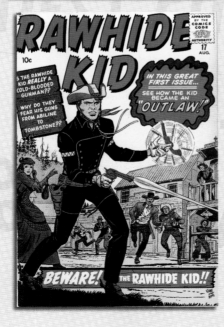

Sugar & Spike #30

Writer: Sheldon Mayer
Artist: Sheldon Mayer
DC (August-September 1960 © 1960 National Comics Publications, Inc.)

Their investigation into the "Mystery of the Funny Faces inna Sand!" leads Sugar and Spike to a meeting with Mayer's other great creation, Scribbly and the now-adult cartoonist's own toddler son. Scribbly hadn't been seen since his title ended in 1951.

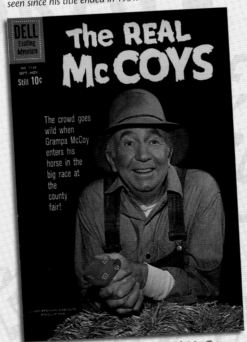

Four Color #1134: The Real McCoys

Writer: uncredited
Artist: Alex Toth
Dell (September-November 1960 © 1960 Brennan-Westgate Productions, image courtesy of Heritage Comic Auctions)

"Rembrandt McCoy" is a hilarious story in which Grandpa McCoy takes the art world by storm with his abstract paintings: paintings created by his brushes accidentally dripping on canvas. **The Real McCoys** *aired on ABC and CBS from 1957 to 1963.*

Batman #134

Writer: Bill Finger
Artist: Sheldon Moldoff
DC (September 1960 © 1960 National Comics Publications, Inc.)

Batman and Robin fought a menacing menagerie of weird beasts in the 1960s, but few were as odd as "The Rainbow Creature." Each colorful component of the South American monster's body gives it a different super-power.

Green Lantern #2

Writer: John Broome
Artists: Gil Kane, Joe Giella
DC (September-October 1960 © 1960 National Comics Publications, Inc.)

Two classic adventures. The cover story introduces the anti-matter universe of Qward, while "Riddle of the Frozen Ghost Town" is the first appearance of Green Lantern friend and confidant Thomas Kalmaku. Both will play key roles for decades to come.

Lassie #51

Writer: Gaylord Du Bois
Artist: Bob Fujitani
Dell (October-December 1960 © 1960 Lassie Programs, Inc., image courtesy of Heritage Comic Auctions)

What's that, Lassie? Timmy's radioactive? I guess he shouldn't have opened the suitcase with the stolen isotopes inside. Kidding aside, Du Bois had a knack for writing edgy stories for all ages. I'm still learning how good he really was.

> ## Du Bois had a knack for writing edgy stories for all ages.

Adventures of Jerry Lewis #61

Writer: uncredited
Artist: uncredited
DC (November 1960 © 1960 Patti Enterprises Inc.)

Lewis split from partner Dean Martin after sharing this comic for 40 issues, but his solo status didn't change the basics of his adventures: outlandishly wacky situations with lots of goofy gags and gorgeous gals.

Rawhide Kid #18

Writer: Stan Lee
Artists: Jack Kirby, Dick Ayers
Marvel (October 1960 ©* 1960 Atlas Magazines, Inc.)

"A Legend Is Born!" when bullies harass the Kid in a saloon, but the gunfighter the eyewitnesses describe bears no resemblance to reality. This clever commentary on perception is one of my all-time favorite comics stories.

Tarzan #121

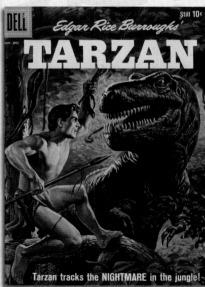

Writer: Gaylord Du Bois
Artists: Jesse Marsh, Russ Manning
Dell (November-December 1960 © 1960 Edgar Rice Burroughs, Inc.)

*George Wilson's cover painting of Tarzan facing down a toothy **T. rex** in the jungle was irresistible to the dinosaur-loving kids of my generation. Du Bois' scripts often made use of both characters and concepts from the original Tarzan novels.*

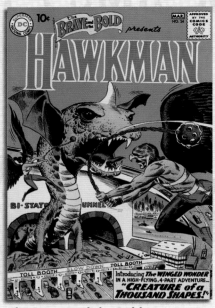

Dennis the Menace Giant #8: Dennis the Menace in Mexico

Writer: Fred Toole
Artist: Al Wiseman
Hallden/Fawcett (Winter 1960 ©* 1960 The Hall Syndicate, Inc.)

Vacations to Mexico weren't in the family budget when I was a kid, but, thanks to Dennis and his family, I got to "visit" our neighbor to the south in a wondrous 100-page comic book filled with fun and fascinating facts.

Showcase #30: Aquaman

Writer: Jack Miller
Artist: Ramona Fradon
DC (January-February 1961 © 1960 National Comics Publications, Inc.)

*After two decades of being a back-up feature in other comics, Aquaman finally gets his shot at stardom. His **Showcase** tryouts won the Sea King his own book. Since then, his appearances on multiple cartoon series have made him a household name.*

The Brave and the Bold #34: Hawkman

Writer: Gardner Fox
Artist: Joe Kubert
DC (February-March 1961 © 1960 National Comics Publications, Inc.)

There's a new Hawkman and Hawkgirl in town. The married duo are police officers from the planet Thanagar who, with the help of police commissioner Emmett, land jobs as the curators of the Midway City Museum.

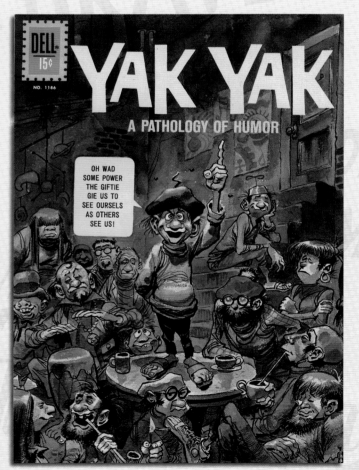

...which, sadly, lasted only two issues.

Four Color #1186: Yak Yak

Writer: Jack Davis
Artist: Jack Davis
Dell (May 1961 © 1961 Western Printing & Lithographing Co.)

Davis drew horror, science fiction, war, and Western stories with uncommon artistry, but his true genius lay in sidesplitting comedy. He wrote, drew, and even edited this "pathology of humor," which, sadly, lasted only two issues.

Gorgo #1

Writer: uncredited
Artist: Steve Ditko
Charlton (May 1961 © 1960 details not given, a King Bros. Productions, Inc. motion picture released by M.G.M. International)

In this adaptation of the 1961 MGM movie, a living prehistoric monster is put on display in London ... until [Spoiler warning!] its even more enormous parent rescues it. Gorgo and his mom continued to appear in often-wacky comic-book adventures through 1965.

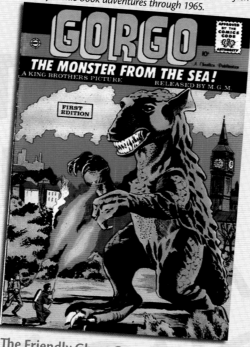

The Friendly Ghost Casper #35

Writer: uncredited
Artist: uncredited
Harvey (July 1961 ©* 1961 Harvey Famous Cartoons, image courtesy of Heritage Comic Auctions)

The scary "Witch of the Mountain Top" sends a hunter into the Enchanted Forest, armed with magical gunpowder that could mean "The End of Casper!" It's a surprisingly suspenseful adventure for the usually gentle world of the Friendly Ghost.

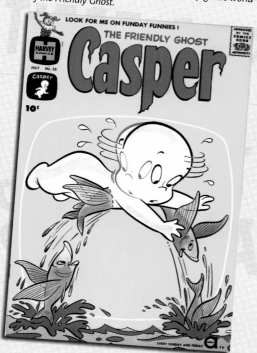

Secret Origins #1

Writers: Edmond Hamilton, Gardner Fox
Artists: Dick Sprang, Mike Sekowsky
DC (Summer 1961 © 1961 Superman, Inc.)

One of the all-time great comics as DC gathered together the origins of the Superman-Batman team, Green Lantern, The Flash, Green Arrow and Speedy, Wonder Woman, The Challengers of the Unknown, and J'onn J'onzz, The Manhunter from Mars.

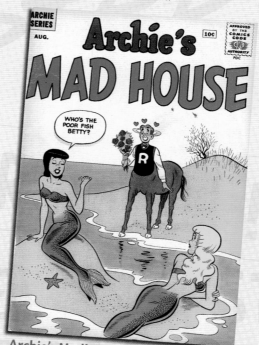

Archie's Madhouse #14

Writers: George Gladir
Artists: uncredited
Archie (August 1961 © 1961 Archie Comics Publications, Inc.)

*This comic book was sort of a gateway drug to **Mad**, but with more emphasis on teenagers and monsters. This issue features "If Teenagers Formed a Union," "Questions Better Left Unanswered," "The Discovery of Girls," and other amusing pieces.*

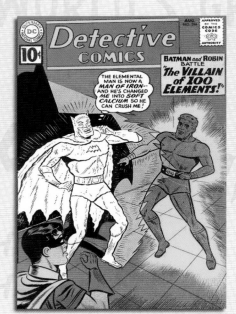

Detective Comics #294

Writer: Bill Finger
Artist: Sheldon Moldoff
DC (August 1961 © 1961 National Periodical Publications, Inc.)

The periodic table of elements was another of my many boyhood fascinations, so a story in which Batman fights a villain who can change into any of those then-100 elements was sure to thrill me. (FYI, there are now 108 elements found in nature.)

Adventures of Little Archie #20

Writer: Bob Bolling
Artist: Bob Bolling
Archie (Fall 1961 © 1961 Archie Comic Publications, Inc.)

The romantic chaos of Riverdale High pales next to what Archie experiences as a kid. Bolling's stories feature mad scientists, Martian visitors, criminal masterminds, and even a dinosaur or two. Sometimes, I think Archie peaked too early.

Showcase #34: The Atom

Writer: Gardner Fox
Artists: Gil Kane, Murphy Anderson
DC (September-October 1961 © 1961 National Comics Publications, Inc.)

Another terrific 1940s super-hero revival from Editor Julius Schwartz and crew, as scientist Ray Palmer discovers a way to shrink his size to battle villains both Earthly and otherworldly and to help his lawyer fiancée, Jean Loring, win her cases.

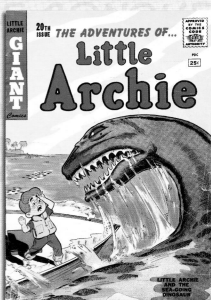

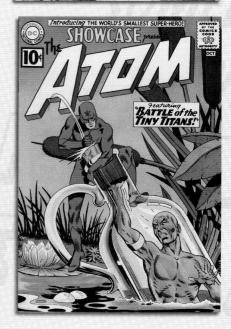

Flash #123

Writer: Gardner Fox
Artists: Carmine Infantino, Joe Giella
DC (September 1961 © 1961 National Comics Publications, Inc.)

The Flash of the 1960s travels to a parallel Earth to team up with the Flash of the 1940s against villains Fiddler, Thinker, and Shade. With this story, Editor Julius Schwartz creates a universe that can encompass all the great DC characters.

Konga #3

Writer: Joe Gill (likely)
Artist: Steve Ditko
Charlton (October 1961 © details not provided)

Each early issue of Konga continued from the previous one. Having survived a volcanic eruption that destroyed one island, the giant ape swims to another, where he battles a sea monster and patches up the troubled marriage of his human co-stars.

Treasure Chest Vol. 17 No. 2

Writer: uncredited
Artist: Reed Crandall
George A. Pflaum (September 28, 1961 © 1961 Geo. A. Pflaum, Publisher, Incorporated)

Designed to warn students about communism, the opening segment of this 10-chapter series offers a chilling portrayal of what life would be in a communist-controlled America. It's the only comic-book story that ever gave me nightmares.

Strange Tales #89

Writer: uncredited
Artists: Jack Kirby, Dick Ayers
Marvel (October 1961 ©* 1961 Vista Publications, Inc.)

This is my favorite of Marvel's giant monster yarns. A quiet, freedom-loving scholar brings a legendary dragon to life to disrupt China's planned invasion of Taiwan. Especially at Marvel, the Cold War was a frequent component of such stories.

...Lee and Kirby changed super-hero comic books forever.

Fantastic Four #1

Writer: Stan Lee
Artists: Jack Kirby, George Klein
Marvel (November 1961 © 1961 Canam Publishers Sales Corp.)

These heroes might have their arguments, but, like the family they are, always come together to do battle with fearsome villains and embark on thrilling adventures. In breaking with tradition, Lee and Kirby changed super-hero comic books forever.

Tales to Astonish #27

Writer: Larry Lieber, Stan Lee
Artists: Jack Kirby, Dick Ayers
Marvel (January 1962 © 1961 Vista Publications, Inc.)

Henry Pym invents a shrinking serum, becoming "The Man in the Ant-Hill" in this typical one-shot science-fiction thriller. But, when Marvel moved into super-hero comics, the better-than-average sales of this issue would earn Pym a promotion.

...Henry Pym invents
a shrinking serum,
becoming "The Man
in the Ant Hill."

Superman #149

Writer: Jerry Siegel
Artists: Curt Swan, Sheldon Moldoff
DC (November 1961 ©* 1961 National Comics Publications, Inc., image courtesy of Heritage Comic Auctions)

"The Death of Superman" might have been an "imaginary story," but its depiction of an alternate reality in which Lex Luthor finally achieves his blackest ambition chilled readers. It's heartrending to see Superman's loved ones file past his casket.

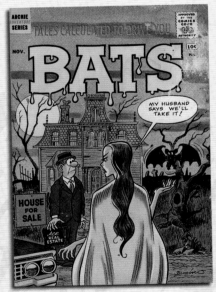

Tales Calculated to Drive You Bats #1

Writer: George Gladir
Artist: Orlando Busino
Archie (November 1961 © 1961 Close-Up, Inc.)

Two of the best and most prolific funny men in comics teamed for this monster-centric humor title featuring such characters as Hugo the Werewolf and Tut-Tut the Mummy. The comic book lasted but seven issues, but every one is a satiric gem.

Amazing Adult Fantasy #9

Writer: Stan Lee
Artist: Steve Ditko
Marvel (February 1962 © 1961 Atlas Magazines, Inc., image courtesy of Heritage Comic Auctions)

"The Magazine That Respects Your Intelligence" featured short, twist-ending fantasy and science fiction tales, which Lee delighted in writing. All eight issues' worth of these stories were drawn by his future Spider-Man collaborator, Steve Ditko.

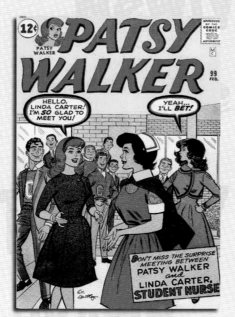

Patsy Walker #99

Writer: Stan Lee
Artist: Al Hartley
Marvel (February 1962 ©* 1961)

My all-time favorite teen humor comic book. Nikita Khrushchev pays a visit to Patsy's town to check out our "pampered" youth. They set him straight. "No matter **how** many bombs and rockets we build, how can anyone **ever** beat those crazy Americans???"

Showcase #37: Metal Men

Writer: Robert Kanigher
Artists: Ross Andru, Mike Esposito
DC (March-April 1962 © 1962 National Periodical Publications, Inc.)

The Metal Men, classic characters of the 1960s, are amazing robots with human personalities. Legend has it that Kanigher created them over a weekend when another planned **Showcase** feature failed to get off the drawing board.

Four Color #1309: 87th Precinct

Writer: uncredited
Artist: Bernard Krigstein
Dell (April-June 1962 © 1962 Ed McBain, image courtesy of Heritage Comic Auctions)

Krigstein's art strives to overcome an odd script wherein a blind portrait painter murders his subjects. For fans of the Ed McBain novels, there's the further absurdity of Steve Carella using his deaf-mute wife Teddy as bait for the insane killer.

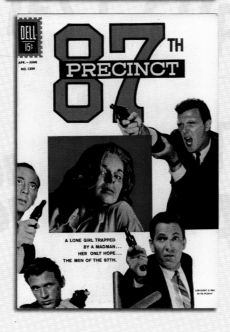

Richie Rich #9

Writer: uncredited
Artist: uncredited
Harvey (March 1962 ©* 1961 Harvey Features Syndicate, image courtesy of Heritage Comic Auctions)

Two members of the supporting cast shine in this issue. Our hero has a tough time buying girlfriend Gloria "Something Simple." Then, in "The Boy and the Butler," Richie learns what a remarkable friend he has in Cadbury.

Kookie #1

Writer: John Stanley
Artists: John Stanley, Bill Williams
Dell (April 1962 © 1961 Dell Publishing Co., Inc.)

Another creation of the prolific Stanley, Kookie is a square chick who works at Mama Pappa's Café Expresso and mingles with its clientele of stereotypical beatniks and other odd Greenwich Village types. Sadly, the title ran but two issues.

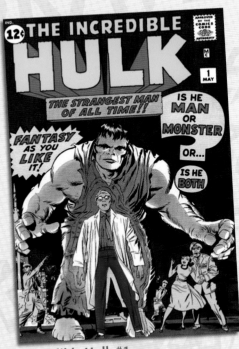

Incredible Hulk #1

Writer: Stan Lee
Artists: Jack Kirby, Paul Reinman
Marvel (May 1962 ©* 1962 Zenith Publishing Corp.)

Scientist Bruce Banner rescues rebellious teenager Rick Jones from certain death on a testing ground, only to be himself caught in the blast of an experimental gamma radiation bomb. It's **Dr. Jekyll and Mr. Hyde,** *updated for the Atomic Age.*

Reptisaurus #4

Writer: uncredited
Artists: Joe Sinnott, Vince Colletta
Charlton (April 1962 © details not printed, image courtesy of Heritage Comic Auctions)

As titles go, "Reptisaurus Meets His Mate" is an alarmingly accurate description of this story: 20 pages of a giant monster in heat, defying military attempts to stop him, and ending with his "wedding night." You can't make this stuff up.

Green Lantern #13

Writer: John Broome
Artists: Gil Kane, Joe Giella
DC (June 1962 © 1962 National Periodical Publications, Inc.)

Their friendship gets off to a rocky start when Green Lantern is brainwashed by aliens into capturing The Flash. They defeat the aliens, reveal their civilian identities to each other, and go on vacation with their girlfriends. Even super-heroes need down time.

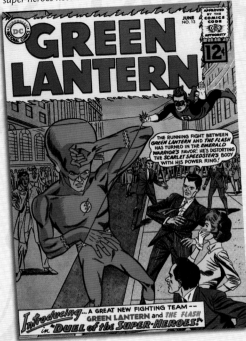

1000 Comic Books You Must Read

Richie Rich #11

Writers: uncredited
Artists: uncredited
Harvey (July 1962 ©* 1962 Harvey Features Syndicate, image courtesy of Heritage Comic Auctions)

Richie visits cousin Rodney Von Snoot in the exclusive (and not even slightly self-consciously named) town of "Snobsdale." It turns out Richie owns the land. He gives it back to its original Native American owners. I love that kid!

Journey into Mystery #83

Writers: Stan Lee, Larry Lieber
Artists: Jack Kirby, Joe Sinnott
Marvel (August 1962 © 1962 Atlas Magazines, Inc.)

A frail physician finds an ancient walking stick in Norway and becomes the mighty Thor, just in time to send "The Stone Men from Saturn" running back to their home planet. Yet another super-hero sensation from the Lee-Kirby team.

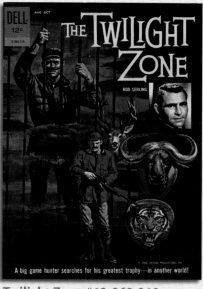

Twilight Zone #12-860-210

Writers: uncredited
Artists: George Evans, Reed Crandall
Dell (August-October 1962 © 1962 Cayuga Productions, Inc., image courtesy of Heritage Comic Auctions)

Don't let the odd number throw you. This is the first issue of a long-running anthology series based on the classic Rod Serling TV series. With its third issue, published after Dell's split with Western, it became a Gold Key Comics title.

> "With great power,
> there must also
> come great
> responsibility."

Amazing Fantasy #15

Writer: Stan Lee
Artist: Steve Ditko
Marvel (August 1962 © 1962 Non-Pareil Publishing Corp.)

One of the greatest origins in comics, as high-school outsider Peter Parker is bitten by a radioactive spider, gains spectacular powers, and learns the harsh lesson that "with great power, there must also come great responsibility."

Ghost Stories #1

Writer: John Stanley
Artists: Ed Robbins, Gerald McCann
Dell (September-November 1962 © 1962 Dell Publishing Co., Inc.)

The unseen "Monster of Dread End" is killing the children of that tenement neighborhood, and the brother of its first victim hunts it. Devoid of any gore, this is still one of the scariest horror stories in comics history.

Wendy Witch World #2

Writers: uncredited
Artists: uncredited
Harvey (September 1962 © 1962 Harvey Famous Cartoons)

*Wendy and Casper meet their evil twins in "Double Trouble." Then, Wendy becomes her **own** evil twin, when her aunts send her away to Miss Viper's School for Ghoulish Girls. Also in this giant issue: Spooky the Tuff Little Ghost.*

Tales to Astonish #35

Writers: Stan Lee, Larry Lieber
Artists: Jack Kirby, Dick Ayers
Marvel (September 1962 © 1962 Vista Publications Inc.)

Scientist Henry Pym gets his second chance at stardom, donning a super-hero costume and battling communists and criminals with his army of obedient ants. Never a success, Pym would be subjected to numerous makeovers over the next few years.

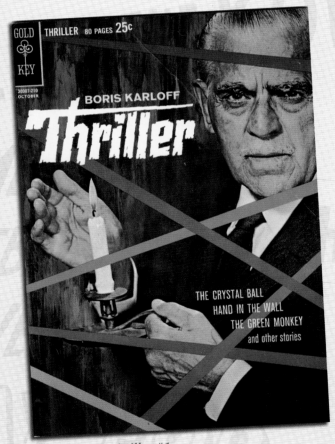

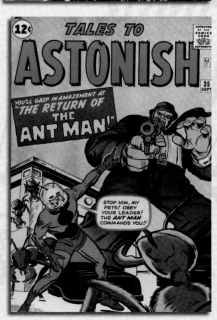

Boris Karloff Thriller #1

Writers: Leo Dorfman, uncredited
Artists: Mike Sekowsky, Alberto Giolitti
Gold Key (October 1962 © 1962 Hubbell Robinson Productions, Inc., image courtesy of Heritage Comic Auctions)

Under its new Gold Key imprint, Western licensed the right to use Boris Karloff as host of this anthology, based on the TV series over which he presided. With its third issue, the series changed its name to **Boris Karloff Tales of Mystery.**

Superman #156

Writer: Edmond Hamilton
Artists: Curt Swan, George Klein
DC (October 1962 © 1962 National Periodical Publications, Inc.)

Superman is dying. His "final" message to mankind — carved on the moon with waning heat vision — sums up everything I love about the greatest comics hero of them all: "Do good to others and every man can be a Superman."

> "Do good to others and every man can be a Superman."

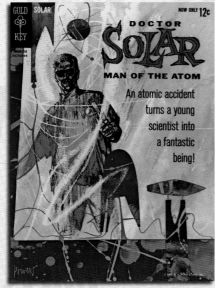

Doctor Solar, Man of the Atom #1

Writer: Paul S. Newman
Artist: Bob Fujitani
Gold Key (October 1962 © 1962 K.K. Publications, Inc.)

"An atomic accident turns a young scientist into a fantastic being!" Though we'd heard that one before, Gold Key's first super-hero was more sophisticated and stylish than most. He even managed to get through four full issues without a super-heroic costume.

Tales from the Tomb #1

Writer: John Stanley
Artists: Frank Springer, Tony Tallarico
Dell (October 1962 © 1962 Dell Publishing Co., Inc.)

Edited by Golden Age veteran L.B. Cole, this one-shot featured a baker's dozen of unforgettable stories, including "Mr. Green Must Be Fed" — with one of the greatest shock endings in comics — "The Mudman," and the single-page "Asphalt Test."

Richie Rich #14

Writers: uncredited
Artists: uncredited
Harvey (November 1962 © 1962 Harvey Features Syndicate)

Confession: I've never read this comic book. I just love the cover. Someone should draw a cover of President Obama reading his Spider-Man and Conan comic books. For more confessions, check out the "Afterword" starting on page 265.

Two-Gun Kid #60

Writer: Stan Lee
Artists: Jack Kirby, Dick Ayers
Marvel (November 1962 ©* 1962 Non-Pareil Publishing Co., image courtesy of Heritage Comic Auctions)

Matt Hawk comes to Tombstone to practice law. A quick study when it comes to cowboy stuff, he also takes up bringing owlhoots to justice as the Two-Gun Kid. This is as much a super-hero strip as it is a Western.

> This is as much a super-hero strip as it is a Western.

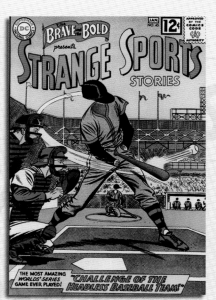

Fantastic Four #9

Writer: Stan Lee
Artists: Jack Kirby, Dick Ayers
Marvel (December 1962 © 1962 Canam Publishers Sales Corp.)

When Mr. Fantastic's investments go really bad, The Fantastic Four find themselves at the economic mercy of their creditors and their then-enemy, The Sub-Mariner. Are super-hero teams eligible for a government bailout?

Justice League of America #16

Writer: Gardner Fox
Artists: Mike Sekowsky, Bernard Sachs
DC (December 1962 © 1962 National Periodical Publications, Inc.)

Justice League members spend the afternoon in their headquarters to beat a deadly trap set by The Maestro, a villain who exists only in a comic book created by a fan. One of the most fun and unusual super-hero stories of the decade.

The Brave and the Bold #45: Strange Sports Stories

Writer: Gardner Fox
Artists: Carmine Infantino, Joe Giella
DC (December-January 1962-1963 © 1962 National Periodical Publications, Inc.)

Strange Sports Stories combined science fiction with all the great American pastimes. Though never a success, its writing and its art were among the most imaginative and inventive to be found in the comic books of this decade.

Strange Tales Annual #1

Writers: Stan Lee, Larry Lieber
Artists: Jack Kirby, Steve Ditko
Marvel (1962 © 1962 Atlas Magazines, Inc.)

Marvel's monsters would soon be eclipsed by the company's new super-hero stars but they receive a last hurrah of sorts in this collection of tales featuring Grottu, King of the Insects; Shagg, the living Sphinx; and other gargantuan menaces.

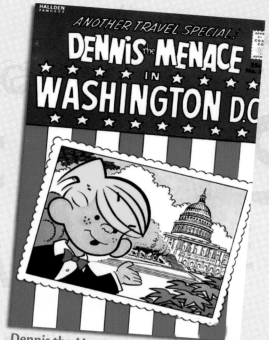

Dennis the Menace Giant #15: Dennis the Menace in Washington, D.C.

Writer: Fred Toole
Artist: Al Wiseman
Fawcett (1963 ©* The Hall Syndicate, Inc.)

The vacation-happy Mitchell family is on the road again, this time to our nation's capital. Dennis sees the sights and meets J. Edgar Hoover. He has a dream adventure with Capt. John Smith and writes a letter to his pal Joey back home.

Magnus, Robot Fighter #1

Writer: Russ Manning
Artist: Russ Manning
Gold Key (February 1963 © 1962 K.K. Publications, Inc.)

In the year 4000 A.D., mankind faces enslavement by the robots on which it has become dependent. One man has the indomitable will and steel-smashing might to stand against these mechanical menaces. A classic comic book with a classic theme.

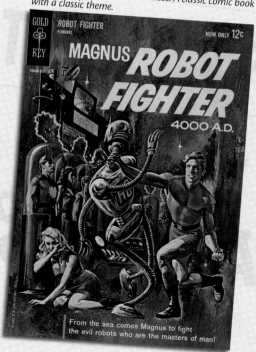

Tales of Suspense #39

Writers: Stan Lee, Larry Lieber
Artist: Don Heck
Marvel (March 1963 © 1962 Vista Publications Inc.)

Mortally wounded in Vietnam, weapons manufacturer Tony Stark creates a life-sustaining suit of armor and joins Marvel's growing ranks of super-heroes as the invincible Iron Man! His origin will be changed periodically to accommodate new wars.

Sgt. Fury #1

Writer: Stan Lee
Artists: Jack Kirby, Dick Ayers
Marvel (May 1963 © 1963 Bard Publishing Corp.)

Lee and Kirby brought the same sensibilities to the "war comic for people who hate war comics" that they'd brought to The Fantastic Four. *Fury and his multi-ethnic, multi-racial band of brothers were as much a family as* The FF.

Thirteen #7

Writer: John Stanley
Artist: John Stanley
Dell (July 1963 © 1963 Dell Publishing Co., Inc.)

As this comic's subtitle, "Going on Eighteen," says, Val and her best friend Judy are just-teens barreling toward young adulthood through one wacky situation after another. The cast also includes older sister Evie and boy next door Billy. The series ran 29 issues.

Batman #156

Writer: Bill Finger
Artists: Sheldon Moldoff, Charles Paris
DC (June 1963 © 1963 National Periodical Publications, Inc.)

Batman watches helplessly as "Robin Dies at Dawn!" It's only a simulation created to test astronauts psychologically, but its hallucinogenic side effects have Batman reliving the death over and over again, threatening his crime-fighting and his sanity.

Dennis the Menace Giant #18: Dennis in Hawaii

Writer: Fred Toole
Artist: Al Wiseman
Hallden/Fawcett (Summer 1963 ©* 1963 The Hall Syndicate, Inc.)

What did Henry Mitchell do *for a living that he could afford to take his family on these fabulous vacations? Toole and Wiseman never asked, probably because they got to go to those same fabulous places to research the comic books.*

THE GREATEST COMIC BOOK OF ALL TIME!

Fantastic Four Annual #1

Writer: Stan Lee
Artists: Jack Kirby, Dick Ayers
Marvel (Summer 1963 © 1963 Canam Publisher Sales Corp.)

Fantastic Four Annual #1 changed my life.

I was not quite 12 years old. My parents were taking us — my sister and brothers — to Oneonta, New York, a small city of roughly 14,000 people, some of them related to my father. It was boredom incarnate, and the only way I managed to get through it was by using my meager vacation savings to buy a comic book or two at every rest stop. It was — thank God — a time when there were comic books at every rest stop.

My parents were annoyed by my purchases. In Oneonta, at the cigar shop owned by my dad's uncle, I made a beeline for the comics. One of my parents — I've clearly repressed the memory of which — told me that whatever I bought was going to be the last comic book I bought on this trip. Defiantly, I bought *Fantastic Four Annual #1*, which cost a quarter. It had 72 big pages, and I planned to savor each and every one of them.

> ## The squabbling between The Human Torch and The Thing was familiar to me...

I don't remember exactly when I first read that annual during the trip. There were hardly any lights in the cabin, so it had to have been the next morning. Odds are I first read the issue sitting on an old chair on the cabin porch. I would read it a dozen more times before we got home.

There was scarcely an open area on the cover. If Kirby and Ayers left any space unadorned with their dramatic illustrations, then Lee filled it with his excited descriptions of the wonders waiting within this annual. And wonders there were.

"Sub-Mariner versus the Human Race" was the longest comic-book story I had ever read. In its 37 pages, there was action and drama aplenty. The squabbling between The Human Torch and The Thing was familiar to me; they were brothers. Having started to notice girls, I was alarmed and intrigued by the passion shown by such characters as Dorma and Namor over loves denied to them. I was thrilled by the vast scope of the story: the centuries-spanning history of Namor's people and the invasion of New York City by the Atlanteans. I was stunned by the courage of Sue Storm, the deadly price she seemed likely to pay for it, and Namor's willingness to sacrifice all to save her. By the time Namor returned to his now-deserted kingdom, abandoned by his own people, I was mentally exhausted.

How could a comic-book story be that good?

The second half of the annual issue wasn't as mind-blowing as the lead but it was still amazing. I didn't know who Spider-Man was but I got a kick out of the six-page "The Fantastic Four Meet Spider-Man" by Lee, Kirby, and Steve Ditko ... and intrigued by the idea that was an expanded version of their original meeting. I think that's when it hit me: **There were real people making comic books, they could tell the stories any way they liked, and making comic books and telling stories was an actual job.**

The feature pages were also a thrill. Seeing the "Gallery of The Fantastic Four's Most Famous Foes" gave me a sense of history. And it wasn't

as intimidating as the history of Superman and Batman and their fellows, which stretched back all the way to when my dad was my age. I wanted to know more about these villains.

There was a two-page section giving personal information about the individual members of The Fantastic Four. That really made the heroes come alive for me.

However, as much as I loved the annual's Sub-Mariner story and its special features, it was the reprinted "Origin of the Fantastic Four" that truly changed my life. Because it wasn't nearly as good as the Sub-Mariner story. It was clearly done by the same people, but they had grown a whole lot better in just a couple of years. This Lee and Kirby were — presumably — adults, but they were still improving on their skills. That was as big an eye-opener as any of the issue's fictional thrills.

If making comic books was a job, then people were hired to do it. If those people could get better at their jobs as they worked at them, then maybe even a kid like me — a kid who loved to write — could learn how to make comic books and get good enough at it that someone would give me a job making comic books. All of a sudden, I knew what I wanted to do when I grew up.

I wanted to make comic books.

I grew up to do just that. I think some of the comic books I made were really good and most of them were pretty good. The ones that weren't pretty good, well, I gave them my best possible effort at the time I made them. I never phoned it in and I never didn't care. I'll never be on anyone's hall of fame list, but, all things considered, the comic books I did represent a body of work of which I'm generally proud.

Fantastic Four Annual #1 changed my life.

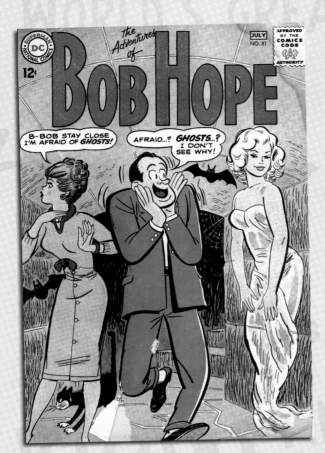

Adventures of Bob Hope #81

Writer: uncredited
Artist: Mort Drucker
DC (June-July 1963 © 1963 Bob Hope)

In 1950, DC had licensed the rights to do a comic book starring the famous comedian. The title was still going strong a dozen years later with its mix of adventure, humor, and, of course, beautiful babes for Hope's comic-book persona to pursue.

> ...mix of adventure, humor, and, of course, beautiful babes...

Konga's Revenge #2

Writer: Joe Gill (likely)
Artist: Steve Ditko
Charlton (Summer 1963 © 1963 details not printed)

A special edition of the ongoing *Konga* title, this hilarious summer special saw the normally enormous ape "shrunk to the size of a human thumb." Ditko added to the humor by including visual gags in the backgrounds of several panels.

My Greatest Adventure #80

Writers: Arnold Drake, Bob Haney
Artist: Bruno Premiani
DC (June 1963 © 1963 National Periodical Publications, Inc.)

The mysterious Chief, a wealthy, reclusive scientific genius, joins three individuals who have become super-powered outcasts — actress Rita Farr, pilot Larry Trainor, sportsman Cliff Steele — to fight for mankind as The Doom Patrol!

Justice League of America #21

Writer: Gardner Fox
Artists: Mike Sekowsky, Bernard Sachs
DC (August 1963 © 1963 National Periodical Publications, Inc.)

It's a cross-dimensional crisis, as The Justice League calls on its parallel-Earth counterparts of The Justice Society to defeat a team of super-villains from both of their worlds. This was a true game-changing moment for super-hero comic books.

Tales to Astonish #44

Writer: Ernest Hart
Artist: Jack Kirby, Don Heck
Marvel (June 1963 © 1963 Vista Publications, Inc.)

In his next makeover, Henry Pym gets a tragic backstory (his wife was murdered by communists) and a partner: beautiful socialite Janet Van Dyne. The flighty Wasp will mature over the years and, at one point, serve as chairman of The Avengers.

Avengers #1

Writer: Stan Lee
Artists: Jack Kirby, Dick Ayers
Marvel (September 1963 © 1963 Vista Publications Inc.)

Second-stringers Ant-Man and Wasp held their own with Iron Man and Thor, but The Hulk quit the team after their second adventure. The ever-changing roster proved to be the team's greatest strength and the key to its continuing success.

Justice League of America #22

Writer: Gardner Fox
Artists: Mike Sekowsky, Bernard Sachs
DC (September 1963 © National Periodical Publications, Inc.)

For comics fans my age, this two-issue thriller was our first look at Dr. Fate, Black Canary, Hourman, and the original Hawkman, Atom, Flash, and Green Lantern. These issues sold so well that the teams continued to meet every summer.

X-Men #1

Writer: Stan Lee
Artists: Jack Kirby, Paul Reinman
Marvel (September 1963 © 1963 Canam Publishers Sales Corp.)

The Marvel Universe had another growth spurt with the debut of these teen heroes: mutants born with extra abilities who learn how to use them at Professor Xavier's School for Gifted Youngsters. Fighting evil mutants was an extracurricular activity.

Strange Tales #115

Writer: Stan Lee
Artist: Dick Ayers
Marvel (December 1963 © Vista Publications, Inc.)

The Human Torch battling The Sandman, one of Spider-Man's most dangerous foes, was a pretty big deal in 1963. But what really put this issue on the map was its second story. Co-created by Ditko, Stephen Strange is an arrogant surgeon. When his hands are damaged in an auto accident, he turns to magic for a cure and finds new purpose for his life, as told in the hitherto-unrevealed "Origin of Dr. Strange."

Action Comics #309

Writer: Edmond Hamilton
Artists: Curt Swan, George Klein
DC (February 1964 © 1963 National Periodical Publications, Inc.)

This tale of Lois and Lana trying to expose Clark Kent as Superman during a live TV broadcast honoring The Man of Steel is remembered for featuring President John F. Kennedy. The issue went on sale one month after Kennedy's assassination.

> ...Lois and Lana trying to expose Clark Kent as Superman...

Treasure Chest of Fun and Fact
Vol. 10 #11

Writer: Barry Reece
Artist: Joe Sinnott
Geo. A. Pflaum (January 30, 1964 © 1964 Geo. A. Pflaum, Publisher, Incorporated)

The six-part "1976 Pettigrew for President" ran for six issues from January through June. The candidate was always drawn in silhouette. In the final chapter, when he won the Democratic Party nomination, readers learned he was an African-American.

Amazing Spider-Man #9

Writer: Stan Lee
Artist: Steve Ditko
Marvel (February 1964 © 1963 Non-Pareil Publishing Corp., image courtesy of Heritage Comic Auctions)

This was my first issue. It introduced Electro (who I thought was very cool) and had Peter Parker struggling with personal problems that seemed very real to me. That was even cooler, especially when Peter came back from defeat to beat Electro.

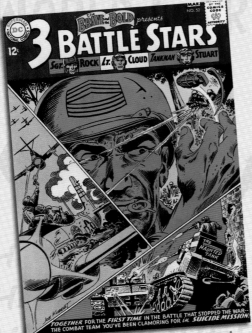

The Brave and the Bold #52: 3 Battle Stars

Writer: Robert Kanigher
Artist: Joe Kubert
DC (February-March 1964 © 1963 National Periodical Publications, Inc.)

Sgt. Rock teams up with Johnny Cloud the Navajo Ace and Jeb Stuart and his Haunted Tank crew to rescue an Allied agent who is revealed to be another DC character. A great story by the best writer-artist team in the company's war comics.

Avengers #4

Writer: Stan Lee
Artists: Jack Kirby, Paul Reinman
Marvel (March 1964 © 1963 Vista Publications Inc., image courtesy of Heritage Comic Auctions)

In a landmark issue, Captain America is found in a block of Arctic ice. He comes out of suspended animation and changes the dynamic of the team forever. For me, The Avengers aren't really The Avengers without Cap on their roster.

She's Josie #1

Writer: Frank Doyle
Artist: Dan DeCarlo
Archie (February 1964 ©* 1963 Archie Comic Publications, Inc.)

Created by DeCarlo for a newspaper strip and based on his own wife, Josie, the level-headed teen starred in funny, masterfully written comic books until the 1969 **Josie and the Pussycats** Saturday morning cartoon show mandated a change in direction.

Mystery in Space #90

Writer: Gardner Fox
Artists: Carmine Infantino, Murphy Anderson
DC (March 1964 © 1964 National Periodical Publications, Inc.)

With its iconic cover, teaming of two popular heroes, and edge-of-your-seat suspense, "Planets in Peril" is a '60s classic. Between his **Brave and the Bold** tryouts and his own series, Hawkman appeared in several issues of this title.

Daredevil #1

Writer: Stan Lee
Artist: Bill Everett
Marvel (April 1964 © 1964 Olympia Publications Inc.)

*Blinded in an accident involving radioactive materials, young Matt Murdock finds his remaining senses enhanced to super-human levels. He becomes a lawyer but does "**pro bono** work" as the masked super-hero Daredevil.*

> Blinded in an accident involving radioactive materials...

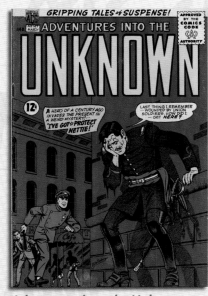

Adventures into the Unknown #147

Writer: Richard E. Hughes
Artists: Ogden Whitney, Pete Costanza
American Comics Group (March 1964 ©* 1963 Best Syndicated Features, Inc.)

*This title survived the 1950s by shifting from horror to clever, frequently whimsical stories of fantasy and science fiction. Under various aliases, Editor Hughes wrote most of the stories here and in companion titles **Forbidden Worlds** and **Unknown Worlds**.*

Fantastic Four #25

Writer: Stan Lee
Artists: Jack Kirby, George Roussos
Marvel (April 1964 © 1963 Canam Publishers Sales Corp.)

***The** classic battle between The Hulk and The Thing. With the former on a rampage and the rest of The Fantastic Four out of action, Ben Grimm stands alone. Pounded and pummeled, he never backs down from the vastly more powerful Hulk.*

Herbie #1

Writer: Richard E. Hughes
Artist: Ogden Whitney
American Comics Group (April-May 1964 © 1964 Best Syndicated Features, Inc.)

Hughes' hilarious masterpiece. Herbie Popnecker, armed with magical lollipops, is Earth's greatest hero, but his clueless dad thinks him a "little fat nothing." Such real-life figures as Lyndon Johnson and Fidel Castro often appeared in Herbie's adventures.

Fantastic Four #26

Writer: Stan Lee
Artists: Jack Kirby, George Roussos
Marvel (May 1964 © 1964 Canam Publishers Sales Corp.)

Continued from the previous issue, The Avengers get all possessive about stopping The Hulk. The two teams argue and then join forces and, doing so, establish the tight continuity that exists among Marvel's super-hero titles to this day.

Detective Comics #327

Writer: John Broome
Artist: Carmine Infantino, Joe Giella
DC (May 1964 © 1964 National Periodical Publications, Inc., image courtesy of Heritage Comic Auctions)

The debut of the "New Look" Batman, modernizing the character for the 1960s. Incoming Editor Julius Schwartz added The Elongated Man to the title, re-imagining the hero as a "stretchable sleuth" who solved mysteries as a hobby.

Captain Storm #1

Writer: Robert Kanigher
Artist: Irv Novick
DC (May-June 1964 © 1964 National Periodical Publications, Inc., image courtesy of Heritage Comic Auctions)

PT boats fascinated the public because President Kennedy had commanded one in World War II. The title hero loses his leg and his first command to a Japanese submarine but fights his way back to active duty, a tour that lasted 18 issues.

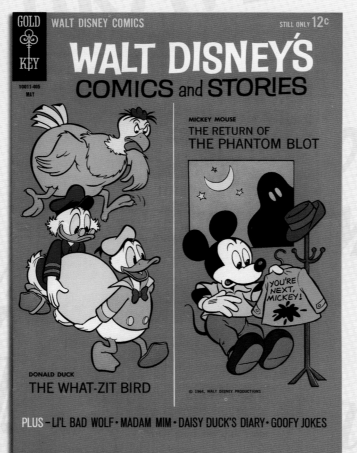

The Blot, arguably Mickey's greatest foe...

Walt Disney's Comics and Stories #284-287

Writer: uncredited
Artist: Paul Murry
Gold Key (May-August 1964 © 1964 Walt Disney Productions)

Introduced in a 1939 comic-strip story by Floyd Gottfredson, The Phantom Blot returned to challenge Mickey Mouse again in a four-issue serial. The Blot, arguably Mickey's greatest foe, then starred in his own comic book for seven issues from 1964 to 1966.

House of Mystery #143

Writer: Jack Miller
Artist: Joe Certa
DC (June 1964 © 1964 National Periodical Publications, Inc., image courtesy of Heritage Comic Auctions)

After nearly a decade as a back-up feature in **Detective Comics**, The Manhunter from Mars moved to this title with his naked alien friend Zook. By adding a super-hero to a fantasy/science-fiction comic, DC was following Marvel's lead.

Mighty Samson #1

Writer: Otto Binder
Artist: Frank Thorne
Gold Key (July 1964 © 1964 K.K. Publications, Inc.)

Centuries after atomic war has turned New York into a mutant-filled jungle, Samson, whose size and strength are likely the result of a more benign mutation, defends the surviving humans. His friends are the lovely Sharmaine and her tinkerer-father Mindor.

Hawkman #4

Writer: Gardner Fox
Artist: Murphy Anderson
DC (October-November 1964 © 1964 National Periodical Publications, Inc.)

Though she isn't on the cover, Zatanna the Magician makes her debut in this issue. She is searching for her missing father, Zatara, who had appeared in **Action Comics** in the 1940s. Her quest continued through several other Schwartz-edited titles.

Our Army at War #147-148

Writer: Robert Kanigher
Artist: Joe Kubert
DC (October-November 1964 © 1964 National Periodical Publications, Inc., image courtesy of Heritage Comic Auctions)

In the two-issue "Generals Don't Die" and "Generals Are Sergeants with Stars," Sgt. Rock must impersonate a slain officer to hold the line against an enemy offensive. The unusual cover designs made it clear this was an exceptional story.

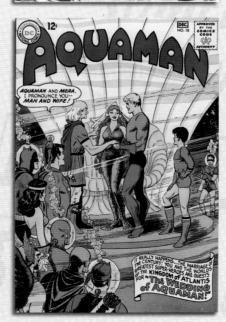

Amazing Spider-Man #18

Writer: Stan Lee
Artist: Steve Ditko
Marvel (November 1964 ©* 1964 Non-Pareil Publishing Corp., image courtesy of Heritage Comic Auctions)

Overwhelmed by Peter Parker's problems and branded a coward, Spidey hangs up his webs ... for half an issue. The most notable scenes are vignettes of citizens, supporting characters, heroes, and villains discussing the hero's fall from grace.

The Brave and the Bold #57: Metamorpho the Element Man

Writer: Bob Haney
Artists: Ramona Fradon, Charles Paris
DC (December-January 1964-1965 © 1964 National Periodical Publications, Inc.)

Exposed to an ancient artifact, Rex Mason is transformed into a being who can control the chemical elements that make up his body. Never a major success, this tragic-but-cocky adventurer was still one of the coolest super-heroes of the 1960s.

Aquaman #18

Writer: Bob Haney
Artist: Nick Cardy
DC (November-December 1964 © 1964 National Periodical Publications, Inc.)

Newly crowned as king of Atlantis, Aquaman must marry an Atlantean woman to keep his throne. He makes girlfriend Mera, a queen in her own water-based dimension, an honorary Atlantean and marries her. When the King does it, it's not illegal!

Sarge Steel #1

Writer: Joe Gill
Artist: Dick Giordano
Charlton (December 1964 © details not printed)

*A hard-boiled detective in the tradition of Mike Hammer, Steel was the first fictional private eye to be a Vietnam veteran. The classy title ran 10 issues, with the last two issues titled **Secret Agent** to reflect the hero's change in occupation.*

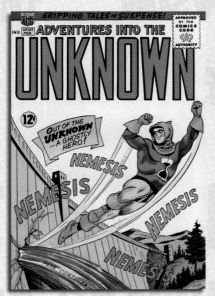

Adventures into the Unknown #154

Writer: Richard E. Hughes
Artist: Pete Costanza
American Comics Group (February 1965 © 1964 Best Syndicated Features, Inc.)

The super-heroes were back! Hughes made Nemesis the lead feature of his longest-running title. Nemesis is a detective murdered by the Mafia but allowed to return to the living to battle crime with his new ghostly powers.

Creepy #1

Writers: Archie Goodwin, Larry Ivie
Artists: Al Williamson, Joe Orlando
Warren (1964 © 1964 Warren Publishing Co.)

A jaw-droppingly good "revival" of E.C. horror in a non-Code-approved black-and-white magazine. The debut issue had Frank Frazetta's last comics story and tales drawn by Williamson, Orlando, Reed Crandall, Gray Morrow, and Angelo Torres.

Our Army at War #151

Writer: Robert Kanigher
Artist: Joe Kubert
DC (February 1965 ©* 1964 National Periodical Publications, Inc., image courtesy of Heritage Comic Auctions)

*That "blazing enemy" is Hans Von Hammer. A man of honor who fought in the "killer skies" of World War I, "Enemy Ace" starred in back-up tales and two issues of **Showcase** before getting the lead in **Star Spangled War Stories**.*

...super-villain
— Nazi scientist
Baron Zemo...

Sgt. Fury #13

Writer: Stan Lee
Artists: Jack Kirby, Chic Stone
Marvel (December 1964 © 1964 Bard Publishing Corp.)

The Howling Commandos faced their first super-villain — Nazi scientist Baron Zemo — a few months prior, but this is their first superhero. Captain America co-creator Kirby returned to do the art for this action-packed issue.

Daredevil #7
Writer: Stan Lee
Artist: Wally Wood
Marvel (March 1965 © 1965 Olympia Publications, Inc.)

Sub-Mariner hires Matt Murdock to sue the human race for its crimes against Atlantis. That goes badly, Namor goes on a rampage, Murdock tries to stop him as Daredevil. A classic tale of a courageous hero battling desperately against overwhelming force.

Sub-Mariner hires Matt Murdock to sue the human race...

Showcase #55:
Doctor Fate and Hourman

Writer: Gardner Fox
Artist: Murphy Anderson
DC (March-April 1965 © 1965 National Periodical Publications, Inc.)

I don't know if DC was seriously considering doing an ongoing title with these heroes, but, with its exciting return of Solomon Grundy and cameo appearance by the original Green Lantern, this was one of the coolest issues of the era.

Journey into Mystery #114-116

Writer: Stan Lee
Artists: Jack Kirby, Chic Stone
Marvel (March-May 1965 © 1965 Atlas Magazines, Inc.)

My favorite Thor serial. It starts with Loki, God of Evil, turning Crusher Creel into The Absorbing Man, who can absorb the power of anything he touches. It ends with "The Trial of the Gods" in fabled Asgard itself.

Avengers #16

Writer: Stan Lee
Artists: Jack Kirby, Dick Ayers
Marvel (May 1965 © 1965 Vista Publications, Inc.)

Iron Man, Thor, Giant-Man, and The Wasp all exit the team, leaving Captain America to lead a new rookie team of villains-turned-heroes Hawkeye, Quicksilver, and Scarlet Witch. This shocking development stunned Marvel's growing fan base.

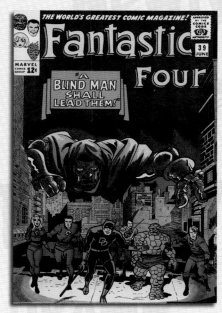

Fantastic Four #39

Writer: Stan Lee
Artists: Jack Kirby, Frank Giacoia
Marvel (June 1965 © 1965 Canam Publishers Sales Corp.)

Their super-powers destroyed by an atomic bomb blast, The Fantastic Four must face their deadliest foe armed with nothing more than their courage, makeshift devices designed by Reed Richards ... and a helping hand from Daredevil.

Total War #1

Writer: uncredited
Artist: Wally Wood
Gold Key (July 1965 © 1965 Western Publishing Company, Inc.)

Unidentified invaders attack every nation on Earth, and the multi-racial M.A.R.S. Patrol comes to America's defense. This issue has a genuine eerie/paranoid/scary vibe with Wood's art setting the dark mood perfectly.

Strange Tales #135

Writers: Jack Kirby, Stan Lee
Artists: Jack Kirby, Dick Ayers
Marvel (August 1965 © 1965 Vista Publications, Inc.)

After the war, Sgt. Fury joined the CIA. In this landmark issue, he solidifies his place in the Marvel Universe by accepting command of S.H.I.E.L.D. and combating the global organization known as Hydra. Eat your heart out, James Bond!

Fantastic Four #40

Writer: Stan Lee
Artists: Jack Kirby, Vince Colletta
Marvel (July 1965 © 1965 Canam Publishers Sales Corp.)

"The Battle of the Baxter Building" ends with a desperate gamble by Mister Fantastic and breathtaking hand-to-hand combat between Dr. Doom and the Thing.

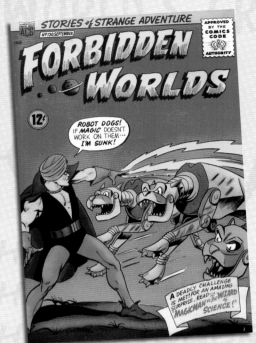

Forbidden Worlds #130

Writer: Richard E. Hughes
Artist: Pete Costanza
ACG (September 1965 © 1965 Best Syndicated Features, Inc., image courtesy of Heritage Comic Auctions)

Magicman had two secret identities: he was the immortal son of the alchemist Cagliostro and Army Private Tom Cargill. "The Wizard of Science" is in the employ of Castro. A later issue would feature Mao Tse Tung in an equally villainous role.

Fantastic Four Annual #3

Writer: Stan Lee
Artists: Jack Kirby, Vince Colletta
Marvel (October 1965 © 1965 Canam Publishers Sales Corp.)

The wedding of Reed Richards and Sue Storm was the social event of the year, attended by darn near every Marvel super-hero and super-villain. Amusingly, creators Lee and Kirby are refused admission to the reception by S.H.I.E.L.D. agents.

Blast-Off #1

Writers: uncredited
Artists: Jack Kirby, Al Williamson
Harvey (October 1965 © 1965 Harvey Features Syndicate)

Though such Harvey's kid-oriented series as Casper and Richie Rich were all doing well, it briefly tested the market for other genres. This one-shot reprinted Kirby's "Three Rocketeers" and non-series tales by Williamson, Howard Nostrand, and Reed Crandall.

Green Lantern #40

Writer: John Broome
Artists: Gil Kane, Sid Greene
DC (October 1965 © 1965 National Periodical Publications, Inc.)

One of the most pivotal stories in the DC Universe. The origin of the Guardians is revealed, as Hal Jordan teams up with the original Green Lantern in a thriller whose events will lead to the equally pivotal Crisis on Infinite Earths in 1985.

Our Army at War #160

Writer: Robert Kanigher
Artist: Joe Kubert
DC (November 1965 © 1965 National Periodical Publications, Inc.)

African-American soldier Jackie Johnson, a prizefighter before the war, gets an unexpected rematch with the German storm trooper who once defeated him. Kanigher was never shy about combating racism in his stories. This one is a classic.

Captain Atom #78

Writer: Joe Gill
Artists: Steve Ditko, Rocco Mastroserio
Charlton (December 1965 © not printed, image courtesy of Heritage Comic Auctions)

Charlton dabbled with super-heroes Blue Beetle and Son of Vulcan before unleashing their big gun. Captain Atom returns in new adventures drawn by original artist Ditko, co-creator of Marvel's Spider-Man and Dr. Strange

Tales of Suspense #71

Writer: Stan Lee
Artists: Don Heck, Wally Wood
Marvel (November 1965 © 1965 Vista Publications, Inc.)

This is the conclusion of Iron Man's three-issue Cold War smackdown with the Soviet Union's Titanium Man. It's got action, all sorts of political and romantic drama, and a heroic sacrifice by a member of the supporting cast.

... A hilarious spoof of what has already become a Marvel cliché...

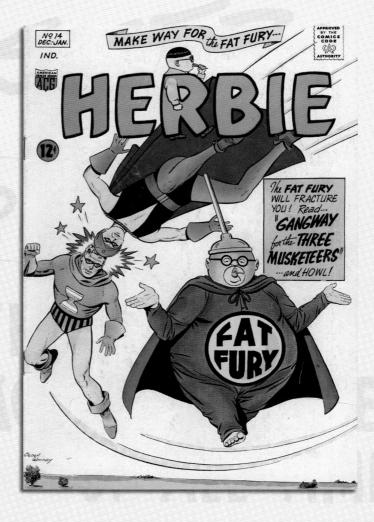

Herbie #14

Writer: Richard E. Hughes
Artist: Ogden Whitney
American Comics Group (December-January 1965-1966 © 1965 Best Syndicated Features, Inc.)

In a hilarious spoof of what has already become a Marvel cliché, Herbie, in his occasional guise as the Fat Fury, meets Magicman and Nemesis. They argue, fight, then beat the villain together with, of course, Herbie outshining his more serious allies.

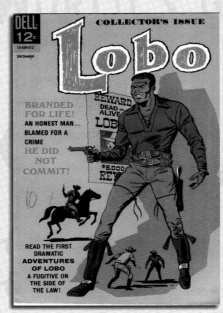

Lobo #1

Writer: Don Arneson
Artist: Tony Tallarico
Dell (December 1965 © 1965 Dell Publishing Co., Inc.)

Created by Tallarico, Lobo is the first black character to have his own comic book. He rides the post-Civil War West helping people and leaving behind wolf-imprinted silver coins. Poor distribution ended the series after just two issues.

House of Mystery #156

Writer: Dave Wood
Artist: Jim Mooney
DC (January 1966 ©* 1965 National Periodical Publications, Inc., image courtesy of Heritage Comic Auctions)

An alien device allows teenager Robby Reed to dial himself into a seemingly endless number of super-hero identities. It was a truly goofy concept, but, Lord help us, we loved it as kids and we still love it today.

Blazing Combat #2

Writer: Archie Goodwin
Artists: Joe Orlando, John Severin
Warren (January 1966 © 1965 Warren Publishing Co., image courtesy of Heritage Comic Auctions)

Publisher James Warren followed **Creepy** *with this title, which, like the E.C. war comics, didn't shy away from including stories about a contemporary war, in this case, Vietnam. The controversial nature of such tales contributed to the magazine's short four-issue run.*

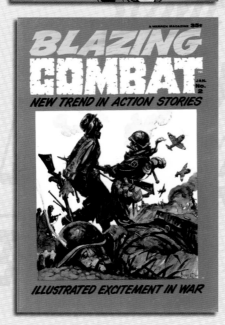

Amazing Spider-Man #33

Writers: Stan Lee, Steve Ditko
Artist: Steve Ditko
Marvel (February 1966 © 1965 Non-Pareil Publishing Corp.)

Pinned by debris, clutching the serum that can save his dying Aunt May, Spidey refuses to surrender to his seemingly inevitable death. This epic sequence that culminates in a hero triumphant is one of the most powerful in comics history.

Mighty Crusaders #4

Writer: Jerry Siegel
Artist: Paul Reinman
Archie (April 1966 published by Radio Comics Inc., no © printed)

In this campy exercise in excess, the newly formed Mighty Crusaders inspire other super-heroes of the 1940s to come out of retirement: 17 different heroes and sidekicks. It was like watching a thousand clowns explode out of a tiny car.

> ... Mighty Crusaders inspire other super-heroes of the 1940s to come out of retirement...

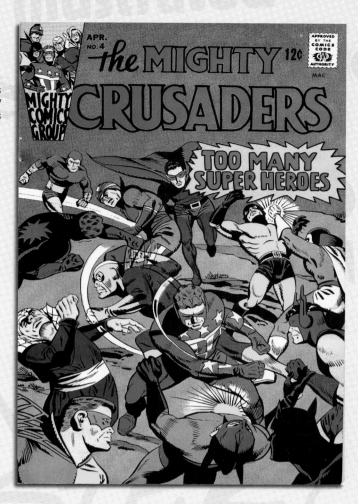

Fantastic Four #48

Writer: Stan Lee
Artists: Jack Kirby, Joe Sinnott
Marvel (March 1966 © 1965 Canam Publishers Sales Corp.)

"The World's Greatest Comic Book" was on a roll in 1965 and 1966. Following the introduction of The Inhumans, the Four return to New York to find the world imperiled by Galactus, a god-like being who devours living planets for food.

Fantastic Four #49

Writer: Stan Lee
Artists: Jack Kirby, Joe Sinnott
Marvel (April 1966 © 1966 Canam Publishers Sales Corp.)

The Fantastic Four goes heads-to-head with The Silver Surfer, who, as the herald of Galactus, shares a portion of his master's power cosmic. Created by Kirby, The Surfer became Lee's favorite vehicle for considering the promise and failings of mankind.

Fantastic Four #50

Writer: Stan Lee
Artists: Jack Kirby, Joe Sinnott
Marvel (May 1966 © 1966 Canam Publishers Sales Corp.)

"The Galactus Trilogy" ends with The Surfer fighting for our world and The Four risking everything to stop Galactus with the Ultimate Nullifier. Afterward, Lee and Kirby provide a down-to-Earth moment via The Human Torch's first day at college.

Fantastic Four #51

Writer: Stan Lee
Artists: Jack Kirby, Joe Sinnott
Marvel (June 1966 © 1966 Canam Publishers Sales Corp.)

How do you follow Galactus? With a story about a nameless scientist who steals the form and power of The Thing and, in doing so, learns the meaning of courage, friendship, and sacrifice. One of the best super-hero comics of all.

How do you follow Galactus?

Eerie #3

Writer: Archie Goodwin
Artists: Steve Ditko, Angelo Torres
Warren (May 1966 © 1966 Warren Publishing Co.)

The long-running companion magazine to Creepy. This issue features the classic Ditko-drawn "Room with a View" as well as stories drawn by Torres, Al Williamson, Rocco Mastro-serio, Jerry Grandenetti, Joe Orlando, Alex Toth, and Gene Colan.

Green Lantern #45

Writer: John Broome
Artists: Gil Kane, Sid Greene
DC (June 1966 © 1966 National Periodical Publications, Inc.)

An alien princess in search of a husband. A brutish suitor. A pair of Green Lanterns and Doiby Dickles, taxi-driving sidekick to the 1940s GL. Who wins the fair princess and why he wins her makes this a sentimental favorite of mine.

Witzend #1

Writers: Wally Wood, Archie Goodwin
Artists: Al Williamson, Angelo Torres
Wallace Wood (Summer 1966 © 1966 Wallace Wood, image courtesy of Heritage Comic Auctions)

Published by Wood with a mission of providing artistic freedom to its contributors, this issue featured "Sinner," a story written and drawn by Goodwin, and tales by Wood, Williamson, science-fiction illustrator Jack Gaughan, and other top talents.

Archie's Girls Betty and Veronica #127

Writers: uncredited
Artists: uncredited
Archie (July 1966 © 1966 Close Up, Inc.)

If it was "in," it was part of the Archie scene. Though Stretchman didn't appear inside this issue, one story had Veronica wearing a then-fashionable "granny dress" and another referenced the Beatles, The Rolling Stones, and The Dave Clark Five.

Fantastic Four #52

Writer: Stan Lee
Artists: Jack Kirby, Joe Sinnott
Marvel (July 1966 © 1966 Canam Publishers Sales Corp.)

Another landmark issue. The Black Panther is T'Challa, king of the green-friendly and technologically advanced nation of Wakanda — and Marvel's first black super-hero. He would get his own book in the 1970s and rise to stardom in the new millennium.

Jughead #134

Writers: uncredited
Artists: uncredited
Archie (July 1966 © 1966 Archie Comic Publications, Inc.)

The Shield, a "real" super-hero from the 1940s, makes an appearance on this cover. Inside, it's Juggy versus the amorous Big Ethel and prankster Reggie — and the United Girls against Jughead, who think he's a bad influence on other boys.

Amazing Spider-Man #39

Writer: Stan Lee
Artists: John Romita, Mike Esposito
Marvel (August 1966 © 1966 Non-Pareil Publishing Corp.)

With the departure of co-creator Ditko, Spidey and his cast get a new look, and The Green Goblin is revealed to be the father of one of Peter Parker's pals. Romita successfully blended Ditko's spidery quirkiness and his own slick style.

1000 Comic Books You Must Read

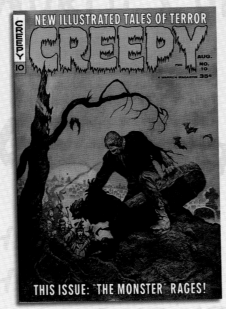

Creepy #10
Writer: Archie Goodwin
Artist: Steve Ditko
Warren (August 1966 © 1966 Warren Publishing Co.)

Ditko left Marvel but he was prolific as ever for other publishers. "Collector's Edition" brilliantly depicts a one-of-a-kind book that reveals the past and the future of its owners. Editor Goodman knew how to match the artist to the story.

Avengers #32
Writer: Stan Lee
Artist: Don Heck
Marvel (September 1966 © 1966 Vista Publications, Inc.)

Replace the Ku Klux Klan's white sheets with snake-motif costumes and you get the Sons of the Serpent. Real-life social concerns were part and parcel of Marvel, and this connected them to high-school, college, and older readers.

T.H.U.N.D.E.R. Agents #7
Writer: uncredited
Artists: Steve Ditko, Wally Wood
Tower (August 1966 © not printed)

In the most memorable scene in this series, Menthor sacrifices his own life to prevent the deaths of his fellow agents. The crackling lightning and pouring rain on the last page intensifies the impact of this classic story.

Fantastic Giants #24
Writers: uncredited
Artist: Steve Ditko
Charlton (September 1966 © details not printed, image courtesy of Heritage Comic Auctions)

*A Ditko spectacular reprinting the original comics adaptations of **Gorgo** and **Konga** alongside two all-new stories. This was one of the few 1960s comics to promote an artist or writer on its cover, perhaps the only one not published by Marvel.*

1000 Comic Books You Must Read

Flash Gordon #1

Writer: Al Williamson
Artist: Al Williamson
King (September 1966 © 1966 King Features Syndicate, Inc., image courtesy of Heritage Comic Auctions)

King Features Syndicate tried to publish comic books of their most popular newspaper strips, but, despite beautifully drawn issues like this one, they never got a foothold in the market and ended up licensing the characters to other publishers.

Fighting American #1

Writers: Joe Simon, Jack Kirby
Artists: Jack Kirby, Joe Simon
Harvey (October 1966 © 1954, 1966 Harvey Features Syndicate, image courtesy of Heritage Comic Auctions)

Harvey continued to test the market with this giant reprint of material from the 1950s. The character started out as a typical patriotic hero but turned into wacky Cold War satire with such villains as Commissar Yutz and Viva Yafata.

The Spirit #1

Writers: Will Eisner, Jules Feiffer
Artists: Will Eisner, Chuck Kramer
Harvey (October 1966 © 1966 Will Eisner)

A new retelling of the Spirit's origin led off this collection of classic stories. By introducing a coming generation of artists and writers to Eisner's genius, this issue became one of the most creatively influential comic books of all.

Mighty Comics #40

Writer: Jerry Siegel
Artist: Paul Reinman
Archie (November 1966 © 1966 Radio Comics, Inc., image courtesy of Heritage Comic Auctions)

In the 1940s, The Web was a grim figure who used his knowledge of criminology to visit harsh justice on lawbreakers. In this revival, he is a henpecked husband who has to sneak past his shrewish wife to fight crime. Oh, those wacky '60s!

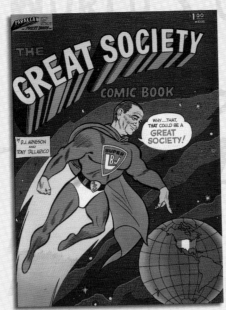

The Great Society Comic Book

Writer: D. J. Arneson
Artists: Bill Fraccio, Tony Tallarico
Parallax Publishing Company, Inc. (1966 © 1966 D.J. Arneson and T. Tallarico)

This odd comic cast political figures as super-heroes and villains: Super LBJ (Lyndon Johnson), Bobman and Teddy (Robert and Ted Kennedy), Gaullefinger (Charles DeGaulle), Dr. Nyet (Nikita Khrushchev), and White-man (George Wallace).

Adventure Comics #353

Writer: Jim Shooter
Artists: Curt Swan, George Klein
DC (February 1967 © 1966 National Periodical Publications, Inc.)

With most of their members on distant missions, the few remaining Legion-naires team with the murderous Fatal Five to save the solar system from The Sun-Eater. When he sold his first stories in 1966, Shooter was only 14 years old.

Thor #136

Writer: Stan Lee
Artists: Jack Kirby, Vince Colletta
Marvel (January 1967 © 1966 Atlas Magazines, Inc.)

The romance between Thor and Jane Foster ends this issue, when the nurse fails Odin's test to become an immortal. From this story on, it became clear Thor was, indeed, the God of Thunder and not merely the transformed Dr. Don Blake.

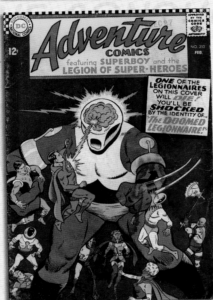

The Spirit #2

Writer: Will Eisner
Artist: Will Eisner
Harvey (March 1967 © 1967 Will Eisner)

This second of Harvey's two collections of Spirit stories featured a new origin story for The Octopus, the hero's most persistent villain, and such classic tales as "Plaster of Paris," "The Deadly Comic Book," and "Rudy the Barber."

Super Green Beret #1

Writer: Otto Binder
Artist: Carl Pfeufer
Lightning Comics (April 1967 © 1966 Milson Publishing Co., Inc.)

When young Tod dons a magical green beret, he changes into an adult super-soldier who bashes commies from Cuba to Vietnam. Canceled after two issues, this grim Captain Marvel wannabe is an example of just how quirky '60s super-heroes could get.

> ...young Tod dons a magical green beret...

Richie Rich #59

Writers: uncredited
Artists: uncredited
Harvey (May 1967 © 1967 Harvey Features Syndicate, image courtesy of Heritage Comic Auctions)

The dominance of the super-hero genre influenced many other kinds of comics, as well. This issue's Ato-man has a typical super-villain origin: a scientist exposed to radiation that increases his envy of his employer, Richie's dad.

Fatman the Human Flying Saucer #1

Writer: Otto Binder
Artist: C.C. Beck
Lightning Comics (April 1967 © 1966 Milson Publishing Co., Inc.)

Somewhat incorrectly billed as the creators of the original Captain Marvel, Binder and Beck re-united for this lighthearted super-hero series. Their stories were charming and entertaining, but the

Adventure Comics #357

Writer: Jim Shooter
Artists: Curt Swan, George Klein
DC (June 1967 © 1967 National Periodical Publications, Inc., image courtesy of Heritage Comic Auctions)

Are Legionnaires being haunted by a fallen com-rade? Nothing is what it seems in this story, but the final page leaves little doubt that friendship can endure beyond the grave. It's a spooky tale with a satisfying conclusion.

Blue Beetle #1

Writers: Steve Ditko, uncredited
Artist: Steve Ditko
Charlton (June 1967 © 1967 details not printed, image courtesy of Heritage Comic Auctions)

Created by Ditko, this incarnation of The Blue Beetle is inventor Ted Kord, who uses his mechanical and scientific know-how to fight crime. In the back-up strip, The Question is a sort of objectivist cousin to Ditko's earlier Mr. A.

Swing with Scooter #7

Writer: uncredited
Artist: uncredited
DC (June-July 1967 © 1967 National Periodical Publications, Inc.)

Born of Beatlemania, Scooter is a British rocker who moves to the U.S. to have a normal life. Apparently, this included being turned into a humanoid vegetable, the experiment mentioned on the cover of this issue. I love the '60s.

Sgt. Fury #45

Writer: Gary Friedrich
Artist: John Severin
Marvel (August 1967 © 1967 Bard Publishing Corp.)

With "The War Lover," Friedrich emerged as Sgt. Fury's best writer. Centering on the excesses of a kill-crazy soldier, it was the first of several "The" stories exploring the larger issues of morality in World War II and in more contemporary conflicts.

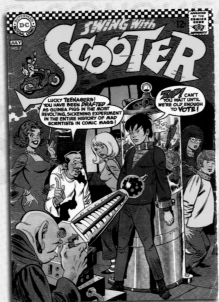

Not Brand Echh #1

Writers: Stan Lee, Roy Thomas
Artists: Jack Kirby, Marie Severin
Marvel (August 1967 © 1967 Leading Magazine Corp., Marvel Comics Group, indicia say only "Brand Echh")

Kirby lets loose his zany side in this hilarious parody of The FF, Doctor Doom, and the Silver Surfer. Stan matches the visuals beat for beat. I laughed out loud when I first read it ... and every time I've read it since.

The Swinging Sixties CHAPTER FOUR

1000 Comic Books You Must Read

Sugar & Spike #72

Writer: Sheldon Mayer
Artist: Sheldon Mayer
DC (August-September 1967 © 1967 National Periodical Publications, Inc.)

Introducing Bernie the Brain. The genius infant was the same age as Sugar and Spike, but his incredible inventions and understanding of the adult world allowed Mayer to expand the scope of his toddlers' adventures in exciting and hilarious ways.

Avengers Annual #1

Writer: Roy Thomas
Artists: Don Heck, George Roussos
Marvel (September 1967 © 167 Vista Publications, Inc., Marvel Comics Group)

Surpassed only by Stan Lee, Thomas quickly became Marvel's second most important writer. He could write every kind of comic book but he excelled at such sprawling super-hero epics as this 49-page battle between The Avengers and The Mandarin.

Fightin' Army #76

Writer: Will Franz
Artist: Sam Glanzman
Charlton (October 1967 ©* 1967 details not printed)

A wrongly convicted American officer of German descent wanders the African desert trying to clear his name while sometimes posing as an enemy soldier. This oft-shocking psychological drama ranks among the best war-comics series of all time.

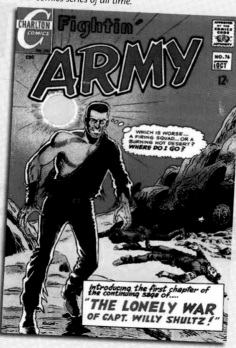

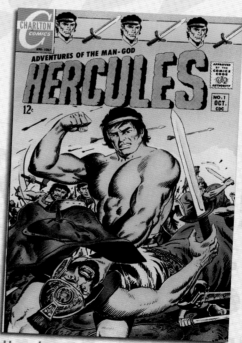

Hercules #1

Writer: Joe Gill
Artist: Sam Glanzman
Charlton (October 1967, no copyright printed)

This is a wondrous and occasionally hilarious retelling of the 12 labors of Hercules. The original legends are sanitized for young readers, the gods speak in modern dialect, and the colorful art is almost psychedelic on occasion.

Strange Adventures #205
Writer: Arnold Drake
Artists: Carmine Infantino, George Roussos
DC (October 1967 © 1967 National Periodical Publications, Inc.)

*Slain by an unknown assassin, circus star Boston Brand must wander the world, possessing the bodies of the living, until he finds his killer. A stylish **noir** thriller.*

> ...Boston Brand must wander the world, possessing the bodies of the living...

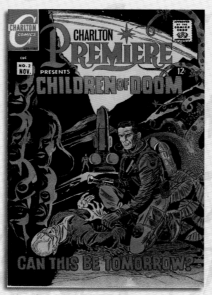

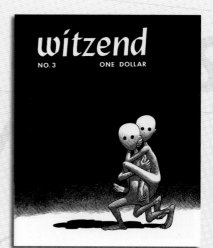

Charlton Premiere Vol. 2 #2
Writer: Denny O'Neil
Artist: Pat Boyette
Charlton (November 1967 © 1967 details not printed, image courtesy of Heritage Comic Auctions)

O'Neil's tale of nuclear doom combine masterfully with Boyette's haunting art. Portions of this story are published in black-and-white, heightening its mood. This quiet classic was a last-minute replacement for the issue's originally planned contents.

Showcase #73: Beware the Creeper!
Writers: Steve Ditko, Don Segall
Artist: Steve Ditko
DC (March-April 1968 © 1968 National Periodical Publications, Inc.)

This title continued to introduce new characters, but, impatient to counter Marvel's growing success, DC would move them to their own titles immediately. Most of these titles, including Ditko's latest creation, were canceled within a year-and-

Witzend #3
Writer: Steve Ditko
Artist: Steve Ditko
Wallace Wood (1967 © 1967 Wallace Wood, image courtesy of Heritage Comic Auctions)

This issue is notable for the first appearance of "Mr. A," Ditko's uncompromising masked vigilante. Ditko embraced the objectivism of author Ayn Rand, and this five-page story was his first attempt to express this philosophy directly in his work.

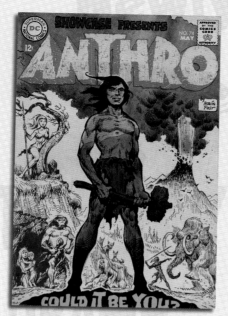

Showcase #74: Anthro
Writer: Howard Post
Artist: Howard Post
DC (May 1968 © 1968 National Periodical Publications, Inc.)

The tragic thing about these **Showcase** *"instant hits" is that most were clever, good, original ideas. The adventures of teenage caveman Anthro have action, drama, humor — and even a bit of social satire.*

His Name Is ... Savage #1
Writers: Gil Kane, Archie Goodwin
Artist: Gil Kane
Adventure House Press (June 1968 © 1968 Adventure House, image courtesy of Heritage Comic Auctions)

Savage is a government agent tracking a renegade American general looking to start a world war. This black-and-white comics magazine was brutal, cool, and smart, but poor distribution and the reaction of actor Lee Marvin (whose likeness was clearly used) killed it after only one issue.

Showcase #75: The Hawk and the Dove
Writers: Steve Ditko, Steve Skeates
Artist: Steve Ditko
DC (June 1968 © 1968 National Periodical Publications, Inc.)

Two brothers — one conservative, one liberal — are given super-powers by a mysterious voice from beyond. A brilliant concept, especially for a time when Americans were torn by Vietnam, but its execution never lived up to the premise.

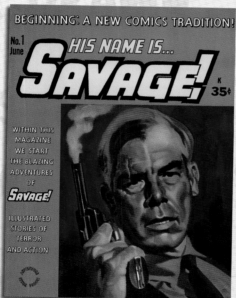

Nick Fury, Agent of S.H.I.E.L.D #1
Writer: Jim Steranko
Artists: Jim Steranko, Joe Sinnott
Marvel (June 1968 © 1968 Olympia Publications, Inc., Marvel Comics Group)

Steranko exploded on the comics scene with the wildest spy capers the industry had ever seen. His stories were exciting, and the ways in which he told them were revolutionary. His work influenced some of the best artists and writers of the 1970s.

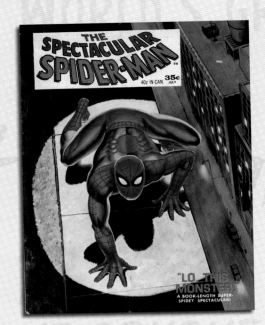

Spectacular Spider-Man #1

Writer: Stan Lee
Artists: John Romita, Jim Mooney
Marvel (July 1968 © 1968 Non-Pareil Publishing Corp.)

Marvel attempted to expand its readership with this black-and-white magazine of its most popular super-hero, but the material was no different from what appeared in the regular comics. The second and final issue of this experiment was in color.

Aquaman #40

Writer: Steve Skeates
Artist: Jim Aparo
DC (July-August 1968 © 1968 National Periodical Publications, Inc.)

Aquaman begins a multi-issue quest to find his kidnapped wife. It was an exciting, imaginative underwater epic. Editor Dick Giordano was a fan favorite for his creative successes at Charlton, and the same excitement followed him to DC.

The Many Ghosts of Dr. Graves #8

Writers: Steve Skeates, uncredited
Artists: Jim Aparo, Pat Boyette
Charlton (August 1968 © 1968 Charlton Press, Inc., image courtesy of Heritage Comic Auctions)

Dr. Graves was the host of this title, but sometimes played a more active role in its stories. The super-heroes hadn't sold well for Charlton, so the company focused on other comics: horror, romance, war, Western, romance, and licensed properties.

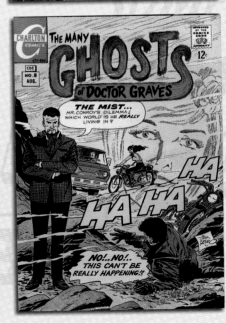

Silver Surfer #1

Writer: Stan Lee
Artist: John Buscema, Joe Sinnott
Marvel (August 1968 © 1968 Official Magazine Corp., Marvel Comics Group)

The Silver Surfer's origin was finally revealed in this first of several double-sized issues. Lee loved the character and used these tales as a vehicle to explore issues of good, evil, and humanity's propensities for both.

Avengers Annual #2

Writer: Roy Thomas
Artists: Don Heck, Werner Roth
Marvel (September 1968 © 1968 Vista Publications, Inc.)

The Avengers travel to an alternate Earth where the original team never broke up but, instead, became the tyrannical rulers of their world. It was the first of countless alternate Earths that continue to appear in Marvel comics to this day.

Mysterious Suspense #1

Writer: Steve Ditko
Artist: Steve Ditko
Charlton (October 1968 © not printed)

A year after Charlton canceled its super-heroes, Ditko's creations perform encores. This book-length tale is a powerful examination of what makes a man a hero, as The Question opposes mobsters trying to silence a controversial TV show.

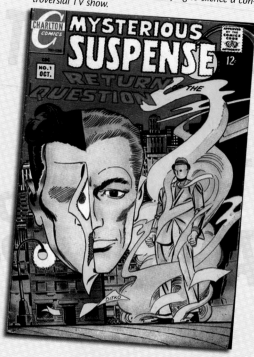

Brother Power, The Geek #1

Writer: Joe Simon
Artist: Al Bare
DC (September-October 1968 © 1968 National Periodical Publications, Inc.)

An abandoned mannequin is struck by lightning, comes to life, and is befriended by hippies. The bizarre concept was doomed to failure by interoffice hostility toward its sympathetic portrayal of the hippie subculture. There were only two issues.

Avengers #57

Writer: Roy Thomas
Artists: John Buscema, George Klein
Marvel (October 1968 © 1968 Vista Publications, Inc.)

The android Vision was created to destroy The Avengers but turned on his creator. In an unforgettable epilogue, a boy plays with the robot Ultron's lifeless head, while captions feature the Percy Bysshe Shelley sonnet "Ozymandias."

Avengers #58
Writer: Roy Thomas
Artists: John Buscema, George Klein
Marvel (November 1968 © 1968 Vista Publications, Inc.)

The Vision joins **The Avengers** *after the team spends an entire issue learning his complicated origin — which grew more complicated over the years. As long as Thomas was writing it, The Avengers was my favorite Marvel super-hero title.*

The Vision joins The Avengers...

Angel and the Ape #1
Writer: uncredited
Artists: Bob Oksner, Henry Scarpelli
DC (November-December 1968 © 1968 National Periodical Publications, Inc., image courtesy of Heritage Comic Auctions)

Angel is a private detective. Her partner, Sam, is a talking gorilla and a comic-book artist who works for Stan Bragg, a parody of Stan Lee. It was a fun concept with gorgeous art but, like other **Show-case** *debuts of those days, it didn't last two years.*

Blue Beetle #5
Writer: Steve Ditko
Artist: Steve Ditko
Charlton (November 1968 © not printed, image courtesy of Heritage Comic Auctions)

The Blue Beetle is inspired by a statue depicting a heroic figure, while the "Destroyer of Heroes" is determined to, well, destroy it. Ditko's objectivist comics would become increasingly heavy-handed, but this story is terrific.

Silver Surfer #3
Writer: Stan Lee
Artists: John Buscema, Joe Sinnott
Marvel (December 1968 © 1968 Official Magazine Corp., Marvel Comics Group)

The demonic Mephisto, pained by the purity of The Silver Surfer's soul, tempts him with earthly pleasures that include reuniting The Surfer with lost love Shalla Bal. It's the temptation of Christ as only mighty Marvel could present it!

Sub-Mariner #8

Writer: Roy Thomas
Artists: John Buscema, Dan Adkins
Marvel (December 1968 © 1968 Atlas Magazines, Inc., Marvel Comics Group)

His boss Stan Lee was cribbing from **The Bible**, *but Thomas turned to* **Peter Pan** *as inspiration, when an enraged Sub-Mariner's battle with The Thing brings Namor to a bittersweet reunion with the woman who loved him in the 1940s.*

Amazing Spider-Man #68-77

Writers: Stan Lee, John Romita
Artists: John Romita, Jim Mooney
Marvel (January-October 1969 © 1969 Magazine Management Co., Inc., Marvel Comics Group)

Crime lords vie for ancient power. Spidey battles to keep them from it. Fast-paced action, surprises galore, intriguing human interest, gorgeous art, and slick scripting. It's one of the greatest Spider-Man adventures ever.

Pussycat #1

Writers: Stan Lee, Larry Lieber
Artists: Jim Mooney, Bill Ward
Marvel (1968 ©* 1968 Magazine Management Co., Inc., image courtesy of Heritage Comic Auctions)

Trying to emulate the success of "Little Annie Fanny" in **Playboy**, *this risqué secret agent appeared in the men's magazines of Marvel Publisher Martin Goodman. The stories were reprinted in this black-and-white one-shot: a first for Marvel.*

House of Mystery #178

Writers: Neal Adams, E. Nelson Bridwell
Artists: Neal Adams, Win Mortimer
DC (January-February 1969 © 1968 National Periodical Publications, Inc., image courtesy of Heritage Comic Auctions)

Once again a horror anthology, **House of Mystery** *served as showcase and training ground for some of the top talents of the 1970s. Adams was already a comics superstar, and "The Game" — a truly scary story with stunning art — showed why.*

Teen Titans #19

Writer: Mike Friedrich
Artists: Gil Kane, Wally Wood
DC (January-February 1969 © 1969 National Periodical Publications, Inc.)

I loved the lighthearted "groovy" Teen Titans comics of the 1960s, but I also loved this more serious tale of a young wannabe villain attempting to work his way up to the big bad-guy leagues by taking out Robin and his fellow sidekicks.

Many Ghosts of Doctor Graves #12

Writer: Steve Skeates
Artist: Steve Ditko
Charlton (February 1969 © 1968 Charlton Press, Inc.)

Host Graves goes all master of the mystic arts, as he stands against a creature from another dimension bent on conquering Earth. Reading "The Ultimate Evil" was like discovering a hitherto unpublished Dr. Strange story. It was even drawn by Ditko!

Captain America #110

Writer: Jim Steranko
Artists: Jim Steranko, Joe Sinnott
Marvel (February 1969 © 1968 Perfect Film & Chemical Corp., Marvel Comics Group)

The Hulk on a rampage, Rick Jones becomes Cap's official partner, and Hydra strikes at the very heart of New York. It's the first of three glorious issues by Steranko, arguably the most talked-about comics creator of the time!

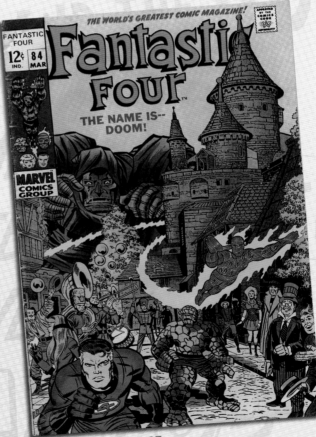

Fantastic Four #84-87

Writer: Stan Lee
Artists: Jack Kirby, Joe Sinnott
Marvel (March-June 1969 © 1968 Magazine Management Co., Marvel Comics Group)

In this Lee-Kirby take on the revolutionary British TV series The Prisoner, The Fantastic Four are stripped of their super-powers and trapped in Latveria, the helpless guests of the country's ruler, their greatest enemy, Doctor Doom!

1000 Comic Books You Must Read   **The Swinging Sixties CHAPTER FOUR**

Motor City Comics #1

Writer: Robert Crumb
Artist: Robert Crumb
Rip Off Press (April 1969 © 1969 R. Crumb Productions, image courtesy of Heritage Comic Auctions)

One of the first underground comix I bought, though I didn't buy it until 1972. It was my introduction to the sensual and wild humor of Robert Crumb via "Lenore Goldberg and her Girl Commandos" and "The Inimitable Boingy Baxter."

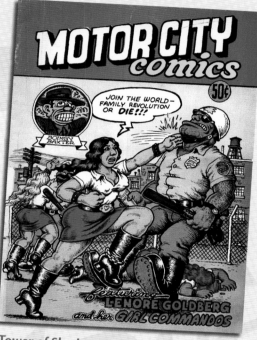

Vampirella #1

Writers: Forest J Ackerman, Don Glut
Artists: Tom Sutton, Billy Graham
Warren (September 1969 © 1969 Warren Publishing Co.)

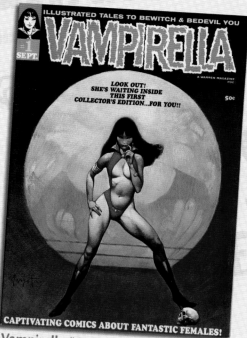

*A sexy companion magazine to **Creepy** and **Eerie**. Its host and title star was a vampire heroine from another planet. The issue featured a Frank Frazetta cover and art by Neal Adams, Ernie Colon, Reed Crandall, Mike Royer, and Tony Tallarico.*

Tower of Shadows #1

Writers: Jim Steranko, Johnny Craig
Artists: Jim Steranko, Johnny Craig
Marvel (September 1969 © 1969 Magazine Management Co., Inc., Marvel Comics Group)

Marvel's first horror anthology in years. The Steranko story is a cinematic chiller, but a misguided editorial decision saw the Craig contribution retouched unto death. The issue also has a tale by Stan Lee and John Buscema.

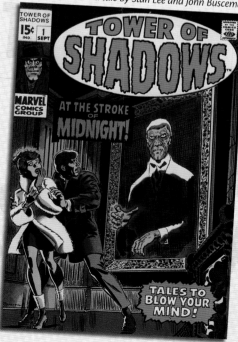

Tower of Shadows #2

Writers: Neal Adams
Artists: Neal Adams, Dan Adkins
Marvel (November 1969 © 1969 Magazine Management Co., Inc., Marvel Comics Group)

How do you follow Steranko? Try "One Hungers" by Neal Adams, a personal favorite about a gelatinous creature in a scary old house! This issue also had stories by Roy Thomas and Don Heck — and Gary Friedrich and John Buscema.

CHAPTER FIVE

Since the 1960s were my personal "Golden Age of Comics," it follows naturally that the 1970s were my "Silver Age." To confuse you even further, many fans and industry professionals refer to the 1970s as the "Bronze Age of Comics."

Eye of the beholder, my friends. Eye of the beholder.

I started out the decade dropping out of Cleveland's John Carroll University after less than one year. I was eager to pursue a career in writing, though working in comics seemed like a distant dream at the time. I wrote for lots of comics fanzines, using them to teach myself how to write comic-book scripts. I began corresponding with industry professionals and unsuccessfully pitched a few plots and stories to them.

I spent a few years in the employ of *The Plain Dealer*, a Cleveland newspaper. It was good money for a single guy. I was able to get my own apartment, attend comics conventions in New York and San Diego, and buy pretty much every new comic book being published.

Among the new comics I bought were *underground comix*. There was a headshop two blocks from my apartment. I didn't use drugs and so had no need for rolling papers and other drug paraphernalia, but the place had an outstanding selection of books by Robert Crumb and other counter-culture cartoonists. I mention these comics because I think we need a disclaimer.

Given the generally family-friendly nature of the volume, I won't go into specifics of the contents of the underground comix included herein. But these comix are important because they influenced the art form on several levels. They allowed creators to retain rights to their own work as a standard operating procedure. They basically created the model the direct market — and we'll talk about that in a bit — would use. They inspired even mainstream creators to expand the possibilities of comics. The underground comix were important, and that's why they have a place in this book.

The 1970s were an exciting decade for fans and professionals. Comic-book publishers were increasing their production, which allowed young artists and writers to find employment in the field at a rate greater than at any time since the 1940s. I was one of those young writers, and you'll even find some of my comics in this book. Which — sigh — means we need another disclaimer of sorts.

Despite my clearly healthy ego, any Isabella-written comics in this tome were suggested by my pals and readers in comicdom. As a sort of warning when these comics appear, they will be marked with one of these smiling "Tony heads" that are used in my **Comics Buyer's Guide** *reviews. Depending on whether or not you like my comics writing, you can consider them a recommendation or a warning. Your call.*

The 1970s were when the traditional methods of comics distribution became increasingly insufficient for publishers and readers alike, leading to the birth of hundreds of comic-book stores throughout the country and the creation of a direct-market distribution system to serve those stores. Comics shops had to buy their comic books on a non-returnable basis but they got better service and much bigger discounts than they could get from regional magazine distributors.

The shops became *so* vital to the comics industry that the industry started producing titles that would be available exclusively in the comic shops … and the very presence of these shops would led to a great many new publishers entering the field in the 1980s and the 1990s.

Comics creators were becoming as much a selling point with comics buyers as the characters who appeared in the comics they wrote and drew. That led to better financial rewards and working conditions from most of the publishers.

Comics creators were being influenced by work from Great Britain, Europe, and Japan. Even in advance of these comics crossing the seas and being sold in America, their influence would begin to be seen in American comic books.

My comics career started in the 1970s. I lived in New York for the better part of four years, then moved back to my native Cleveland and continued to write for Marvel, DC, and other publishers. By the decade's end, I was still writing comics and also writing columns and cartoons for *Comics Buyer's Guide*. I had also become the owner and operator of a comic-book store in downtown Cleveland, assuring myself of a continuous supply of comic books. There was a lesson to be learned from all this — and, if I hadn't been so darn busy wearing so many hats, I might have learned it.

The 1970s were an exciting decade for comics. Here are some of the reasons …

Sgt. Fury #75

Writer: Gary Friedrich
Artists: Dick Ayers, John Severin
Marvel (February 1970 © 1969 Magazine
Management Co., Inc.)

The most powerful of the "The" stories in which
Friedrich explored issues of mortality in wartime. "The Deserter" was inspired by the real-life
case of Eddie Slovik, the only American soldier
executed for cowardice since the 1900s.

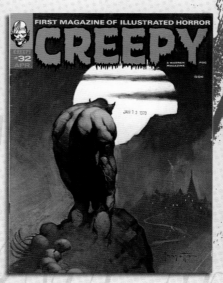

Creepy #32

Writer: Harlan Ellison
Artist: Neal Adams
Warren (April 1970 © 1970 Warren Publishing Co.)

Inspired by the Frank Frazetta cover painting, Ellison's "Rock God" is one of the great comics horror
stories. The Adams art chillingly conveys the horrors
of the dim past and of an ancient god rising in the
heart of a modern metropolis.

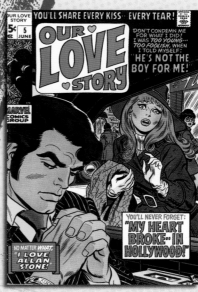

Our Love Story #5

Writer: Stan Lee
Artist: Jim Steranko
Marvel (June 1970 © 1970 Magazine Management
Co., Inc.)

The Steranko art for "My Heart Broke in Hollywood" has a wonderful Peter Max vibe to it,
but the story is a stupidly sexist tale of a director
who passes over an actress for a role so that he
can cast her as his wife.

Green Lantern #76

Writer: Denny O'Neil
Artist: Neal Adams
DC (April 1970 © 1970 National Periodical Publications, Inc.)

With the title facing cancellation, Editor Julius Schwartz
okayed a bold new direction in which GL and Green Arrow
explored real-life issues. This is the story that added the
phrase "social relevance" to the comics lexicon.

...a bold new direction in which Green Lantern and Green Arrow explored real-life issues.

Aquaman #53

Writer: Steve Skeates
Artist: Jim Aparo
DC (September-October 1970 © 1970 National Periodical
Publications Inc.)

*Environmental concerns outlined here foreshadowed devel-
opments that would come in Aquaman's 2003-2006 series.*

Superman's Pal, Jimmy Olsen #133

Writer: Jack Kirby
Artists: Jack Kirby, Vince Colletta
DC (October 1970 © 1970 National Periodical Publications,
Inc., image courtesy of Heritage Comic Auctions)

*DC kicked off the decade with a major coup: hiring
Kirby away from Marvel. Olsen acquires his own sidekicks — updated versions of the 1940s Newsboy Legion
— and would soon be embroiled in a war between the
warring "gods" of two distant worlds.*

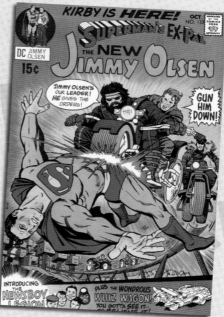

Hot Wheels #5

Writers: Alex Toth, Len Wein
Artists: Alex Toth, Ric Estrada, Dick Giordano
DC (November-December 1970 © 1970 Ken Snyder
Properties, Inc.)

*Based on a Saturday morning cartoon which was little
more than a half-hour commercial for the popular die-cast
toy cars, this issue is notable for "The Case of the Curious
Classic," a masterpiece of comics cinematography.*

Superman's Girl Friend, Lois Lane #106

Writer: Robert Kanigher
Artists: Werner Roth, Vince Colletta
DC (November 1970 © 1970 National Periodical Publications,
Inc., image courtesy of Heritage Comic Auctions)

*Lois uses a Kryptonian machine to become a black woman
for a day, the better to write a story about the African-
American community. It's heavy-handed, but its good inten-
tions and optimistic ending overcome that awkwardness.*

Vampirella #8

Writer: Archie Goodwin
Artist: Tom Sutton
Warren (November 1970 © 1970 Warren Publishing Co., image courtesy of
Heritage Comic Auctions)

*Vampire hunters Conrad and Adam Von Helsing and The Cult of Chaos
become part of Vampirella's world, as the beautiful alien returns to starring
in her own adventures while continuing to introduce the other stories in
her magazine.*

O.G. Whiz #1

Writer: John Stanley
Artist: John Stanley
Gold Key (February 1971 © 1970 Western
Publishing Company, Inc.)

*The hero is an 8-year-old boy who trades his
shoeshine kit for a failing toy company and turns
it into a roaring success. It was an entertaining
concept, but, sadly, this issue was Stanley's last
original work for comics.*

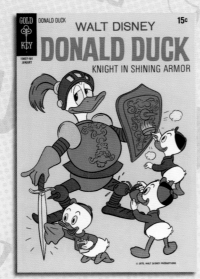

Donald Duck #135

Writer: Carl Barks
Artist: Carl Barks
Gold Key (January 1971 © 1970, © 1959, © 1957, © 1952
Walt Disney Productions)

*A stirring tale of heroism, "Knight in Shining Armor"
was reprinted from **Walt Disney's Comics and Stories** #198 (March 1957). I include it here because it
was the first Barks story I read and remains one of
my favorites.*

The Forever People #1

Writer: Jack Kirby
Artists: Jack Kirby, Vince Colletta
DC (February-March 1971 © 1971 National Periodical Publications, Inc.)

*They dress like flower children of the 1960s, but these five young "gods" from
New Genesis have come to Earth to oppose the forces of Apokolips. This
is one of three connected titles that made up Kirby's ambitious "Fourth
World" saga.*

Asterix the Gaul

Writer: René Goscinny translated by Anthea Bell, Derek Hockridge
Artist: Albert Uderzo
William Morrow and Company (1970 © 1969 Brockhampton Press Ltd.
French edition © 1961 Dargaud S.A.)

50 B.C.: Caesar has conquered all Gaul, except for a small village whose residents have a magic potion that turns fighting Romans into a sport. The hilarious Franco-Belgian comic strip had come to America, the best gift since the Statue of Liberty!

Asterix and Cleopatra

Writer: René Goscinny translated by Anthea Bell, Derek Hockridge
Artist: Albert Uderzo
William Morrow and Company (1970 © 1969 Brockhampton Press Ltd.,
French edition © 1965 Dargaud S.A.)

The Gauls go to Egypt to help its queen win a bet with Caesar. It's a parody of the 1963 movie starring Elizabeth Taylor but much, much funnier. It's my favorite Asterix album with a killer running joke about the beauty of Cleo's nose.

Aquaman #56
Writer: Steve Skeates
Artist: Jim Aparo
DC (March-April 1971 © 1971 National Periodical Publications, Inc.)

Many of DC's super-heroes had fallen on hard times, but Aquaman's first series went out on a high note with a sharp tale dealing with such matters as vigilantism and unrestricted technology's threat to the environment.

...many of DC's super-heroes had fallen on hard times....

The New Gods #1

Writer: Jack Kirby
Artists: Jack Kirby, Vince Colletta
DC (February-March 1971 © 1972 National Periodical Publications, Inc.)

Orion, a child of Apokolips raised on New Genesis, fights against the despotic Darkseid. This was the cornerstone of Kirby's "Fourth World" saga, and its characters and concepts continue to shape today's DC Universe.

Eerie #32

Writer: Steve Skeates
Artist: Tom Sutton
Warren (March 1971 © 1970 Warren Publishing Co.)

"Superhero" is Skeates' hilariously subversive take on a renowned caped crusader. Other contributors to this issue included Gardner Fox, Frank Bolle, Gerry Conway, Richard Corben, Jack Sparling, Don Glut, Mike Royer, and Bill Dubay.

Mister Miracle #1

Writer: Jack Kirby
Artists: Jack Kirby, Vince Colletta
DC (April 1971 © 1971 National Periodical Publications, Inc.)

The aptly named Scott Free is a child of New Genesis raised on Apokolips. He resists all that dark world's attempts to break his spirit, breaks free of his captivity there, and travels to Earth to become our world's greatest escape artist.

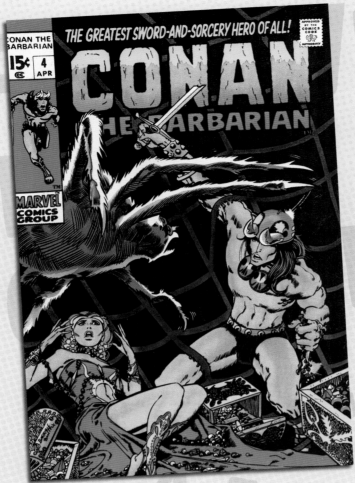

Conan the Barbarian #4

Writer: Roy Thomas
Artists: Barry Windsor-Smith, Sal Buscema
Marvel (April 1971 © 1971 Magazine Management Co., Inc.)

Created by Robert E. Howard, Conan is one of the most iconic heroes in fantasy fiction. This issue's adaptation of Howard's "The Tower of the Elephant" is a dazzling display of swords-and-sorcery at its finest.

Batman #232

Writer: Denny O'Neil
Artists: Neal Adams, Dick Giordano
DC (June 1971 © 1971 National Periodical Publications, Inc., image courtesy of Heritage Comic Auctions)

The O'Neil-Adams team revitalized Batman in the 1970s with stories that emphasized his courage, intelligence, and sense of justice in a dark world. Their greatest additions to the mythos were Ra's al Ghul and his daughter, Talia.

Avengers #89

Writer: Roy Thomas
Artists: Sal Buscema, Sam Grainger
Marvel (June 1971 © 1971 Magazine Management Co.)

This issue kicks off "The Kree-Skrull War," a nine-issue epic that would feature dozens of heroes, two warring extraterrestrial races, and battles that range from the cornfields of Earth to the distant reaches of our galaxy.

Our Army at War #233

Writer: Bob Kanigher
Artist: Joe Kubert
DC (June 1971 © 1971 National Periodical Publications, Inc., image courtesy of Heritage Comic Auctions)

*"Head Count" is a fictional World War II parallel to the 1968 "My Lai Massacre" of hundreds of unarmed South Vietnamese civilians by U.S. soldiers. The issue was featured on the cover of **The New York Times Sunday Magazine**.*

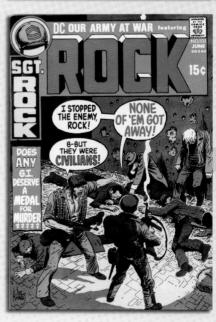

In the Days of the Mob #1

Writer: Jack Kirby
Artists: Jack Kirby, Vince Colletta
DC (Fall 1971 © 1971 Hampshire Distributors, image courtesy of Heritage Comic Auctions)

This one-shot black-and-white magazine echoed the true-life crime comics of earlier decades. Besides stories of Ma Barker and Pretty Boy Floyd, there are cartoons by Sergio Aragonés and text pieces by Mark Evanier and Steve Sherman.

Avengers #93

Writer: Roy Thomas
Artists: Neal Adams, Tom Palmer
Marvel (November 1971 © Magazine Management Co., Inc., Marvel Comics Group)

The Kree-Skrull War rages on with the heroes scattered across Earth and space. To repair The Vision, Hank Pym shrinks to ant-size and makes repairs from within the android's body. This issue knocked me out then and still thrills me today.

Spirit World #1

Writer: Jack Kirby
Artist: Jack Kirby, Vince Colletta
DC (Fall 1971 © 1971 Hampshire Distributors, image courtesy of Heritage Comic Auctions)

*Kirby's second one-shot black-and-white comics magazine, this focuses on ghosts and other paranormal themes. Two romance titles — **Divorce** and **Soul Love** — were planned and partly completed — but neither was ever published.*

Green Lantern #87

Writers: Denny O'Neil, Elliot S! Maggin
Artists: Neal Adams, Dick Giordano
DC (January 1972 © 1971 National Periodical Publications, Inc.)

Two solo adventures. The GL tale introduces John Stewart, the first black Green Lantern and a future member of The Justice League, while the Green Arrow story is Maggin's first professional sale. He would become an important Superman writer.

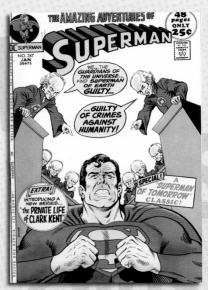

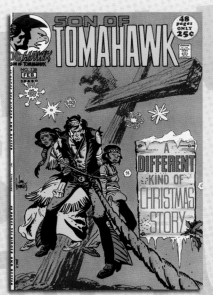

Superman #247

Writer: Elliot S! Maggin, Denny O'Neil
Artist: Curt Swan, Murphy Anderson
DC (January 1972 © 1971 National Periodical
Publications, Inc.)

Maggin's cover story is a classic in which The Man of Steel ponders whether his good works might be impeding the progress of mankind, while O'Neil's "The Private Life of Clark Kent" offers a look at Kent's apartment and neighbors.

Tomahawk #138

Writer: Robert Kanigher
Artist: Frank Thorne
DC (January-February 1972 © 1971 National
Periodical Publications, Inc.)

After 130 issues fighting the British and an occasional monster, Tomahawk moves west, marries a Native American, and starts a family. His son, Hawk, became the star of the title, but Tomahawk made frequent appearances.

Eerie #38

Writer: Don McGregor
Artist: Tom Sutton
Warren (February 1972 © 1971 Warren Publishing
Co.)

Since the start of his career, McGregor has been one of the most distinctive, original voices in comics. "The Night the Snow Spilled Blood!" is a razor-smart combination of detectives, horror, Peanuts references, and even holiday cheer.

...he was a mysterious hero who battled occult menaces.

The Phantom Stranger #17

Writer: Len Wein
Artist: Jim Aparo
DC (January-February 1972 © 1971 National Periodical Publications, Inc.)

Introduced in a short-lived 1950s series, he was a mysterious hero who battled occult menaces. His adventures were chronicled by some of the best young writers of the era: Gerry Conway, Len Wein, David Michelinie, and Paul Levitz.

Marvel Spotlight #2

Writers: Roy and Jean Thomas, Gerry Conway
Artist: Mike Ploog
Marvel (February 1972 © 1971 Magazine Management Co., Inc., Marvel Comics Group, image courtesy of Heritage Comic Auctions)

Once the Comics Code eased its restrictions on the use of classic horror creatures, Marvel delivered this stylish tale of a teenage werewolf. Ploog, who had worked with Will Eisner, proved himself an instant master of modern moody atmosphere.

> ...an instant master of modern moody atmosphere.

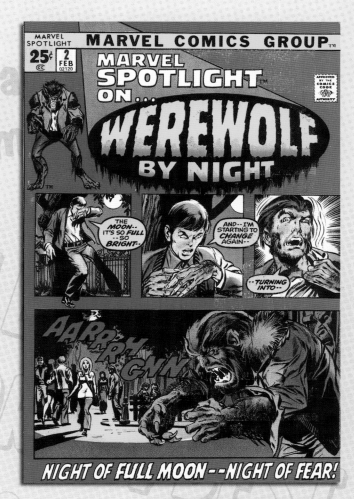

Avengers #97

Writer: Roy Thomas
Artist: John Buscema, Tom Palmer
Marvel (March 1972 © 1971 Magazine Management Co., Inc., Marvel Comics Group)

In the epic conclusion to the Kree-Skrull War, an Avenger is lost, several little-known super-heroes from the 1940s join the fray, and shocking secrets are revealed about the alien combatants — and the ultimate potential of mankind.

Binky Brown Meets the Holy Virgin Mary

Writer: Justin Green
Artist: Justin Green
Last Gasp (March 1972 © 1972 Justin Considine Green)

Through his comics alter ego, Green examines his upbringing in the Roman Catholic Church in bold and humorous fashion. This comic book has been called sacrilegious but it's also been praised as must reading for neurotics of every faith.

House of Mystery #201

Writers: Joe Orlando, John Albano
Artist: Jim Aparo
DC (April 1972 © 1972 National Periodical Publications, Inc.)

A young boy with magical powers regularly embarrasses and frightens his parents, who take extreme measures to restore normalcy to their family. This jaw-dropping short story is on a par with the very best of E.C.'s horror comics.

The New Gods #8

Writer: Jack Kirby
Artists: Jack Kirby, Mike Royer
DC (April–May 1972 © 1972 National Periodical
Publications, Inc.)

"Terrible" Turpin, a tough Metropolis cop, takes a
stand against the "gods" waging war in his city. For
all the cosmic elements of his saga, Kirby never lost
sight of the courage and determination of the humans
caught up in that war.

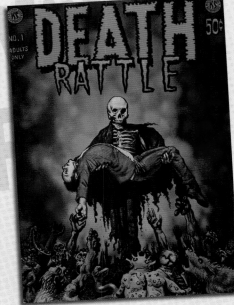

Death Rattle #1

Writers: Richard Corben, Tim Boxell
Artists: Richard Corben, Tim Boxell
Kitchen Sink (June 1972 © 1972 Krupp Comic Works, Inc.)

Denis Kitchen, himself a cartoonist, published three
issues of this underground comix horror anthology in
the 1970s. Other contributors included John Pound and
Pete Poplaski. The series would return for an 18-issue
run in the 1980s.

Tomb of Dracula #1

Writer: Gerry Conway
Artist: Gene Colan
Marvel (April 1972 © 1971 Magazine Management Co., Inc.,
Marvel Comics Group)

This title started out slow, with Hammer Films and **Dark
Shadows** riffs but, after writer Marv Wolfman and inker Tom
Palmer joined Colan on the series, **Tomb of Dracula** became
a top contender for best comic-book horror series ever.

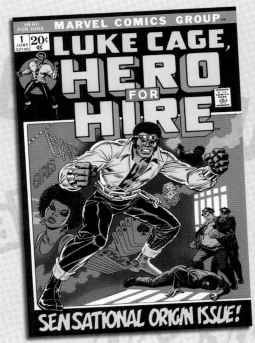

Hero for Hire #1

Writer: Archie Goodwin
Artists: George Tuska, Billy Graham
Marvel (June 1972 © 1972 Magazine Management Co., Inc.,
Marvel Comics Group)

A government experiment brought invulnerability and
tremendous strength to an unjustly convicted prisoner.
Breaking out of jail and using the assumed name Luke
Cage, he becomes a hero-for-hire and the first African-
American super-hero to headline his own title.

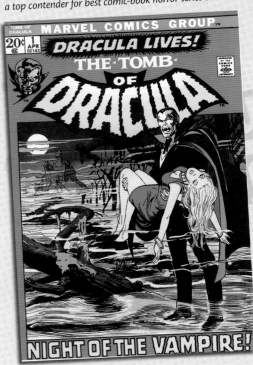

1000 Comic Books You Must Read

Incredible Hulk #140

Writers: Harlan Ellison, Roy Thomas
Artists: Herb Trimpe, Sam Grainger
Marvel (June 1972 © 1971 Magazine Management Co., Inc.,
Marvel Comics Group)

Shrunken to such a degree he enters a micro-world, The
Hulk regains Bruce Banner's intelligence and rescues a
beautiful princess. As a nod to Ellison, Thomas worked
the titles of several of the noted writer's stories into this
issue's captions.

Avengers #101

Writers: Harlan Ellison, Roy Thomas
Artists: Rich Buckler, Dan Adkins
Marvel (July 1972 © 1972 Magazine Management Co., Inc.,
Marvel Comics Group)

Another terrific plot, but this one came with a history. In the
1960s, Ellison pitched it to DC Comics editor Julius Schwartz
as a Hawkman story. Schwartz rejected it, and the short
story was published, instead, in the fanzine **Comic Art**. A
decade later, Thomas reworked it into this Avengers story.

The Demon #1

Writer: Jack Kirby
Artists: Jack Kirby, Mike Royer
DC (August 1972 © 1972 National Periodical Publications,
Inc.)

The demon Etrigan is bound to human Jason Blood,
forcing the former to fight for good and granting virtual
immortality to the latter. I loved the combination of the
horror genre with Kirby's slam-bang action. The title ran
for 18 issues.

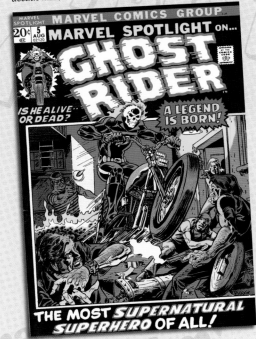

Marvel Spotlight #5

Writer: Gary Friedrich
Artist: Mike Ploog
Marvel (August 1972 © 1972 Magazine Management Co., Inc.,
Marvel Comics Group)

Stunt-cyclist Johnny Blaze sells his soul to the devil to save
a man who is like a father to him. Bonded with a demon,
he is cursed to ride the night, punishing evildoers in Satan's
name while searching for his own salvation.

Mister Miracle #9

Writer: Jack Kirby
Artists: Jack Kirby, Mike Royer
DC (August 1972 © 1972 National Periodical Publications, Inc.)

Though Scott Free grew up in a "terror orphanage," he was secretly tutored by the rebel Himon. This issue tells of Scott's childhood and subsequent escape from Apokolips and is my pick for the best installment of this title's 18-issue run.

Kamandi, the Last Boy on Earth #1

Writer: Jack Kirby
Artists: Jack Kirby, Mike Royer
DC (October-November 1972 © 1972 National Periodical Publications, Inc.)

After an unidentified "Great Disaster," Kamandi fights to survive on a devastated future Earth ruled by talking animals. This was the most successful of Kirby's DC books, continuing for two years after he left the company to return to Marvel.

Wimmen's Comix #1

Writers: Aline Kominsky, Trina Robbins
Artists: Aline Kominsky, Trina Robbins
Last Gasp (November 1972 © 1972 Michelle Brand, Lee Marrs, Lora Fountain, Patricia Moodian (Editor), Sharon Rudall, Shelby, Aline Kominsky, Trina, Karen Marie Haskell, and Janet Wolfe Stanley)

This first issue of the groundbreaking underground comix anthology produced and jointly edited by women features "A Neurotic Woman," "A Teenage Abortion," "Sandy Comes Out," and other stories, many of them focusing on feminist issues.

Swamp Thing #1

Writer: Len Wein
Artist: Bernie Wrightson
DC (October-November 1972 © 1972 National Periodical Publications, Inc., image courtesy of Heritage Comic Auctions)

This was the year for horror. After a pilot of sorts in House of Secrets, this humanoid plant-man received his own title. The first 10 issues of the series by its creators are rightly considered to be among the best comic books of the decade.

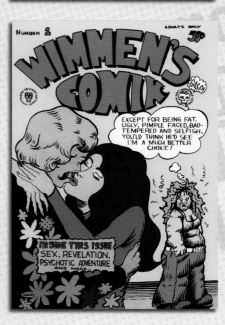

Captain Marvel #25
Writers: Mike Friedrich, Jim Starlin
Artists: Jim Starlin, Chic Stone
Marvel (March 1973 © 1972 Magazine Management Co., Inc., Marvel Comics Group)

Reformed space invader Mar-Vell received a cosmic revamp courtesy of Starlin. He became the "Protector of the Universe" and battled such foes as Thanos, a worshiper of Death, who was herself (itself?) portrayed as a humanoid being.

...Mar-Vell received a cosmic revamp courtesy of Starlin.

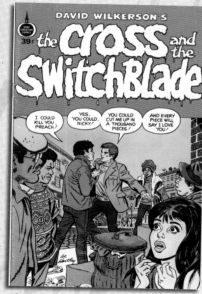

The Cross and the Switchblade
Writer: Al Hartley
Artist: Al Hartley
Spire (1972 © 1972 Fleming H. Revell Company)

Marvel and Archie artist Hartley adapted this comic from evangelist David Wilkerson's book about his work with New York drug addicts. It was hoped the Spire comics line would help bring the Christian faith into the everyday lives of their readers.

Conan the Barbarian #24
Writer: Roy Thomas
Artist: Barry Windsor-Smith
Marvel (March 1973 © 1972 Magazine Management Co., Inc., Marvel Comics Group)

Windsor-Smith leaves the Conan comic with a beautifully drawn tale set during the multi-issue "Siege of Makkalet." But there are more than pretty pictures here, as Thomas provides a character-defining story for the newly introduced Red Sonja.

Conan the Barbarian #25
Writers: Roy Thomas, Barry Windsor-Smith
Artists: John Buscema, Sal Buscema
Marvel (April 1973 © 1973 Marvel Comics Group)

Incoming artist Buscema made Conan his own, establishing the look of the barbarian for decades to come. The issue also has a brief flashback with King Kull, another Robert E. Howard creation who appeared in his own Marvel title.

Amazing Spider-Man #121

Writer: Gerry Conway
Artists: Gil Kane, John Romita
Marvel (June 1973 © 1973 Marvel Comics Group)

Many believe this issue (in which Gwen Stacy, Peter's girlfriend, is murdered by The Green Goblin) marked the end of innocence in the Marvel Age of Comics. It was certainly one of the most talked-about comic books of the year and remains a matter of controversy, at least to some older fans.

Tomb of Dracula #10

Writer: Marv Wolfman
Artists: Gene Colan, Jack Abel
Marvel (July 1973 © 1973 Marvel Comics Group)

Blade's mother gave birth to him while she was being drained by a vampire. As a result, he grew up with quasi-vampiric abilities and an immunity to vampirism. Besides comic books, the vampire hunter has appeared in three theatrical movies and a TV series.

Jungle Action #6

Writer: Don McGregor
Artists: Rich Buckler, Klaus Janson
Marvel (September 1973 © 1973 Marvel Comics Group, image courtesy of Heritage Comic Auctions)

The Panther gets his own series, albeit in this unfortunately named book. His throne was challenged by would-be usurper Erik Killmonger in a two-year story that was equal parts character studies, gritty adventure, and old-time movie serial.

Plop! #1

Writers: Sergio Aragonés, Frank Robbins
Artists: Sergio Aragonés, George Evans
DC (September-October 1973 © 1973 National Periodical Publications Inc.)

"The Magazine of Weird Humor" warped the minds of its readers for two-dozen hilarious issues. Contributing to its debut were Sheldon Mayer, Alfredo Alcala, Steve Skeates, and Bernie Wrightson — and, on the cover, the legendary Basil Wolverton.

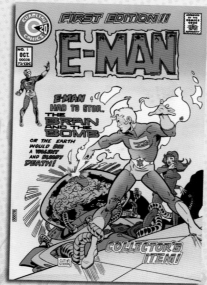

Prez #1

Writer: Joe Simon
Artist: Jerry Grandenetti
DC (September 1973 © 1973 National Periodical Publications, Inc.)

When the voting age is lowered, teen Prez Rickard — his mother had high hopes for him — is elected president and clashes with corrupt power-brokers. This wacky way-out-there political satire deserved more than its meager four-issue run.

E-Man #1

Writer: Nicola Cuti
Artist: Joe Staton
Charlton (October 1973 © 1973 Charlton Publications, Inc.)

Thrown off from a nova, a sentient glob of energy takes on human form and becomes a super-hero on Earth. His wondrously lighthearted adventures continued to appear from other publishers long after the demise of Charlton.

Savage Tales #2

Writers: Roy Thomas, Robert E. Howard
Artist: Barry Windsor-Smith
Marvel (October 1973 © 1973 Marvel Comics Group)

Thomas and Windsor-Smith begin an epic adaptation of Howard's "Red Nails," as Conan becomes the star of this magazine. The issue also features a comics version of the Howard poem "Cimmeria" and a King Kull story by Thomas and Bernie Wrightson.

The Shadow returns in a comics series faithful to his pulp magazine and radio adventures.

The Shadow #1

Writer: Denny O'Neil
Artist: Michael W. Kaluta
DC (October-November 1973 © 1973 National Periodical Publications, Inc.)

The Shadow returns in a comics series faithful to his pulp magazine and radio adventures. The work of O'Neil and Kaluta was critically acclaimed, but #5, #7, #8, and #9 featured art by Frank Robbins. I loved both versions.

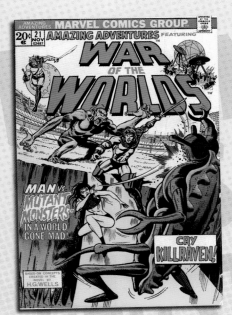

Amazing Adventures #21

Writer: Don McGregor
Artists: Herb Trimpe, Yolande Pijcke
Marvel (November 1973 © 1973 Marvel Comics Group)

A futuristic sequel to the classic H.G. Wells novel. McGregor makes Killraven an inspirational free-dom-fighter, adds a supporting cast that readers take to their hearts, and masterfully blends human interest with science-fiction adventure and horror.

Swamp Thing #7

Writer: Len Wein
Artist: Bernie Wrightson
DC (November-December 1973 © 1973 National Periodical Publications Inc.)

Swamp Thing travels to Gotham City to rescue friends Abby and Matt from the Conclave. Not surprisingly, he comes to the attention of you-know-you and, while their meeting is combative, The Batman soon reconsiders his initial impression of the swamp-man.

Special Marvel Edition #15

Writers: Steve Englehart, Jim Starlin
Artists: Jim Starlin, Al Milgrom
Marvel (December 1973 © 1973 Marvel Comics Group)

Following the then-current martial-arts craze, Marvel introduced a new hero: Shang Chi, master of kung fu and soon-to-be-estranged son of Sax Rohmer's Fu Manchu. Two issues later, the series changed its title to **Master of Kung Fu**.

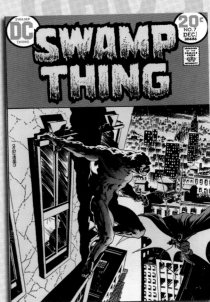

1000 Comic Books You Must Read

Astonishing Tales #21

Writer: Tony Isabella
Artist: Dick Ayers
Marvel (December 1973 © 1973 Marvel Comics Group)

I took a 1960s Marvel monster and turned him into a super-hero with the usual Marvel angst. People either make jokes about this short-lived series or tell me how much fun they thought it was. I believe both reactions are legitimate.

Man-Thing #1

Writer: Steve Gerber
Artists: Val Mayerik, Sal Trapani
Marvel (January 1974 © 1973 Marvel Comics Group, image courtesy of Heritage Comic Auctions)

The title character's origin and the timing of its first appearance were eerily and coincidentally similar to those of DC's Swamp Thing, but, as the series continued, Gerber would push the envelope of what mainstream comics could be.

...eerily and coincidentally similar to those of DC's Swamp Thing...

Archie's Clean Slate

Writer: Al Hartley
Artist: Al Hartley
Spire (1973 © 1973 Fleming H. Revell Company)

Due to Hartley's association with Archie Comics, he obtained permission to use the company's characters in his Christian comics. Archie and his pals express their faith in 19 issues, including **Archie's One Way** *and* **Jughead's Soul Food**.

Mr. A #1

Writer: Steve Ditko
Artist: Steve Ditko
Comic Art Publishers (1973 © 1973 Steve Ditko)

Mr. A is the ultimate expression of Ditko's objectivist philosophy in the form of an uncompromising vigilante. Several Mr. A stories ran in fanzines, and two of them — "Right to Kill!" and "When Is a Man to Be Judged Evil?" were reprinted here.

Hansi, the Girl Who Loved the Swastika

Writer: Al Hartley
Artist: Al Hartley
Spire (1973 © 1973 by Tyndale House Publishers and assigned to Maria Anne Hirschmann)

Hartley adapted this comic from the book by Maria Anna Hirschmann. He did 13 biographical or autobiographical comics for Spire comics, among them: **Hello, I'm Johnny Cash** *and* **Tom Landry and the Dallas Cowboys**.

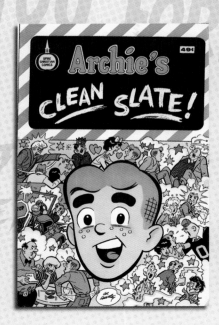

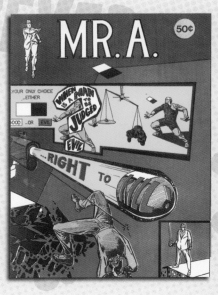

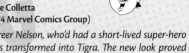

Giant-Size Creatures #1

Writer: Tony Isabella
Artists: Don Perlin, Vince Colletta
Marvel (July 1974 © 1974 Marvel Comics Group)

Mortally wounded, Greer Nelson, who'd had a short-lived super-hero career as The Cat, was transformed into Tigra. The new look proved popular with readers, and Tigra has continued to appear in Marvel titles ever since.

> Mortally wounded,
> Greer Nelson...
> was transformed
> into Tigra.

Captain America #175

Writer: Steve Englehart
Artists: Sal Buscema, Vince Colletta
Marvel (July 1974 © 1974 Marvel Comics Group)

Captain America follows a criminal conspiracy to the White House. The shocking events of the conclusion of this multi-issue storyline shook the hero's faith in his country. He abandoned his traditional garb and adopted the identity of Nomad.

Tomb of Dracula #25

Writer: Marv Wolfman
Artists: Gene Colan, Tom Palmer
Marvel (October 1974 © 1974 Marvel Comics Group)

In a title known for great supporting characters, Hannibal King was my favorite. Slain by a vampire, the hard-boiled detective refused to feed on living humans. His undead nature was not revealed until the end of this first appearance.

Ghost Rider #9

Writer: Tony Isabella
Artists: Jim Mooney, Sal Trapani
Marvel (December 1974 © 1974 Marvel Comics Group)

I'd written myself into a "Satan is going to claim the hero's soul" corner, when Steve Gerber suggested I have God save Johnny Blaze. It worked. This and subsequent appearances of "The Friend" are among the proudest moments of my career.

Incredible Hulk #182

Writer: Len Wein
Artist: Herb Trimpe
Marvel (December 1974 © 1974 Marvel Comics Group)

The best issue of Wein's impressive run, as The Hulk finds a friend in Crackajack Jackson. Though the kindly hobo only appears in this one issue, he had a profound effect on The Hulk and on yours truly. A classic unforgettable tale.

Supernatural Thrillers #10

Writers: Tony Isabella, Len Wein
Artists: Val Mayerik, Dan Adkins
Marvel (December 1974 © 1974 Marvel Comics Group)

An African chief condemned to monstrous immortality, N'Kantu roams the Middle East. In this story, co-plotted by Mayerik and scripted by Wein, he fights alongside an Israeli soldier. Another favorite, though Val and Len deserve all the credit.

The Crusaders #1

Writer: Jack Chick
Artist: Fred Carter
Chick Publications (1974 ©* 1974 Jack Chick, image courtesy of Heritage Comic Auctions)

Carter and Emerson go on missions for the Lord around the world. This series by evangelical pamphleteer Chick became increasingly virulent in its later issues, accusing Catholics of cannibalism and consorting with the Devil.

The Sandman #1

Writer: Joe Simon
Artists: Jack Kirby, Mike Royer
DC (Winter 1974 © 1973 National Periodical Publications, Inc.)

Decades after they closed their studio, the fabled Simon and Kirby team reunited for one last story. This version of The Sandman is the master of a dream dimension whose mission is to protect kids from nightmare monsters.

Tales of the Zombie #9

Writers: Tony Isabella, Chris Claremont
Artists: Virgilio Redondo, Alfredo Alcala
Marvel (January 1975 © 1974 Marvel Comics
Group, image courtesy of Heritage Comic Auctions)

*Since this was supposed to be the last issue, Chris Clare-
mont and I wrote a story bringing the undead life of zombie Simon Garth to a satisfying conclusion. Sadly, even
the undead don't seem to stay dead in comic books.*

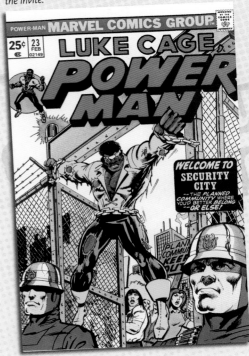

Power Man #23

Writer: Tony Isabella
Artists: Ron Wilson, Dave Hunt
Marvel (February 1975 © 1974 Marvel Comics Group)

*Inspired by an obnoxious TV ad for a "planned commu-
nity," I wrote this issue and parodied the ad in my story.
The company running the community in the ad invited
me to visit it. That was creepy enough for me to decline
the invite.*

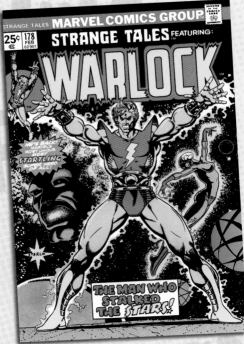

Strange Tales #178

Writer: Jim Starlin
Artist: Jim Starlin
Marvel (February 1975 © 1975 Marvel Comics Group)

*Adam Warlock had appeared in various Marvel comics
and in his own short-lived series, but Starlin made him
a fan favorite with this cosmic adventure involving a
corrupt intergalactic religious empire and Warlock's evil
future self.*

Unknown Worlds of Science Fiction #2

Writers: various
Artists: various
Marvel (March 1975 © 1975 Magazine Management Co., Inc.)

*During its six-issue run, this black-and-white anthology
featured original tales as well as adaptations of stories
by Alfred Bester, Harlan Ellison, Frank Herbert, Michael
Moorcock, Larry Niven, Bob Shaw, Robert Silverberg, and
John Wyndham.*

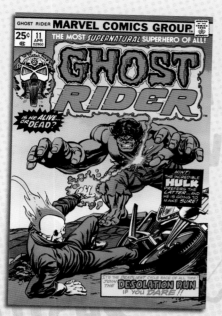

Ghost Rider #11

Writer: Tony Isabella
Artists: Sal Buscema, John Tartaglione
Marvel (April 1975 © 1975 Marvel Comics Group

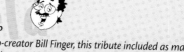

Written shortly after the death of Batman co-creator Bill Finger, this tribute included as many Finger-isms as possible, especially his bringing together troubled characters and letting them work out their problems during an adventure.

Giant-Size Man-Thing #4

Writer: Steve Gerber
Artists: Ed Hannigan, Frank Brunner
Marvel (May 1975 © Marvel Comics Group)

Gerber's "The Kid's Night Out" is a brilliantly gut-wrenching tale of hypocrisy and prejudice exploring the death of a bullied kid. The issue's second story is cult favorite Howard the Duck's first solo adventure.

Shadow #11

Writer: Michael Uslan
Artist: E.R. Cruz
DC (June-July 1975 © 1975 National Periodical Publications, Inc.)

A once-in-a-lifetime — so far, anyway — meeting between The Shadow and The Avenger, a fellow pulp magazine vigilante. The Avenger also appeared in a four-issue series with stories by Denny O'Neil and art by Alden McWilliams and Jack Kirby.

Casper's Ghostland #85

Writer: uncredited
Artist: uncredited
Harvey (July 1975 © 1975 Harvey Famous Cartoons, image courtesy of Heritage Comic Auctions)

"The Search for Wendy" leads Casper to the strange Vice-Versa Land, where everyone acts the opposite of their usual selves, including our hero and heroine. Rounding off the issue is a solo adventure of Spooky the Tuff Little Ghost.

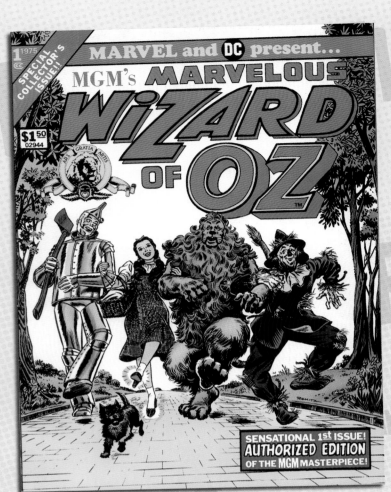

MGM's Marvelous Wizard of Oz #1

Writer: Roy Thomas
Artists: John Buscema, Tony DeZuniga
DC/Marvel (1975 © 1975 Marvel Comics Group, a division of Cadence Industries Corporation and National Periodical Publications, Inc. Based on material © 1939 Loew's Inc., Renewed © 1966 Metro-Goldwyn-Mayer, Inc.)

I was working at Marvel when this tabloid-sized adaptation of the classic movie was published and never did understand how DC got a piece of the action. But the wonderful story and the bonus features made this one of the best comics of the year.

...one of the best comics of the year.

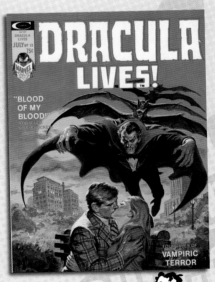

Dracula Lives #13

Writer: Tony Isabella
Artist: Tony DeZuniga
Marvel (July 1975 © 1975 Magazine Management Co., Inc.)

I pitched "Bounty for a Vampire" to Editor Marv Wolfman as a "Dracula Meets Jonah Hex" issue, and he was smart enough to get the original Jonah Hex artist to draw it. Unfortunately, this was the last issue of the magazine.

Howard the Duck #1

Writer: Steve Gerber
Artist: Frank Brunner, Steve Leialoha
Marvel (January 1976 © 1975 Marvel Comics Group)

Trapped in a world he never made and living in Cleveland to boot, Gerber's signature character gets his own series and meets girlfriend Beverly. The title melded oft-biting social satire with parodies of genre fiction, including comic books.

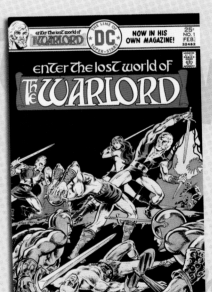

The Warlord #1

Writer: Mike Grell
Artist: Mike Grell
DC (January-February 1976 © 1975 National Periodical Publications, Inc., image courtesy of Heritage Comic Auctions)

Pilot Travis Morgan enters a hole in the Earth's crust and crashes in Skartaris, where he fights dinosaurs, tyrants, and wizards. Grell's knack for science-fantasy and two-fisted action made this series one of the few DC successes of the 1970s.

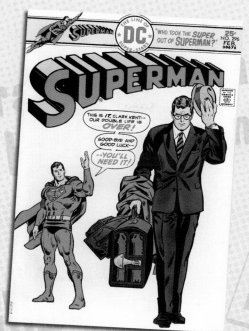

Master of Kung Fu #45

Writer: Doug Moench
Artists: Paul Gulacy, Pablo Marcos
Marvel (October 1976 © 1976 Marvel Comics Group)

This begins a six-issue story in which each issue is narrated by a different character. The Moench-Gulacy team made this title their own by smartly combining espionage thrills and martial-arts action with riveting character interactions.

Superman #296

Writers: Elliot S! Maggin, Cary Bates
Artists: Curt Swan, Bob Oksner
DC (February 1976 © 1975 National Periodical Publications, Inc.)

Maggin and Bates, DC's top Superman writers, collaborated on many stories. This issue kicks off a four-issue arc that explores the possibilities of a relationship between Lois Lane and a temporarily non-powered Clark Kent.

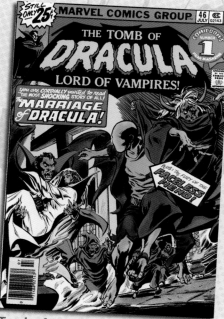

Fantastic Four #176

Writer: Roy Thomas
Artists: George Pérez, Joe Sinnott
Marvel (November 1976 © 1976 Marvel Comics Group)

The impish Impossible Man from the planet Poppup hits the Big Apple and goes to the Marvel offices to demand his own comic book. Impy's shape-shaping antics and lots of "in" jokes made this the funniest comic book of the year.

Tomb of Dracula #46

Writer: Marv Wolfman
Artist: Gene Colan, Tom Palmer
Marvel (July 1976 © 1976 Marvel Comics Group)

Dracula takes a mortal woman for his bride. As the multi-issue arc unfolds, she gives birth to Dracula's son. The kid is possessed by an angel, grows to adulthood, and battles Dracula in a story that constantly challenged and surprised its readers.

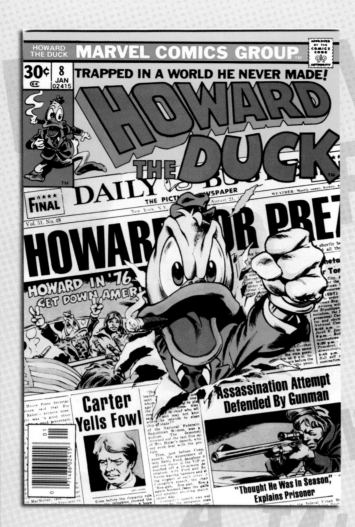

Howard the Duck #8

Writer: Steve Gerber, David Anthony Kraft, Don McGregor
Artist: Gene Colan, Steve Leialoha
Marvel (January 1977 © 1976 Marvel Comics Group)

Get down, America! In one of his finest moments, Howard campaigns for president as the candidate of the All-Night Party. "Mad Genius Associates" — Gerber and some industry pals — even sold buttons and other merchandise to the duck's supporters.

...Howard campaigns for president as the candidate of the All-Night Party.

American Splendor #1

Writer: Harvey Pekar
Artist: Robert Crumb
Harvey Pekar (1976 ©* 1976 Harvey Pekar and Robert Crumb, image courtesy of Heritage Comic Auctions)

"Comics are words and pictures. You can do anything with words and pictures." That creative philosophy made Pekar the comics voice of the average Joe and, three decades later, he's still the best man for that job. He's an American treasure.

Superman vs. the Amazing Spider-Man

Writer: Gerry Conway
Artists: Ross Andru, Dick Giordano
DC/Marvel (1976 © 1976 National Periodical Publications, Inc. and The Marvel Comics Group)

Literary agent David Obst suggested to Marvel's Stan Lee and DC's Carmine Infantino that Superman and Spider-Man should meet. This 100-page tabloid-size spectacular was the result ... and the first of dozens of DC-Marvel crossovers in the ensuing years.

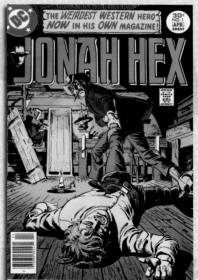

Jonah Hex #1

Writer: Michael Fleisher
Artist: Jose Luis Garcia-Lopez
DC (March-April 1977 © 1976 National Periodical Publications, Inc., image courtesy of Heritage Comic Auctions)

Hex was a disfigured Confederate officer turned bounty hunter after the Civil War. Fleisher didn't create Hex but he wrote more of his stories than any other writer and made the character one of the few DC success stories of the late 1970s.

Welcome Back, Kotter #3

Writer: Tony Isabella
Artists: Ric Estrada, Bob Oksner
DC (March 1977 © 1976 The Wolper
Organization, Inc. and the Komack
Co., Inc.)

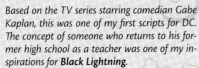

*Based on the TV series starring comedian Gabe Kaplan, this was one of my first scripts for DC. The concept of someone who returns to his former high school as a teacher was one of my inspirations for **Black Lightning**.*

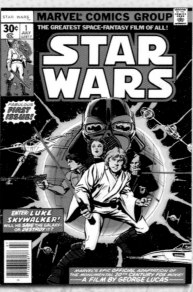

Star Wars #1

Writer: Roy Thomas
Artist: Howard Chaykin
Marvel (July 1977 © 1977 Twentieth Century Fox Film Corporation. The advertising and editorial material appearing on pages 12, 18, 20, 28, and 29 © 1977 Marvel Comics Group.)

The first part of a six-issue adaptation of the now-classic movie was published before the film had been released. George Lucas' characters and Marvel were a successful match, and the title ran for 107 issues plus annuals and reprints.

Detective Comics #471

Writer: Steve Englehart
Artists: Marshall Rogers, Terry Austin
DC (August 1977 © 1977 DC Comics Inc., image courtesy of Heritage Comic Auctions)

The start of a six-issue story that brought back a villain from the 1940s, introduced a new love for Bruce Wayne, dealt with political intrigue in Gotham, and gave us The Joker's wildest scheme ever. A classic Batman adventure.

Black Lightning #1

Writer: Tony Isabella
Artists: Trevor Von Eeden, Frank Springer
DC (April 1977 © 1977 DC Comics Inc.)

Jefferson Pierce becomes a costumed vigilante to fight, without endangering his students, the criminals who target them. Created to address the lack of positive African-Americans in the comics of the time, he remains my proudest creation.

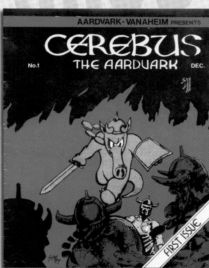

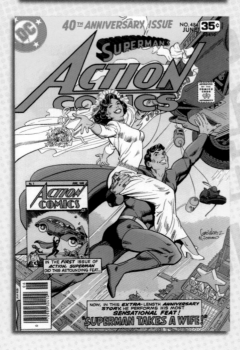

Howard the Duck #16

Writer: Steve Gerber
Artists: various
Marvel (September 1977) © 1977 Marvel Comics Group

This was Gerber's year. Faced with the "Dreaded Deadline Doom," he wrote "Zen and the Art of Comic Book Writing." A brilliant riff on the creative process, it consists of text pieces and illustrations by some of Marvel's finest artists.

Cerebus #1

Writer: Dave Sim
Artist: Dave Sim
Aardvark-Vanaheim (1977 © 1977 Dave Sim, image courtesy of Heritage Comic Auctions)

The first issue of the longest-running English language comic book by a single creative team. The life of Sim's misanthropic humanoid aardvark unfolded over 300 issues, encouraging hundreds of comics creators to self-publish their work.

Action Comics #484

Writer: Cary Bates
Artists: Curt Swan, Joe Giella
DC (June 1978 © 1978 DC Comics Inc.)

*In this 40th anniversary issue of **Action Comics**, Superman marries Lois! OK, it's the Superman of Earth-2, and he marries her during a period when The Wizard has caused him to forget he is Superman, but it's **still** a way cool story!*

Marvel Comics Super Special: Kiss

Writer: Steve Gerber
Artist: Alan Weiss, others
Marvel (September 1977, image courtesy of Heritage Comic Auctions)

*The hottest rock-and-roll band of the 1970s performed in invented comic-book personas. So starring in their own comic was as natural as Gerber's writing it. This issue was touted as being "printed in real KISS blood," but presumably not a **lot** of it.*

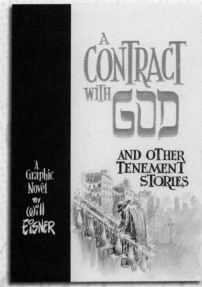

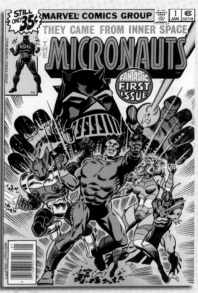

Richie Rich Cash #25

Writer: uncredited
Artist: uncredited
Harvey (September 1978 ©* 1978 Harvey Features Syndicate, image courtesy of Heritage Comic Auctions)

From 1961 to 1993, Richie Rich starred in more titles than any other comics character. There were 44 different titles, including **Richie Rich Millions, Richie Rich Success Stories, Richie Rich Bank Book,** *and* **Richie Rich and The New Kids on the Block.**

A Contract with God

Writer: Will Eisner
Artist: Will Eisner
Baronet Publishing (1978 © 1978 Will Eisner)

Not a graphic novel, **per se**, *but an anthology of four tales drawn from Eisner's experiences in the Bronx of the 1930s, this is a pivotal work in American comics. As he had in the 1940s, Eisner set the standard for a new kind of comic book.*

Micronauts #1

Writer: Bill Mantlo
Artist: Michael Golden, Joe Rubinstein
Marvel (January 1979 © 1978 Marvel Comics Group. Micronauts © 1978 by Mego Corp.)

Impressed by his son's Christmas presents, Mantlo convinced Marvel to license the Micronauts. He created personas for the figures, as well as new characters and their subatomic universe. The series was one of the most beloved series of the 1970s and 1980s.

...Larry Gonick's explanation of how corporations avoid taxes.

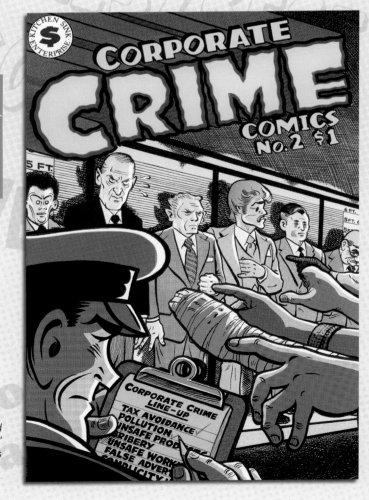

Corporate Crime Comics #2

Writers: various
Artists: various
Kitchen Sink (April 1979 © 1979 Leonard Rifas (editor) and respective contributing artists)

Created by activist cartoonist Leonard Rifas, this title was a good two decades ahead of its time. This issue included Trina Robbins' account of the Triangle Shirtwaist Co. tragedy and Larry Gonick's explanation of how corporations avoid taxes.

ElfQuest #1

Writers: Wendy Pini, Richard Pini
Artist: Wendy Pini
Warp (April 1978 © 1978 Wendy and Richard Pini)

The Pinis "met" on the letters page of a Silver Surfer comic book, married, and gave birth to this epic series about elves and other races trying to coexist on a primitive planet. I'd rank *ElfQuest* as one of the top 10 American comics of all time.

ROM #1

Writer: Bill Mantlo
Artist: Sal Buscema
Marvel (December 1979 © 1979 Parker Brothers. All other material © 1979 Marvel Comics Group)

As a toy, ROM the Space Knight was a failure. But Mantlo created an exiting scenario of heroic cyborgs fighting the evil Dire Wraiths on our own planet. The series ran 75 issues and long outlasted the toy. It's my favorite Mantlo series.

CHAPTER SIX

The 1970s, especially the second half of that surprising decade, were clearly a transitional period for American comics. The changes might have been a tad tentative, but the creators and the industry built on them, refined them, and took comic books in exciting new directions.

New writers and artists continued to come into the field, and there were new publishers to welcome them. Chief among these publishers were Comico, Dark Horse, Eclipse, First, and Pacific, though only Dark Horse survives and thrives to this day.

Several existing publishers fell by the wayside. By the middle of the decade, Charlton, Gold Key, and Warren would publish their last comics. Harvey struggled in the 1990s, publishing its last issue of Richie Rich in 1994.

Comics continued to be sold on newsstands and other traditional venues, but the direct-market distribution system was quickly becoming the industry standard. The direct-market leaders were Capital City Distribution and Diamond Comic Distributors, with several smaller outfits also supplying comic books and related items to the growing network of comics specialty stores.

Comics creators continued their gains. They were as big a selling point as the characters they wrote and drew, especially in the fan-oriented direct market. Their page rates and their benefits grew, including royalty payments based on sales and reprints of their work. Some creators became millionaires. Most didn't fare as well but were still better off than their predecessors. On the downside, some new publishers would default on payments to creators, and some publishers would continue to practice the old business models for dealings with creators whenever they figured they could get away with it.

> ## ...the direct-market distribution system was quickly becoming the industry standard.

Creators were still being influenced by comics from Great Britain, Europe, and Japan. In the 1980s, those comics started coming to the United States in their original form, in reprints designed for the American market, and, in the case of Japanese comics, in English-language translations.

Comics aficionados, I give you the 1980s …

Hembeck: The Best of Dateline: @!!?#

Writer: Fred Hembeck
Artist: Fred Hembeck
FantaCo (December 1980 © 1979 Fred G. Hembeck)

Hembeck has done countless strips spoofing his favorite comic books and with himself as a featured character. This collection includes both new material and reprints of earlier material. His work would later appear in DC and Marvel comic books.

Detectives Inc.: A Remembrance of Threatening Green

Writer: Don McGregor
Artist: Marshall Rogers
Eclipse (May 1980 © 1980 Don McGregor and Marshall Rogers)

In this gripping mystery-drama, a midwife hires Denning and Rainier to find out who killed her female lover. McGregor brings tremendous skill and sensitivity to the subject matter and to the friendship between the interracial detectives.

...gripping
mystery-drama... |

Action Comics #507-508

Writer: Cary Bates
Artist: Curt Swan, Frank Chiaramonte
DC (May-June 1980 © 1980 DC Comics Inc.)

The late Pa Kent is miraculously restored to life, spending quality time with his son before everything returns to the status quo. This heartwarming tale is one of the last great Superman stories before The Man of Steel's 1986 reboot.

Action Comics #510-512

Writer: Cary Bates
Artist: Curt Swan, Frank Chiaramonte
DC (August-October 1980 © 1980 DC Comics Inc.)

Luthor reforms — or seems to — in this terrific three-issue story. Bates crafted a brilliantly convincing scenario that I wish hadn't been undone in its finale. What a wasted opportunity for shaking up the Superman titles!

What If? #24

Writer: Tony Isabella
Artists: Gil Kane, Frank Giacoia
Marvel (December 1980 © 1980 Marvel
Comics Group)

This title showed how Marvel Universe events, in parallel worlds, might have happened differently. This issue is one of my personal favorites; readers liked it so much they wanted to see the story continue in its own title.

X-Men #141-142

Writers: Chris Claremont, John Byrne
Artists: John Byrne, Terry Austin
Marvel (January-February 1981 © 1980 Marvel Comics Group)

They had made The X-Men a fan favorite, but the volatile Claremont and Byrne collaboration was ending. Their final story was the two-issue "Days of Future Past," which showed a chilling future for Marvel's mutants.

Daredevil #168

Writer: Frank Miller
Artists: Frank Miller, Klaus Janson
Marvel (January 1981 © 1980 Marvel Comics Group)

*Matt Murdock is reunited with his college girlfriend Elektra, who's now a contract killer. Miller's **noir** story and his creation of one of the great **femmes fatales** in modern comics established him as the Eisner of the 1980s.*

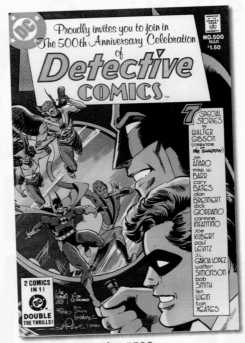

Detective Comics #500

Writers: Alan Brennert, various
Artists: Dick Giordano, various
DC (March 1981 © 1980 DC Comics Inc.)

This 84-page special starts with Batman visiting a parallel world where a thief had not murdered his parents. It continues with seven additional stories by many of DC's best writers and artists. One of the best comics of the decade.

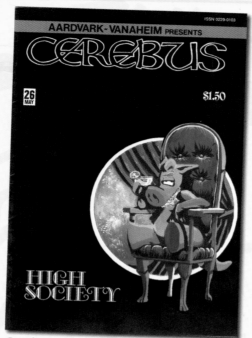

Cerebus #26

Writer: Dave Sim
Artist: Dave Sim
Aardvark-Vanaheim (May 1981 © 1981 Dave Sim, image courtesy of Heritage Comic Auctions)

The aardvark enters the world of parliamentary politics in this first part of a 25-issue story. With this masterful satiric drama, Sim firmly established himself as one of the most original comics creators of our time.

Mendy and the Golem #1

Writer: Leibel Estrin
Artist: Dovid Sears
Mendy Enterprises (1981 © 1981 Mendy Enterprises)

The self-pronounced "world's only kosher comic book" featured the comical adventures of an Orthodox Jew-ish boy and the Golem he found in his rabbi father's synagogue. After its original 19 issues, the comic briefly returned in 2003.

Fantastic Four #236

Writer: John Byrne
Artist: John Byrne
Marvel (November 1981 © 1981 Marvel Comics Group)

In this classic issue, The Fantastic Four are caught in Doom's most diabolic trap ever. Byrne's run on the title is rightly celebrated as one of the best in its history. I rank it second only to that by Stan Lee and Jack Kirby.

Destroyer Duck #1

Writers: Steve Gerber, others
Artists: Jack Kirby, others
Eclipse (February 1982 Entire contents © 1982 by Eclipse Enterprises. Cover and Destroyer Duck © 1982 by Steve Gerber and Jack Kirby. Great Moments in Comic Book History © 1982 by Mark Evanier and Dan Spiegle. Gimme My Check © 1982 by Martin Pasko, Joe Staton, and Scott Shaw! The Adventures of Thelma Ironthighs © 1982 by Shary Flenniken. Groo the Wanderer © 1982 by Sergio Aragonés. FOOG Marching Ducks illustration © 1982 by Gordon Kent)

The title hero sought revenge for the death of his best friend at the hands of the soulless "Godcorp." This anthology comic book was published to help Gerber raise funds for his lawsuit against Marvel over ownership of Howard the Duck.

Daredevil #181

Writer: Frank Miller
Artists: Frank Miller, Klaus Janson
Marvel (April 1982 © 1982 Marvel Comics Group)

Assassins Bullseye and Elektra battle to the death in a double-size special that would change Daredevil's life. Miller's influence on his fellow and future comics creators continued to grow throughout the 1980s.

Marvel Two-in-One #86

Writer: Tom DeFalco
Artist: Ron Wilson, Chic Stone
Marvel (Apr 1982 © 1982 Marvel Comics Group)

The Thing finds the Sandman in a bar and the two foes ... have a beer together. The dispirited Sandman tells the Thing the sad story of his life with surprising results. This change-of-pace issue is one of my all-time favorite super-hero comics.

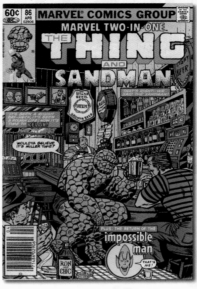

Doctor Strange #52

Writer: Roger Stern
Artists: Marshall Rogers, Terry Austin
Marvel (June 1982 © 1982 Marvel Comics Group)

Time-traveling to find a friend's lost soul shards, Strange ends up in ancient Egypt and the middle of a 1963 Fantastic Four adventure. It's a big, fun issue from one of the best runs in the good doctor's long and mystic career.

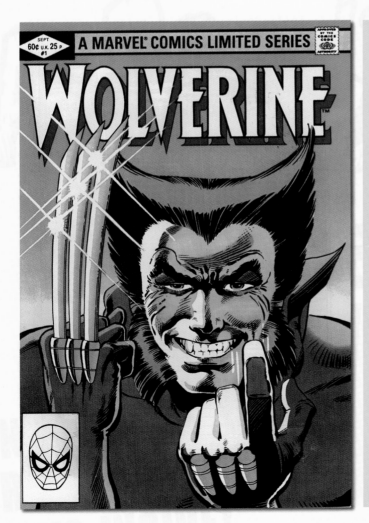

Wolverine #1-4

Writer: Chris Claremont
Artist: Frank Miller, Joe Rubinstein
Marvel (September-December 1982 © 1982 Marvel Comics Group)

In a character-defining series, Wolverine goes to Japan and battles scores of ninjas to win the woman he loves. It's also where he gets his signature phrase: "I'm the best there is at what I do, but what I do isn't very nice."

I'm the best there is at what I do...

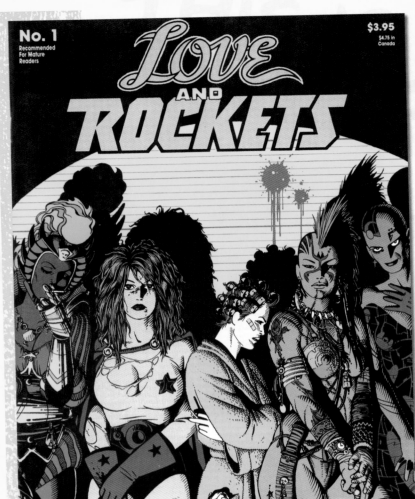

Love and Rockets #1
Writers: Jamie Hernandez, Gilbert Hernandez
Artists: Jamie Hernandez, Gilbert Hernandez
Fantagraphics (Fall 1982 © 1982 Fantagraphics Books, Inc. All characters, stories, and art © 1982 Los Bros. Hernandez, image courtesy of Heritage Comic Auctions)

*This anthology featured several ongoing series with characters of Hispanic origin and stories informed by cultural, economic, sexual, and real-life issues. It's **the** most important alternative comic book of the 1980s and remains just as vital today.*

> It's *the* most important alternative comic book of the 1980s.

Camelot 3000 #1
Writer: Mike W. Barr
Artist: Brian Bolland, Bruce Patterson
DC (December 1982 © 1982 DC Comics, Inc.)

Arthur returns to defend Earth from an alien invasion commanded by Morgan le Fay. This thrilling science-fiction take on the classic legend was DC's first "maxi-series" and one of its first projects offered exclusively to the direct market.

Groo the Wanderer #1
Writers: Sergio Aragonés, Mark Evanier
Artist: Sergio Aragonés
Pacific (December 1982 © 1982 Sergio Aragonés)

Delightful characters, hilarious situations, witty writing, swords, sorcery, satire, slapstick ... these are the elements that have taken Groo through five publishers and more than 150 issues of what's arguably the funniest comic book on the planet!

I Saw It!
Writer: Keiji Nakazawa
Artist: Keiji Nakazawa
Educomics (1982 © 1982 Keiji Nakazawa)

In this autobiographical comic, Nakazawa, a young survivor of the atomic bombing of Hiroshima, tells of his life in the days directly after the attack and into adulthood. It is a stark, uncompromising, unforgettable tale of war's horror.

Marvel Graphic Novel #5: X-Men

Writer: Chris Claremont
Artist: Brent Anderson
Marvel (1982 © 1982 Marvel Comics Group)

A preacher uses religion to provoke hatred of and violence toward mutants. The X-Men have long served as metaphors for bigotry based on race and sexual orientation, but never so powerfully as in this landmark graphic novel.

Jon Sable, Freelance #1

Writer: Mike Grell
Artist: Mike Grell
First (June 1983 © 1983 First Comics, Inc.)

An Olympic athlete and a safari organizer whose family was murdered by poachers, Sable is a mercenary who also writes children's books. The rugged adventure series was one of First Comics' launch titles and ran for 56 issues in its original run.

Journey #1

Writer: William Messner-Loebs
Artist: William Messner-Loebs
Aardvark-Vanaheim (March 1983 © 1983 Bill Loebs)

The adventures of 19th century Michigan frontiersman "Wolverine" MacAlistaire. The stories were sometimes funny, sometimes serious, and always entertaining. The series ran 31 issues with additional tales appearing here and there since.

The Badger #1

Writer: Mike Baron
Artist: Jeffrey Butler
Capital Comics (September 1983 © 1983 Capital Publications, Inc.)

This sometimes-dark comedy stars a Vietnam veteran with multiple personalities, of which The Badger is the most dominant. It mixes the super-hero genre with fantasy and martial arts. As was the case with **Nexus**, it was later published by First Comics.

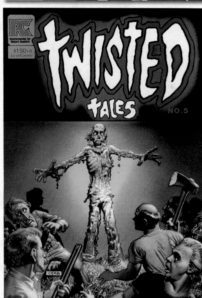

American Flagg! #1

Writer: Howard Chaykin
Artist: Howard Chaykin
First (October 1983 © 1983 First Comics, Inc. and Howard Chaykin, Inc.)

TV actor Reuben Flagg is drafted to become a cop in the corporate-dominated USA of 2030. Chaykin combined satire, science fiction, sex, slick art, acerbic wit, and a fascinating supporting cast to create this raucously revolutionary series.

Twisted Tales #5

Writer: Bruce Jones
Artist: Rand Holmes
Pacific (October 1983 © 1983 Bruce Jones Associates)

"Banjo Lessons" may be the most controversial horror story ever to appear in comics. Its elements of gore, extreme violence, racism, and such are so unsettling that, to this day, I don't know if it's a classic or an abomination.

Thor #337

Writer: Walt Simonson
Artist: Walt Simonson
Marvel (November 1983 © 1983 Marvel Entertainment Group, Inc.)

With the introduction of Beta Ray Bill, an alien worthy to hold the hammer of Thor, Simonson's justly praised run in this title got off to a great start. Simonson would write and draw the series through #367 and write it through #382.

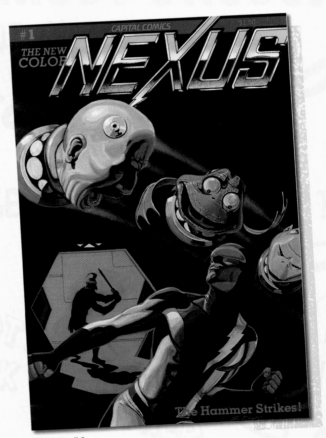

Nexus #1

Writer: Mike Baron
Artist: Steve Rude
Capital Comics (1983 © 1983 Capital Publications, Inc.)

Nexus was a man granted extraordinary powers by an alien entity in exchange for assassinating mass murderers. Baron and Rude combined the super-hero and science-fiction genres with human drama and moral quandaries. A classic of the 1980s.

Amazing Spider-Man #248

Writer: Roger Stern
Artists: Ron Frenz, Terry Austin
Marvel (January 1984 © 1983 Marvel Comics Group)

Stern is noted for excellent runs on this title, **The Avengers**, and many others, but this Eisneresque human-interest tale of Spider-Man's greatest fan ranks among the very best super-hero stories in the history of comics.

Mars #1

Writers: Mark Wheatley, Marc Hempel
Artists: Mark Wheatley, Marc Hempel
First (January 1984 © 1983 First Comics, Inc.)

This 12-issue tale of humans terraforming our red-planet neighbor invokes the classic science-fiction pulps of the 1930s and 1940s with its Martian mysteries, its brilliant, gutsy heroine, and art that virtually **flows** from panel to panel.

Betty and Me #137

Writer: uncredited
Artist: uncredited
Archie (January 1984 © 1984 Close-Up, Inc.)

Dan DeCarlo's eye-catching cover illustrates a story in which our heroine enters a **Flashdance**-inspired dance contest. It demonstrates how, by utilizing contemporary themes, Archie has kept its comics fresh and fun through the decades.

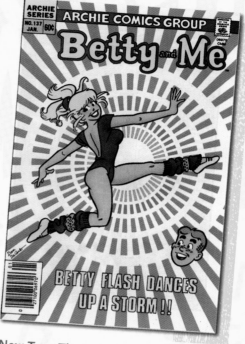

New Teen Titans #38

Writers: Marv Wolfman, George Pérez
Artists: George Pérez, Romeo Tanghal
DC (January 1984 © 1983 DC Comics, Inc.)

Wonder Girl was an impossibility. In her first appearances, she was a teen Wonder Woman, somehow existing simultaneously with her adult self. Wolfman and Pérez made her real, and this issue exploring the mystery of her youth was key to that.

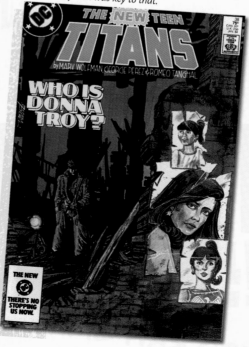

normalman #1

Writer: Jim Valentino
Artist: Jim Valentino
Aardvark-Vanaheim (January 1984 © 1984 Valentino)

*Shot into space as an infant by his crazy dad, "Norm" was the only person on planet Levram without super-powers. The hilarious series over the years spoofed all kinds of comics and characters, **Star Wars**, **The Wizard of Oz**, and even **Spirit** creator Will Eisner.*

Saga of the Swamp Thing #21

Writer: Alan Moore
Artists: Stephen R. Bissette, John Totleben
DC (February 1984 © 1983 DC Comics Inc.)

Alan Moore's "The Anatomy Lesson" changes Swamp Thing forever with its startling revelation that the plant-man has never been human. The British writer would quickly become one of the most respected creators in the history of comics.

G.I. Joe, A Real American Hero #21

Writer: Larry Hama
Artists: Larry Hama, Steve Leialoha
Marvel (March 1984 © 1983 Hasbro Industries, Inc.)

The comic-book adventures of the Hasbro action fig-ures were featured in one of Marvel's most successful 1980s titles. Starring the popular Snake-Eyes character, this brilliant story is told without captions, dialogue, or sound effects.

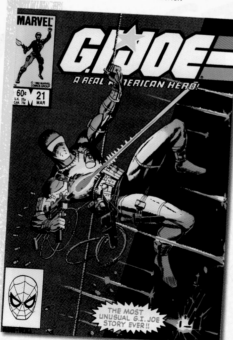

Action Comics #544

Writer: Cary Bates, Marv Wolfman
Artist: Curt Swan, Gil Kane
DC (April 1984 © 1983 DC Comics, Inc.)

The 45th anniversary issue features new looks for classic Superman villains Luthor and Brainiac, special contribu-tions from Superman co-creators Jerry Siegel and Joe Shus-ter, and design pin-ups by George Pérez and Ed Hannigan.

Zot! #1

Writer: Scott McCloud
Artist: Scott McCloud
Eclipse (April 1984 © 1984 Silver Linings)

As comics grew darker, McCloud went bright with the adventures of this teenage hero from an alternate Earth. It was one of the first American comic books influenced by Japanese manga, specifically the Astro Boy stories of Osamu Tezuka.

Adventures of a teenage hero from an alternate Earth.

Manhunter #1

Writer: Archie Goodwin
Artist: Walt Simonson
DC (May 1984 © 1984 DC Comics, Inc.)

Killed on safari, this 1940s hero is revived by a secret society but he opposes it after discovering its true nature. The stories originally appeared in Detective Comics #437-443 and were collected for the first time in this 76-page special.

Marvel Super Heroes Secret Wars #1

Writer: Jim Shooter
Artists: Michael Zeck, John Beatty
Marvel (May 1984 © 1984 Marvel Comics Group)

This 12-issue series featuring heroes and villains duking it out on an artificial world was created to tie in with a toy line. Though a commercial success, the writing is excruciatingly bad, with many players acting wildly out of character.

Batman Special #1

Writer: Mike W. Barr
Artists: Michael Golden, Mike DeCarlo
DC (June 1984 © 1984 DC Comics Inc.)

Batman's parents were upstanding citizens killed by a robber, while The Wrath's parents were burglars accidentally killed by a police officer. Shaped by these tragedies, these mirror images clash in one of the best Batman stories of all.

Writer: Max Allan Collins
Artists: Terry Beatty, Gary Kato
Aardvark-Vanaheim (August 1984 © 1984 Max Collins and Terry Beatty)

Michael Tree took over her murdered husband's business and quickly became my favorite comic-book private eye. This issue is printed in black and white with red ink highlights, a look that suits the hard-boiled stories particularly well.

Grimjack #1

Writer: John Ostrander
Artist: Timothy Truman
First (August 1984 © 1984 First Comics, Inc.)

Sword-for-hire John Gaunt makes his home base in Cynosure, a city that connects to all dimensions and whose laws of nature change from neighborhood to neighborhood. It was one of the toughest, coolest series of the 1980s.

Marvel Team-Up #145

Writer: Tony Isabella
Artists: Greg LaRocque, Mike Esposito
Marvel (September 1984 © 1984 Marvel Comics Group)

Spider-Man and Iron Man battle Blacklash. It's one of my favorites, because it focuses on the villain, a "hometown boy" suffering from manic-depression, and because it is set in Cleveland. My father's bakery even makes an appearance.

Power Pack #1

Writer: Louise Simonson
Artists: June Brigman, Bob Wiacek
Marvel (August 1984 © 1984 Marvel Comics Group)

The preteen Power siblings are given super-powers and a sentient starship by a dying alien. Their adventures often addressed serious issues, and, during the course of their run, they fought alongside many other Marvel super-heroes.

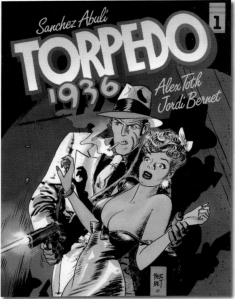

Torpedo 1936 #1

Writer: Sanchez Abuli
Artists: Alex Toth, Jordi Bernet
Catalan Communications (October 1984 © 1982 by Enrique Sanchez Abuli, Alex Toth and Jordi Bernet, text material © 1984 by David H. Rosenthal and Will Eisner, English language edition © 1984 Catalan Communications)

Luca Torelli is a contract killer operating in New York during the Great Depression. Originally published in Spain, these dozen darkly humorous short stories are superbly realized by the black-and-white artistry of Toth and Bernet.

Fantastic Four #275

Writer: John Byrne
Artist: John Byrne
Marvel (February 1985 © 1984 Marvel Comics Group)

*Temporary member She-Hulk tries to prevent a sleazy publisher from running **au naturelle** sunbathing photos of her. Byrne did a number of wonderful single-issue FF tales, and this one, with its very clever funny resolution, has always tickled me.*

Doc Stearn ... Mr. Monster #1

Writer: Michael T. Gilbert
Artists: Michael T. Gilbert, William F. Loebs
Eclipse (January 1985 © 1985 Michael T. Gilbert and William Loebs)

Take an obscure Canadian hero of the 1940s, add Gilbert's sense of the grimly wacky, and you get Doc Stearn, heir to a monster-busting tradition that stretches back for decades and decades, and one of the true delights of the 1980s.

Teenage Mutant Ninja Turtles #1

Writers: Kevin Eastman, Peter Laird
Artists: Kevin Eastman, Peter Laird
Mirage (1984 © 1984 Mirage Studios)

*It began as a self-published spoof of Frank Miller's **Daredevil** and **Ronin**, and became an entertainment empire. Leonardo, Michelangelo, Raphael, and Donatello are among the most beloved characters ever to appear in comics, cartoons, and movies.*

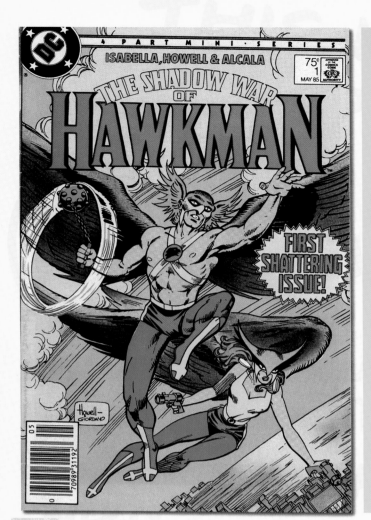

The Shadow War of Hawkman #1-4
Writer: Tony Isabella
Artists: Richard Howell, Alfredo Alcala
DC (May-August 1985 © 1985 DC Comics, Inc.)

Hawkman's homeworld declares war on Earth, and no one knows it except for him, Hawkwoman, and the human pawns of the secret invaders. It's a super-hero story wrapped in dark paranoid science fiction, and I loved writing it.

It's a super-hero story wrapped in dark paranoid science fiction...

Ambush Bug #1-4
Writers: Keith Giffen, Robert Fleming
Artists: Keith Giffen, Bob Oksner
DC (June-September 1985 © 1985 DC Comics, Inc.)

This intentionally silly character defies description and even what passes for reality in the DC Universe. All I know for sure is that, every time I read one of his comic-book misadventures, I laugh out loud. Which is good enough for me.

Wordsmith #1
Writer: Dave Darrigo
Artist: R.G. Taylor
Renegade (August 1985 © 1985 Dave Darrigo)

Pulp writer Clay Washburn struggles to make ends meet in the Great Depression. His life and the stories he writes are intertwined in this stylish six-issue series, a terrific example of the creativity and variety found in the 1980s.

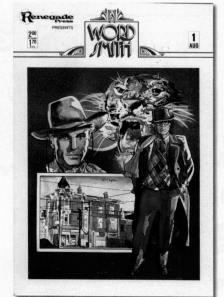

Heroes for Hope Starring The X-Men #1
Writers: various
Artists: various
Marvel (December 1985 © 1985 Marvel Comics Group)

This profits from this "jam" issue went to African famine relief. Dozens of writers and artists contributed to the issue, including Chris Claremont, Stephen King, Alan Moore, Harlan Ellison, Bernie Wrightson, and Jim Starlin.

Superman Annual #11

Writer: Alan Moore
Artist: Dave Gibbons
DC (1985 © 1985 DC Comics, Inc.)

On his birthday, Superman is trapped in a dream of a Krypton that never was, courtesy of a gift from space tyrant Mongul. Guest stars Batman, Robin, and Wonder Woman also show up for the party in this classic thriller by the co-creators of Watchmen.

'Mazing Man #1

Writer: Bob Rozakis
Artists: Stephen DeStefano, Karl Kesel
DC (January 1986 © 1985 DC Comics, Inc.)

Sweepstakes millionaire Hunch lives in Queens, New York, and does good deeds in his neighborhood while dressed in a homemade costume. He's a touch off his nut, but his short-lived title was an honestly charming and good-hearted super-hero comic book.

Star Trek #22-23

Writer: Tony Isabella
Artists: Tom Sutton, Ricardo Villagran
DC (January-February 1986 © 1985 Paramount Pictures Corporation. All other material © 1985 DC Comics, Inc.)

A sequel to Robert Bloch's "Wolf in the Fold," one of the very best episodes of the original series. I've written several Trek stories since, but this two-issue tale, inspired by the work of an admired author, is probably my favorite.

Daredevil #227-233

Writer: Frank Miller
Artist: David Mazzucchelli
Marvel (February-August 1986 © 1985, 1986 Marvel Comics Group)

The Kingpin strips Daredevil of everything he holds dear and makes The Man without Fear more of a threat to the criminal overlord than ever. The gritty "Born Again" is the finest "street-level" super-hero adventure of all time.

Writer: William Messner-Loebs
Artists: Wendy Pini, Joe Staton
Comico (July 1986 © 1986 Hanna-Barbera
Productions, Inc.)

The hitherto-unrevealed story of how Jonny's
mother died and Race Bannon became his
bodyguard and tutor. Based on the 1960s Hanna-Barbera cartoon created by Doug Wildey,
this 31-issue series is one of the few high points
of Comico's brief history.

Sgt. Rock #408

Writer: Robert Kanigher
Artist: Andy Kubert
DC (February 1986 © 1985 DC Comics, Inc.)

Dedicated to Sheldon Mayer, creator of *Scribbly* and
Sugar & Spike and an editor instrumental in shaping
such young talents as Editor Joe Kubert. Fittingly, the
story is drawn by Kubert's son, and the issue features
back-ups by other young artists.

Mr. Monster's Super Duper Special #3

Writers: Michael T. Gilbert, Jack Cole
Artists: Michael T. Gilbert, Jack Cole
Eclipse (September 1986 © 1986 Michael T. Gilbert and
Eclipse Enterprises, Inc.)

This anthology series reprinted horror, crime, science fiction,
and just plain weird stories from the 1940s and 1950s. In
this issue, editor Gilbert reprinted three crime stories by legendary Plastic Man creator Jack Cole.

Heroes Against Hunger

Writers: various
Artists: various
DC (August 1986 © 1986 DC Comics Inc.)

Another "jam" to benefit hunger relief in Africa. Its
contributors included Neal Adams, Robert Bloch, Jim
Starlin, Bernie Wrightson, Paul Levitz, Curt Swan, John
Byrne, Doug Moench, and George Pérez.

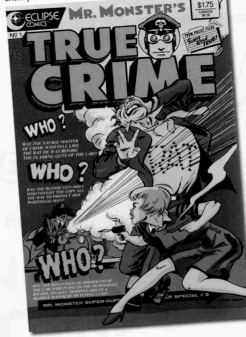

Watchmen #1

Writer: Alan Moore
Artist: Dave Gibbons
DC (September 1986 © 1986 DC Comics Inc.)

*Taking place in an alternate Earth of 1986 — Nixon is serving his **fifth** term as President — this landmark 12-issue series energized the super-hero genre. It has remained in print for two decades and continues to influence comics creators.*

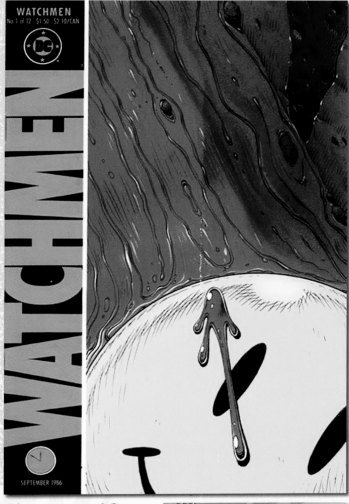

It has remained in print for two decades...

D.P.7 #1

Writer: Mark Gruenwald
Artists: Paul Ryan, Romeo Tanghal
Marvel (November 1986 © 1986 Marvel Comics Group

Marvel's attempt to create a "New Universe" was commercially and creatively unsuccessful, but this excellent series about a group of seven "displaced paranormals" on the run was the best written and most interesting of the bunch.

Hawkman #4

Writer: Tony Isabella
Artists: Richard Howell, Don Heck
DC (November 1986 © 1986 DC Comics Inc.)

The most self-indulgent comic I ever wrote, filled with things I love: Zatanna, a robot pteranodon, a goofy old Batman villain, and lots of humor, as I gleefully revealed that The Kite-Man's civilian identity was ... Charles Brown.

The 'Nam #1

Writer: Doug Murray
Artists: Mike Golden, Armando Gil
Marvel (December 1986 © 1986 Marvel Comics Group)

Set during America's military involvement in Vietnam, this series was told from the perspective of soldiers, mixing personal stories with the larger events of the war. It was an exceptional title and ran for 84 issues.

The Dreamer

Writer: Will Eisner
Artist: Will Eisner
Kitchen Sink (1986 © 1986 Will Eisner)

This "fictional autobiography" is based on Eisner's early career, the people he worked with, and the never-ending conflict between art and commerce. Eisner wrote many masterful graphic novels, but this one is a favorite of mine.

...this one is a favorite of mine.

Maus: A Survivor's Tale #1

Writer: Art Spiegelman
Artist: Art Spiegelman
Pantheon (1986 © 1973, 1980, 1981, 1982, 1983, 1984, 1985, 1986 Art Spiegelman)

*Collecting material earlier serialized in **Raw**, this Pulitzer Prize-winning graphic novel relates how Spiegelman's father survived the Nazi persecution of Jews. It's a soul-chilling narrative and one of the most important works in the comics art form.*

Batman #404-407

Writer: Frank Miller
Artist: David Mazzucchelli
DC (February-May 1987 © 1987 DC Comics Inc.)

*"Batman: Year One" relates the beginning of Batman's career and the arrival in Gotham City of future Police Commissioner James Gordon. As was the case with **Batman: The Dark Knight**, this grim-and-gritty retelling would set the tone for future Batman comics.*

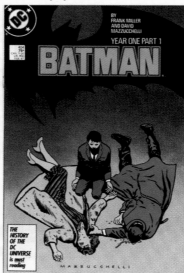

Death Rattle #9

Writers: Robert M. Ingersoll, Basil Wolverton
Artists: Rand Holmes, Basil Wolverton
Kitchen Sink (February 1987 © 1987 Kitchen Sink Press, Inc.)

Now more mainstream than underground, this issue of the anthology cover-featured "Child of the Media," a sharp topical tale about the trivialization of violence, and a reprint of a classic 1950s science-fiction horror tale by Basil Wolverton.

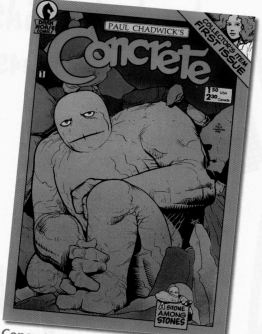

Concrete #1

Writer: Paul Chadwick
Artist: Paul Chadwick
Dark Horse (April 1987 © 1987 Paul Chadwick)

Abducted by aliens, his brain transplanted into a stone-like body, Concrete undertakes the adventures he could never have had in his previous life in stories that often address such social issues as overpopulation and the environment.

Lone Wolf and Cub #1

Writer: Kazuo Koike
Artist: Goseki Kojima
First (May 1987 © 1997 Cazuo Koieke and Goseki Kojima; English translation © First Comics, Inc. and Global Communications Corporation; cover illustration and introduction © 1987 Frank Miller)

Disgraced executioner Ogami Itto travels the path of the assassin with his son, seeking vengeance on the clan that falsely accused him. The popular samurai epic spans 28 volumes and has been adapted for movies, plays, and TV.

Deadface #1

Writer: Eddie Campbell
Artist: Eddie Campbell
Harrier (April 1987 © 1987 Harrier Publishing)

*The title hero is Bacchus, Roman god of wine. The series combines adventure, mythology, and satire. After eight issues from British publisher Harrier, Bacchus and creator Campbell moved to **Dark Horse Presents**, **Cheval Noir**, and other venues.*

Detective Comics #575-578

Writer: Mike W. Barr
Artists: Alan Davis, Paul Neary
DC (June-September 1987 © 1987 DC Comics Inc.)

*The Reaper, Gotham's first costumed vigilante, returns, and Batman confronts the man who murdered his parents. "Batman: Year Two" is a follow-up to Frank Miller's successful "Year One" and is the basis of the animated movie **Batman: Mask of the Phantasm**.*

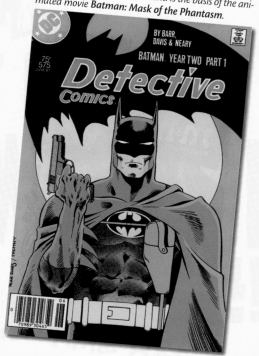

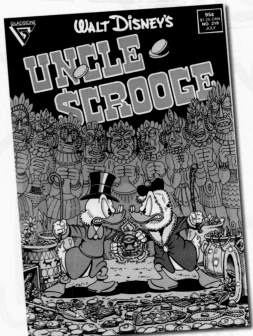

Walt Disney's Uncle Scrooge #219

Writer: Don Rosa
Artist: Don Rosa
Gladstone (July 1987 © 1987 The Walt Disney Company)

Rosa's first Scrooge story became an instant classic with its sharp writing, detailed art, and use of Scrooge's more redeeming traits. With frequent homages to Carl Barks in his work, Rosa is the second-most-popular Scrooge storyteller in the world.

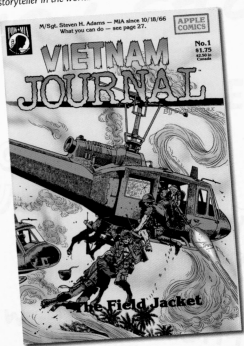

Vietnam Journal #1

Writer: Don Lomax
Artist: Don Lomax
Apple (November 1987 © 1987 Don Lomax)

In this gritty companion to Marvel's The 'Nam, correspondent Scott "Journal" Niethammer covers the conflict on the ground, learning oft-conflicting truths about himself and the war. In a tough field, it's the best of the Vietnam War comics.

Marvel Graphic Novel #32: The Death of Groo

Writer: Mark Evanier
Artist: Sergio Aragonés
Marvel (November 1987 © 1987 Sergio Aragonés)

Dragon, tyrant who hates Groo, laws compelling people to hate Groo, tavern brawl, chase scene, dragon, alleged death, funeral, hooded hero, identity confusion, mass mayhem, dragon, satisfying finish. Total: one hilarious graphic novel.

Cartoon History of the Universe #1

Writer: Larry Gonick
Artist: Larry Gonick
Rip Off Press (1987 © 1987 Larry Gonick)

Self-described "overeducated cartoonist" Gonick takes his readers from the Big Bang and to the entrance of human beings. His comics on history and science span a dozen volumes and are all wonderfully informative and entertaining.

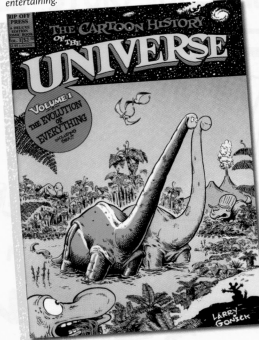

Marvel Graphic Novel: A Sailor's Story

Writer: Sam Glanzman
Artist: Sam Glanzman
Marvel (1987 © 1987 Sam Glanzman)

Glanzman's short autobiographical tales of his World War II service on the **U.S.S. Stevens** *appeared in DC war comics in the 1970s. This is the first of two graphic novels continuing the series to the end of the war.*

The Sacred and the Profane

Writer: Dean Motter
Artist: Ken Steacy
Eclipse (1987 © 1987 Dean Motter and Ken Steacy)

Religion thrives in a future when Roman Catholic space missions travel to distant worlds to colonize them and convert their inhabitants. Serialized in anthology titles from other publishers, this stunning hardcover collects the entire graphic novel.

Aliens #1

Writer: Mark Verheiden
Artist: Mark A. Nelson
Dark Horse (May 1988 © 1988 Twentieth Century Fox Film Corp.)

A sequel to the 1986 movie, this scary six-issue tale was the first of many **Aliens** *limited series and one-shots. Because the third movie contradicted this story, later printings changed the names of the lead characters.*

Walt Disney's Uncle Scrooge Adventures #5

Writer: Don Rosa
Artist: Don Rosa
Gladstone (June 1988 © 1988, 1986 The Walt Disney Company)

"Last Sled to Dawson" is a sequel to the classic Carl Barks story "Back to the Klondike." It's the first of more than a dozen sequels Rosa would do in a brilliantly realized quest to chronicle the life and times of his favorite character.

Cerebus #114
Writer: Dave Sim
Artists: Dave Sim, Gerhard
Aardvark-Vanaheim (September 1988 © 1988 Dave Sim)

The prologue to a 23-issue story focusing on the love of Cerebus' life in which the aardvark is more supporting character than star. Though Sim's work would become misogynist as the series continued, the moving "Jaka's Story" is a comics classic.

Spiral Cage
Writer: Al Davison
Artist: Al Davison
Renegade Press (September 1988 © 1988 Al Davison)

When he was born in 1960 with spina bifida, doctors said Davison would never live a meaningful life. This stirring autobiographical comic says otherwise. Besides continuing to write and draw comic books, Davison teaches and holds a black belt in karate.

Wolverine #1
Writer: Chris Claremont
Artists: John Buscema, Al Williamson
Marvel (November 1988 © 1988 Marvel Entertainment Group, Inc.)

As if being in the X-Men isn't enough, Wolverine leads a second life on the exotic and dangerous island of Madripoor. Though this title didn't focus exclusively on his adventures there, the issues that did are my favorites.

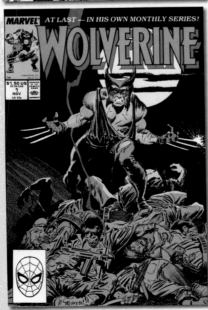

The Maze Agency #1
Writer: Mike W. Barr
Artists: Adam Hughes, Rick Magyar
Comico (December 1988 © 1988 Michael W. Barr. All other material, unless otherwise specified, © 1988 Comico the Comic Company)

Starring ex-CIA private eye Jennifer Mays and her mystery novelist boyfriend Gabriel Webb, this shrewd series played mostly fair with its readers by giving sufficient clues to solve the mysteries being investigated by the detectives.

The Sandman #1

Writer: Neil Gaiman
Artists: Sam Kieth, Mike Dringenberg
DC (January 1989 © 1988 DC Comics, Inc.)

Morpheus is the personification of dreams. This title's 75 issues form a breathtaking panorama of drama, fantasy, and mythology. It's the only comic book to win the World Fantasy Award and one of the few to make **The New York Times** *bestseller List.*

Damage Control #1-4

Writer: Dwayne McDuffie
Artists: Ernie Colon, Bob Wiacek
Marvel (May-August 1989 © 1989 Marvel Entertainment Group, Inc.)

Damage Control is the construction company that cleans up after the heroes battle the villains, repairing the damage both leave behind. It's one of those absolutely brilliant ideas that other writers wish they had come up with first.

Walt Disney's Donald Duck Adventures #12

Writer: Don Rosa
Artist: Don Rosa
Gladstone (May 1989 © 1989, © 1955, © 1952, © 1938 The Walt Disney Company)

"Return to Plain Awful" was a sequel to Barks' "Lost in the Andes" and one of the last stories Rosa did for Gladstone. Fortunately, he started doing stories for Danish publisher Egmont, and most of those stories have been reprinted in this country.

Sensational She-Hulk #1

Writer: John Byrne
Artists: John Byrne, Bob Wiacek
Marvel (May 1989 © 1989 Marvel Entertainment Group, Inc.)

Byrne gave us a She-Hulk who knew she was a comic-book character and who regularly broke the "fourth wall" to address her readers. The stories were exciting and hilarious; no one who followed Byrne managed that trick half as well.

Zot! #28-36

Writers: Scott McCloud, Ivy Ratafia
Artist: Scott McCloud
Eclipse (September 1989-July 1991 © 1989, ©1990, © 1991 Scott McCloud)

Zot is stranded on our world. The stories in this sequence are more character-oriented and down-to-earth than those in previous issues. One consists of Zot and girlfriend talking about sex, while another focuses on a character's lesbianism.

Zot is stranded on our world.

THE NOISY NINETIES

Be careful what you wish for.

Those six words describe the comics industry of the 1990s as well as any. At the decade's start, *Maus* was receiving critical acclaim outside of comicdom, and such titles as *Batman: The Dark Knight Returns* and *Watchmen* were getting decent outside-the-industry press, as well. The previous decade had ended with the successful *Batman* film starring Michael Keaton as The Caped Crusader and Jack Nicholson as The Joker.

Comic books were on the public radar in a manner not seen since the anti-comics outcry of the 1950s — only, this time, the coverage was largely positive. Especially when the media reported on the large profits being made from the sale of back-issue comics.

The fortuitous confluence of DC's "The Death of Superman" storyline with a slow news day put comic-book shops on the map, as thousands of civilians flocked to buy the "rare" issue they foolishly thought would put their kids through college. There were multiple printings of the issue, with variant covers as identification and a boost to perceived "collectibility."

Be careful what you wish for.

The comic-book boom was on. New publishers. New sales gimmicks that usually involved either variant covers (die-cut, metallic, and even press-on figures) or storylines that stretched, willy-nilly, from one title to another. Collect them all!

Collectibles speculators, both professional and amateur, saw money to be made from comics. Several new price guides hit the market, some of them published by folks who owned comics retail operations and who, thus, stood to gain from high prices "commanded" by recent back issues. This conflict of interest didn't seem to faze the new speculators. Comics were a sure thing, right?

New comics publishers were releasing some terrific material, though most of it was in the super-hero genre. Valiant had rights to the Gold Key characters of the 1960s and, alongside new characters, re-imagined *Doctor Solar, Magnus Robot Fighter,* and *Turok, Son of Stone* for a new generation of readers.

Published by DC, Milestone released a line of high-quality comics featuring more diverse heroes (African-American, Latina, gay, *etc.*) than had previously been seen from an individual publisher in the industry.

Several of Marvel's most popular young artists, unhappy with their working conditions, editorial constraints, and share of the profit pie, left the company to form Image Comics. Ironically, the success of the new organization might not have been possible without the fame and large royalties its members' association with Marvel had brought them.

Topps, the country's leading maker of collectible sports and non-sports trading cards, got into the comic-book business, as well, with adaptations of *Bram Stoker's Dracula, The X-Files,* and *Xena Warrior Princess* — and several titles created by writer-artist Jack Kirby but written and drawn by others.

Comics sales were high, and creator paychecks were getting bigger.

Then, the speculator-driven boom went bust.

Sales dropped faster than the stock market in 2008. Publishers went out of business, often owing money to creators. Comics shops closed their doors. Comics creators who, just months earlier, had had all the work they could handle, found themselves effectively unemployed.

Marvel Comics cut back on its staff, canceled one title after another, and, in 1997, declared bankruptcy. It continued to publish comics while recovering from its financial crisis.

DC Comics cut fewer staffers, canceled as many titles, but never hit bottom as hard as Marvel had. Many credit the smart management of current President and Publisher Paul Levitz for DC's weathering that particular storm.

Even comics distribution took a hit. By the end of the decade, only one major direct-marker distributor — Diamond Comic Distributors — was left standing: not the best circumstance for an industry that had always thrived on competition.

The 1990s. The Boom. The Bust. Here are some of the best and most intriguing comics of that decade …

Classics Illustrated #2: Great Expectations

Writer: Rick Geary
Artist: Rick Geary
First (February 1990 © 1990 The Berkeley Publishing Group
and First Publishing, Inc.)

Two decades after the end of the original **Classics Illus-**
trated run from Gilberton, a new series was launched
with some of the industry's top creators on board.
Geary's adaptation of this challenging Dickens novel is a
particular favorite of mine.

Aliens vs. Predator #1

Writer: Randy Stradley
Artists: Phill Norwood, Karl Story
Dark Horse (June 1990 © 1990 Twentieth Century Fox Film
Corporation)

Dark Horse capitalized on the continuing success of its
Aliens comics by combining the franchise with **Preda-**
tor, another popular horror and science-fiction film series. It would take Hollywood until 2004 to release its
first **Aliens vs. Predator** movie.

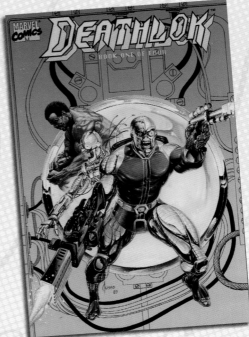

Deathlok #1-4

Writers: Dwayne McDuffie, Gregory Wright
Artists: Jackson Guice, Scott Williams
Marvel (July-October 1990 © 1990 Marvel Entertainment
Group, Inc.)

McDuffie and Wright re-imagined this obscure 1970s
cyborg hero for a classy mini-series that mixed high-
tech adventure with compelling human drama. A
subsequent ongoing series ran 34 issues; its version of
Deathlok continues to appear in other Marvel comics.

Spider-Man #1

Writer: Todd McFarlane
Artist: Todd McFarlane
Marvel (August 1990, © 1990 Marvel Entertainment Group, Inc.)

Given the chance to launch a new Spider-Man title, super-
star artist McFarlane delivered phenomenal sales. As had
happened the year before with DC's Batman: Legends of
the Dark Knight, four initial versions were released, and
other printings followed. The event had much to do with
starting the decade's speculation craze.

The Sandman #18
Writer: Neil Gaiman
Artists: Kelley Jones, Malcolm Jones III
DC (August 1990 © 1990 DC Comics, Inc.)

An unusual story even for this title, "A Dream of a Thousand Cats" has a cat for its focal character. The issue notes the universality of dreams and a central theme of the series: that dreams are shaped by their dreamers.

The Sandman #19
Writer: Neil Gaiman
Artist: Charles Vess
DC (September 1990 © 1990 DC Comics, Inc.)

*Almost every issue of **Sandman** could be justifiably included in this book, but none more than "A Midsummer Night's Dream," which reveals that it was Morpheus who commissioned the Shakespeare play. This story won the 1991 World Fantasy Award.*

From Hell #1
Writer: Alan Moore
Artist: Eddie Campbell
Mad Love Publishing (March 1991 © 1991 Alan Moore and Eddie Campbell)

This chilling look at the Jack the Ripper murders was meticulously researched with art so detailed I felt as if I were living in those grim times. Whether or not you agree with Moore's theory of the killings, this is an unforgettable story.

...flashback tale reveals that adamantium was bonded to Wolverine's bones...

Marvel Comics Presents #72
Writer: Barry Windsor-Smith
Artist: Barry Windsor-Smith
Marvel (March 1991 © 1991 Marvel Entertainment Group, Inc.)

Serialized over 13 issues of this anthology title, Windsor-Smith's stunning flashback tale reveals that adamantium was bonded to Wolverine's bones in a Canadian government project to turn people into living weapons.

Classics Illustrated #27: The Jungle

Writer: Peter Kuper
Artist: Peter Kuper
First (June 1991 © 1991 First Publishing, Inc.)

A brilliant adaptation by the versatile Kuper of the Upton Sinclair novel about corruption in the American meatpacking industry in the early 20th century. Kuper has drawn covers for **Time** magazine and "Spy vs. Spy" for Mad.

Flash #54

Writer: William Messner-Loebs
Artists: Greg LaRocque, Jose Marzan Jr.
DC (September 1991 © 1991 DC Comics Inc.)

A stewardess is sucked out of an airplane, and The Flash (who can't fly, by the way) leaps after her. Done in one issue, "Nobody Dies" is a glorious affirmation of why optimistic super-hero comics still have something to say to us.

The Twilight Zone Premiere #1

Writer: Harlan Ellison
Artist: Neal Adams
Now (October 1991 © 1991 CBS Entertainment, Inc.)

A con man sells his soul to the devil, then enlists a slick mobster to help regain said soul. Adapted from the screenplay for a 1989 episode of **The Twilight Zone** that starred Anthony Franciosa, it's the high point of this publisher's brief existence.

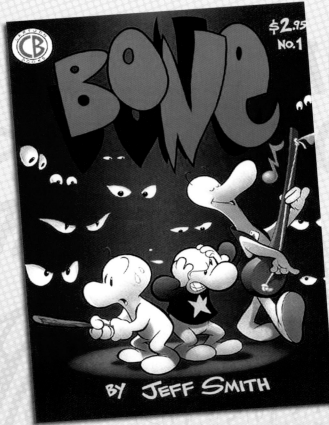

Bone #1

Writer: Jeff Smith
Artist: Jeff Smith
Cartoon Books (July 1991 © 1991 Jeff Smith)

In this epic fantasy, three cousins have exciting adventures in a mysterious valley filled with terrors and wonders. Its 55 issues have been compiled into a magnificent 1,332-page volume, befitting one of the greatest graphic novels of all time.

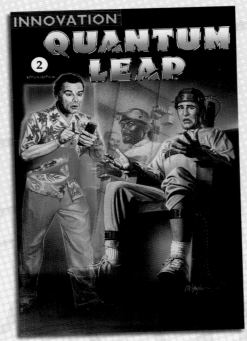

Quantum Leap #2

Writer: Bob Ingersoll
Artist: Rob Davis
Innovation (December 1991 © 1991 Universal City Studios,
Inc. Other editorial material TM & © 1991 Innovative Corp.)

Based on the TV series, **Quantum Leap** *featured a time-
lost scientist who leaps into the lives of others. In this
story, he's a death-row convict who must somehow prevent a crime on the outside. The writer is an attorney, a
comics writer, and a novelist.*

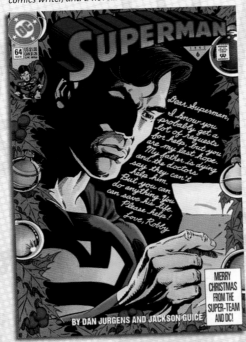

Superman #64

Writer: Dan Jurgens
Artist: Jackson Guice
DC (February 1992 © 1991 DC Comics Inc.)

*Superman and Lois read his mail; then, the big guy flies
off to make Christmas dreams come true for some of
the folks who wrote him. An utterly heartwarming super-hero story then, and I'd like to see many more like
it today.*

To the Heart of the Storm

Writer: Will Eisner
Artist: Will Eisner
Kitchen Sink (1991 © 1991 Will Eisner)

*A thinly disguised autobiographical graphic novel
examines an era when America was heading toward
war while struggling with its own ethnic, racial, and
religious demons. Many Eisner works could be in this
book; this one's a favorite of mine.*

Ms. Tree Quarterly #8

Writer: Max Allan Collins
Artist: Terry Beatty
DC (Summer 1992 © 1992 Max Allan Collins and Terry
Beatty)

*After a long run at small publishers, Ms. Tree moved to
DC Comics for eight double-sized issues. This final issue
has a very pregnant Michael wrapping up old business
before the birth of her baby. It was an excellent sign-off
for a great character.*

The Demon #26-29

Writer: Dwayne McDuffie
Artists: Val Semeiks, Bob Smith
DC (August-November 1992 © 1992 DC Comics, Inc.)

In this hilariously satiric four-issue arc, Etrigan the Demon becomes involved in the 1992 presidential election. Stop snickering. It's not as if we haven't done worse! Depending on your political bent, these issues could explain a lot.

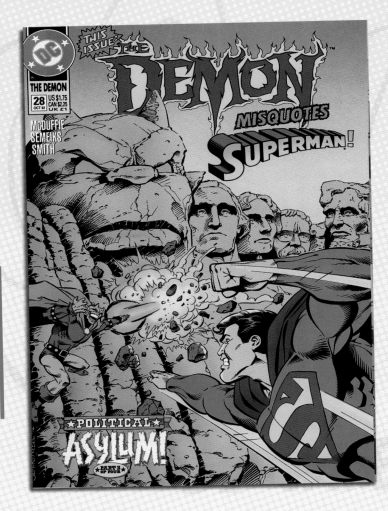

Etrigan the Demon becomes involved in the 1992 presidential election.

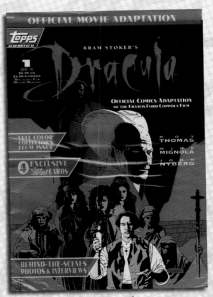

Bram Stoker's Dracula #1

Writer: Roy Thomas
Artist: Mike Mignola, John Nyberg
Topps (October 1992 © 1992 Columbia Pictures Industries, Inc.)

Topps' first comic book begins a four-issue adaptation of the 1992 movie produced and directed by Francis Ford Coppola. The original novel was adapted for the screen by James V. Hart. As was the case with all initial Topps releases, this one was bagged with trading cards.

Elfquest: Hidden Years #3

Writers: Wendy Pini, Richard Pini
Artist: Wendy Pini
WaRP Graphics (October 1992 © 1992 Warp Graphics, Inc.)

Adopted by Tyleet after being abandoned as a child, Little Patch is the first human to live among the Wolfriders. Though he eventually rejoins his own tribe and becomes their chief, he returns to Tyleet in the second of two bittersweet issues.

Elfquest: Hidden Years #4

Writers: Wendy Pini, Richard Pini
Artist: Wendy Pini
WaRP Graphics (November 1992 © 1992 Warp Graphics, Inc.)

Elfquest is among the most beloved series in comics history. The original series ran for 20 issues with dozens of sequels and spin-offs since. Republished by Marvel in the 1980s and DC in the 2000s, it's an adventure I hope never ends.

Flash #73

Writer: Mark Waid
Artists: Greg LaRocque, Roy Richardson
DC (February 1993 © 1992 DC Comics)

At the end of a wonderful Christmas team-up between the Golden Age Flash and current Flash Wally West, we got a surprise that knocked fandom on its butt. Waid, now recognized as one of the best writers in comics, made his name on this title.

Hardware #1

Writer: Dwayne McDuffie
Artists: Denys Cowan, Jimmy Palmiotti
DC/Milestone (April 1993 © 1993 Milestone Media Inc.)

Genius inventor Curtis Metcalf changes his status as a cog in the machine after learning his boss is a crime boss. A terrific super-hero comic, *Hardware* is most notable for the character development of its lead as the series progressed.

Icon #1

Writer: Dwayne McDuffie
Artists: M.D. Bright, Mike Gustovich
DC/Milestone (May 1993 © 1993 Milestone Media Inc.)

An alien who has lived as a black man since 1839 gets an unlikely Jiminy Cricket in an idealistic teen who convinces him to become a super-hero with her as his sidekick. One of the best super-hero comics of all and my favorite Milestone title.

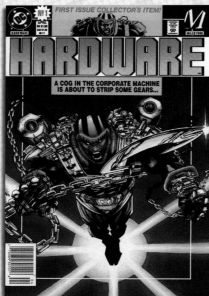

Prime #1

Writers: Gerard Jones, Len Strazewski
Artist: Norm Breyfogle
Malibu (June 1993 © 1993 Malibu Comics Entertainment, Inc.)

A 13-year-old boy can become an adult super-hero in this 1990s take on the original Captain Marvel. Malibu's "Ultraverse" universe of super-hero titles included **Firearm**, **Hardcase**, **Mantra**, **The Night Man**, and **The Strangers**.

The Sandman #50

Writer: Neil Gaiman
Artist: P. Craig Russell
DC/Vertigo (June 1993 © 1993 DC Comics)

This is a tale of Baghdad, the greatest city of the ancient world, and why its legend will endure for all time. The issue is written, drawn, and lettered in the Arabic tradition, proof of the amazing artistry and variety contained in this series.

Static #1

Writer: Dwayne McDuffie, Robert L. Washington III
Artists: John Paul Leon, Steve Mitchell
DC/Milestone (June 1993 © 1993 Milestone Media Inc.)

During a gang war, Virgil Hawkins is exposed to an experimental gas that gives him electromagnetic powers. But what makes this series one of the best is watching the teenager address and deal with the problems that most modern kids face.

Satan's Six #4

Writer: Tony Isabella
Artists: John Cleary, Armando Gil
Topps (July 1993 © 1993 Jack Kirby; Wolff and Byrd © Batton Lash; Jason © 1993 New Line Cinema Corp; all other material © 1993 Topps Comics, Inc.)

*Created by the legendary Jack Kirby and developed by not-legendary me into an action-comedy, **Satan's Six** was about lost souls trying to earn their place in Hell. They weren't very bright, they weren't really evil, but they sure were fun to write.*

Marvels #1

Writer: Kurt Busiek
Artist: Alex Ross
Marvel (January 1994 © 1993 Marvel Entertainment Group, Inc.)

Depicted through Ross' dramatic painted art, we see super-heroes and villains as seen by news photographer Phil Sheldon. The four-issue series poignantly presents an Everyman's perspective of the fantastic Marvel Universe.

1000 Comic Books You Must Read

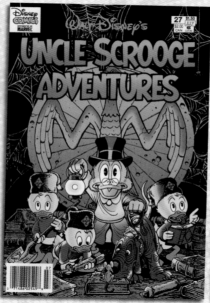

The Power of Shazam!

Writer: Jerry Ordway
Artist: Jerry Ordway
DC (January 1994 © 1994 DC Comics)

This hardcover graphic novel revamped Captain Marvel for the 1990s. Though not the lighthearted entertainment of the Golden Age, it was an exciting, heroic portrayal of the classic comics character with art as powerful as its story.

Walt Disney's Uncle Scrooge Adventures #27

Writer: Don Rosa
Artist: Don Rosa
Gladstone (July 1994 © 1994 The Walt Disney Company)

Spanning the ages and the world, "Guardians of the Lost Library" is a rousing adventure centering on Scrooge's quest for knowledge and profit with a star turn for the Junior Woodchucks, the organization of which Huey, Dewey, and Louie are members.

The Tale of One Bad Rat #1

Writer: Bryan Talbot
Artist: Bryan Talbot
Dark Horse (October 1994 © Bryan Talbot)

Originally published as a four-issue mini-series, Talbot's quietly powerful graphic novel follows the journey of Helen Potter, a child-abuse victim and teenage runaway. The children's books of writer-artist Beatrix Potter play a key role in Helen's story.

...his battle against cancer as shared by his wife...

Our Cancer Year

Writers: Joyce Brabner, Harvey Pekar
Artist: Frank Stack
Publisher (October 1994 © 1994 Joyce Brabner and Harvey Pekar)

Pekar's first book-length comic book is an account of his battle against cancer as shared by his wife, Joyce. Their struggle is framed by the year's events, which include Desert Storm. It's an incredible work, one of the best graphic novels of any year.

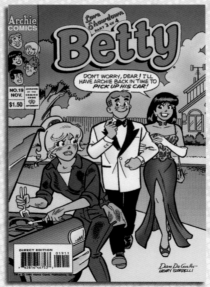

Archie #429

Writers: Dan Parent
Artists: Stan Goldberg, Dan DeCarlo
Archie (November 1994 © 1994 Archie Comic
Publications, Inc.)

*The "eternal triangle" of Archie, Betty, and Ve-
ronica is shaken to its core when Archie receives
a mysterious love letter. Each of the girls believes
the other wrote the letter. The four-issue story
continued in* Betty *#19.*

Betty #19

Writer: Bill Golliher
Artists: Doug Crane, Ken Selig
Archie (November 1994 © 1994 Archie Comic
Publications, Inc.)

*Betty and Veronica declare an all-out war to win
Archie's heart for once and always. The "Love
Showdown" serial was extremely popular with
the readers, promising that, at its conclusion, Archie would, indeed, make a choice.*

Betty and Veronica #82

Writer: Dan Parent
Artists: Dan DeCarlo, Alison Flood
Archie (December 1994 © 1994, Archie Comic
Publications, Inc.)

*Archie is pressed to choose between Betty and
Veronica, as the "Love Showdown" draws to its
conclusion. The story continues in* Veronica *#39,
wherein we learn the letter was written by …*

One of 17 magnificently entertaining anthologies...

The Big Book of Urban Legends

Writer: Jan Harold Brunvand, various
Artists: various
DC/Paradox (November 1994 © 1994 Jan Harold Brunvand.
All other material © 1994 Paradox Press)

*One of 17 magnificently entertaining anthologies cover-
ing a variety of topics as drawn by a dizzying array of
some of the best artists in comicdom. An 18th book,*
The Big Book of Wild Women, *is largely completed but
was not yet published as of the start of 2009.*

Veronica #39

Writer: Bill Golliher
Artists: Stan Goldberg, Henry Scarpelli
Archie (December 1994 © 1994 Archie Comic
Publications, Inc.)

… *Cheryl Blossom, a red-haired beauty from several 1980s stories. She's a student at Pembrook Academy, an elite private school. In a surprising turn of events, Archie chooses the vivacious Ms. Blossom over Betty and Veronica!*

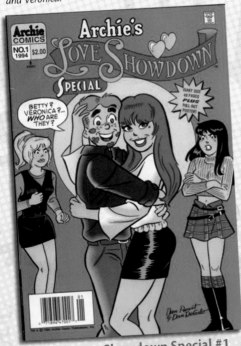

Archie's Love Showdown Special #1

Writers: Dan Parent, Bill Golliher
Artists: Dan Parent, Bill Golliher
Archie (1994 ©* 1994 Archie Comic Publications, Inc.)

In this 56-page special combining new material with reprints, the "eternal triangle" is more or less restored. Cheryl will continue to date Archie on occasion and proves popular enough to headline her own series for the next few years.

Deathwish #1

Writers: Adam Blaustein, Yves Fezzani
Artists: J.H. Williams III, Jimmy Palmiotti
DC/Milestone (December 1994 © 1995 DC Comics)

The sole survivor of a gang rape of his family, Deathwish becomes a vigilante obsessed with sex crimes. The four-issue mini-series is notable for its use of a preoperative transsexual police detective as the focus of the storyline.

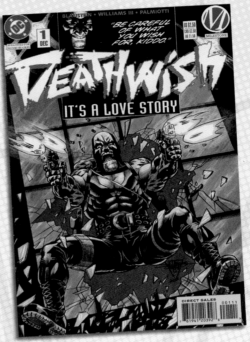

Black Lightning #1

Writer: Tony Isabella
Artists: Eddy Newell, Ron McCain
DC (February 1995 © 1994 DC Comics)

Jefferson Pierce confronts crime and gang violence as a high-school teacher and super-hero. In returning to my creation, I wanted to tell stories that were grittily realistic but still optimistic. I consider it the best work of my career.

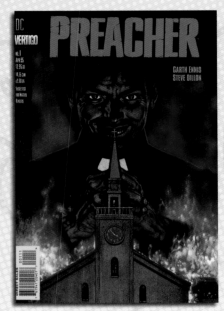

Preacher #1

Writer: Garth Ennis
Artist: Steve Dillon
DC/Vertigo (April 1995 © 1995 Garth Ennis and Steve Dillon)

Its title character is a down-and-out preacher with supernatural powers who's looking to get answers from God ... directly. The controversial series is noted for its religious themes, violence, and dark humor.

Black Lightning #5

Writer: Tony Isabella
Artist: Eddy Newell
DC (June 1995 © 1995 DC Comics)

Jeff Pierce spends the entire issue in a hospital recovering from a gunshot wound and contemplating the nature of heroism. Partially illustrated in breathtaking black-and-white, "Blowed Away" might be the best story I ever wrote.

Impulse #3

Writer: Mark Waid
Artists: Humberto Ramos, Wayne Faucher
DC (June 1995 © 1995 DC Comics)

Born in the future, Bart Allen is the grandson of the Silver Age Flash. In this funny, warm-hearted tale, Waid takes us through Bart's school day, which, for an impatient young speedster, seems to drag on forever.

Kurt Busiek's Astro City #1

Writer: Kurt Busiek
Artist: Brent Anderson
Image (August 1995 © 1995 Juke Box Productions)

Astro City features a variety of characters, both human and super-human, in stories told from many perspectives and addressing many genre themes. Brilliantly written, beautifully drawn, it's one of the best super-hero comics of all time.

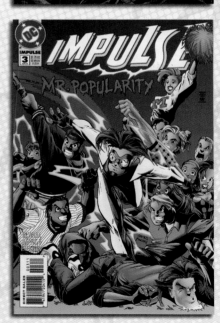

Untold Tales of Spider-Man #1

Writer: Kurt Busiek
Artists: Pat Olliffe, Al Vey
Marvel (September 1995 © 1995 Marvel Entertainment Group, Inc.)

This 25-issue series presented new Spider-Man stories set in the early years of his career and taking place between his previously published adventures. Despite its low 99¢ price tag, this title never achieved the commercial success it deserved.

> ...this title never achieved the commercial success it deserved.

Akiko on the Planet Smoo #1

Writer: Mark Crilley
Artist: Mark Crilley
Sirius (December 1995 © 1995 Mark Crilley)

A 10-year old girl is whisked away to a distant world to rescue its kidnapped prince. Filled with exciting action, great characters, science-fiction wonderment, and laugh-out-loud humor, it's a terrific comic book for kids of all ages.

Akiko #1

Writer: Mark Crilley
Artist: Mark Crilley
Sirius (March 1996 © 1995 Mark Crilley)

The ongoing series kicked off with "The Menace of Alia Rellapor," an 18-issue epic. As each issue came out, I would read it with/to my son Eddie and daughter Kelly. Those times may be favorites in a lifetime of loving comic books.

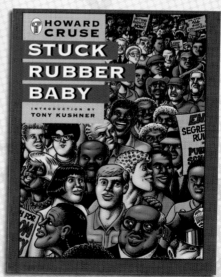

Stuck Rubber Baby

Writer: Howard Cruse
Artist: Howard Cruse
DC/Paradox (1995 © 1995 Howard Cruse)

Set in Alabama, this outstanding coming-of-age graphic novel tells of a young white man from a working-class background who struggles to accept his homosexuality while rejecting the racism around him. One of the most moving comics of all.

The Sandman #75

Writer: Neil Gaiman
Artist: Charles Vess
DC/Vertigo (March 1996 © 1996 DC Comics)

*Once more with Shakespeare. For the finale of the ongoing series, Gaiman channels **The Tempest** in a story that examines Morpheus/Dream intimately and echoes the play's themes of change, endings, and new beginnings. It's a curtain call that left me breathless.*

Supreme #41

Writer: Alan Moore
Artists: Joe Bennett, Norm Rapmund
Image (August 1996 © 1996 Rob Liefeld, Inc.)

*It started out as a cheesy "Superman" knock-off, but, for the 12 issues written by Moore, **Supreme** became a glorious, imaginative celebration of the "white hat" heroes with which Moore and readers of my generation had grown up.*

Leave It to Chance #1

Writer: James Robinson
Artist: Paul Smith
Image/Homage (October 1996 © 1996 James Robinson and Paul Smith)

1996 was a good year for adventurous girls. Chance Falconer, the daughter of a famous paranormal investigator and owner of a pet dragon, appeared in 13 wonderful issues over a four-year-span. The title has won several industry awards.

An anthology
featuring Ellison
as its host...

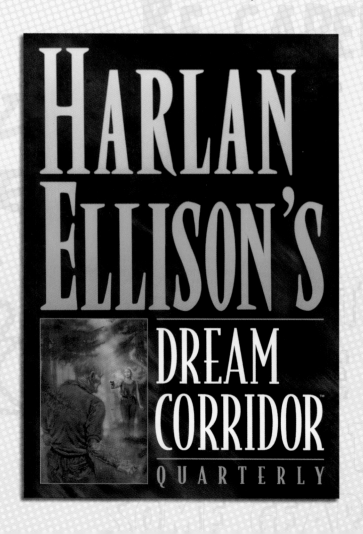

Harlan Ellison's Dream Corridor Quarterly #1

Writers: Harlan Ellison, others
Artists: Eric Shanower, others
Dark Horse (August 1996 © 1996 The Kilimanjaro Corporation. Original Harlan Ellison stories from which these graphic adaptations have been taken are variously © 1956, © 1957, © 1967, © 1969, and © 1970 by Harlan Ellison. Renewed © 1984, © 1985, and © 1995 by Harlan Ellison)

An anthology featuring Ellison as its host and comics adaptations of stories by the celebrated author, including "One Life, Furnished in Early Poverty," "The Voice in the Garden," "Gnomebody," and "Opposites Attract."

Fax from Sarajevo

Writer: Joe Kubert
Artist: Joe Kubert
Dark Horse (November 1996 © 1996 Joe Kubert & Strip Art Features)

Based on the faxes sent by European comics agent Ervin Rustemagic during the two-and-a-half years of the Serbian siege of Sarajevo. This compelling non-fiction graphic novel won both the Eisner and Harvey Awards, the industry's highest honors.

Daddy's Girl

Writer: Debbie Drechsler
Artist: Debbie Drechsler
Fantagraphics (1996 © Debbie Drechsler)

Drechsler's semi-autobiographical account of a pre-teen/adolescent girl's abuse at the hands of her father is so painfully honest it brought to me to tears when I read it, one of only two comic books or graphic novels that have ever done that.

It's a Good Life, if You Don't Weaken

Writer: Seth
Artist: Seth
Drawn & Quarterly (1996 © 1993, 1994, 1995, 1996 Seth)

*Originally published in **Palookaville**, this "autobiographical" work is actually a fictional account of Seth's search for an obscure **New Yorker** cartoonist. Rich in nostalgic images, the tale **feels** true — and isn't that the mark of great fiction?*

Thunderbolts #1

Writer: Kurt Busiek
Artists: Mark Bagley, Vince Russell
Marvel (April 1997 © 1997 Marvel Characters, Inc.)

With The Avengers and The Fantastic Four missing in action, a new band of super-heroes stepped up ... except they were secretly super-villains. In 40 years reading comics, 25 years writing them, I still never saw this coming.

Transmetropolitan #1

Writer: Warren Ellis
Artist: Darick Robertson, Jerome K. Moore
DC/Helix (September 1997 © 1997 Warren Ellis and Darick Robertson)

Spider Robinson, renegade journalist of the future, takes on, not one, but two presidents in a never-ending battle against abuse of power and corruption and his own growing popularity. It's perhaps the edgiest science-fiction comic of all.

> It's perhaps the edgiest science-fiction comic of all.

What If ... ? #105

Writers: Tom DeFalco, Ron Frenz
Artists: Ron Frenz, Bill Sienkiewicz
Marvel (February 1998 © 1997 Marvel Characters, Inc.)

In an alternate future world, the daughter of Peter Parker (now a police scientist) and Mary Jane Watson inherits her dad's powers and becomes Spider-Girl. The character was so well received she got her own ongoing series six months later.

Desperadoes #5

Writer: Jeff Mariotte
Artist: John Cassaday
Image (June 1998 © 1998 Aegis Entertainment)

Four outlaws ride through a post-Civil War West that's not merely wild, it's downright weird. Unjustly accused by a vengeful sheriff, Gideon Brood and his crew contend with dark forces in this stylish supernatural Western series.

The Amazing "True" Story of a Teenage Single Mom
Writer: Katherine Arnoldi
Artist: Katherine Arnoldi
Hyperion (September 1998 © 1998 Katherine Arnoldi)

Arnoldi's courageous real-life story of her life as a poor teenage mom trying to build a future for herself and her daughter. I picked this as the best graphic novel of the year and have recommended it to friends ever since.

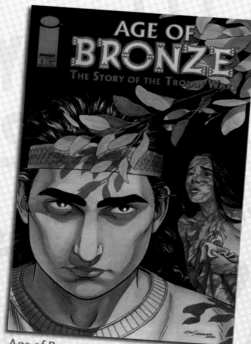

Age of Bronze #1
Writer: Eric Shanower
Artist: Eric Shanower
Image (November 1998 © 1998 Eric Shanower)

Eisner Award-winning cartoonist Shanower brings the epic story of the Trojan War to comic-book life with amazing attention to detail, a sure handle on characterization, and a classic, yet modern, sense of storytelling.

Spider-Girl #1
Writer: Tom DeFalco
Artists: Pat Olliffe, Al Williamson
Marvel (October 1998 © 1998 Marvel Characters, Inc.)

Her first series ran 101 issues, her second 30, and her manga-sized reprints have sold better than any other Marvel heroes reprinted in that format. Marvel's most successful super-heroine, Spider-Girl began appearing in **Amazing Spider-Man Family** *in 2009.*

A Patty Cake Christmas

Writer: Scott Roberts
Artist: Scott Roberts
Permanent Press (1999 © 1996, 1999 Scott Roberts)

Originally published in 1996, this extended version is a Christmas classic, eliciting laughs and tears as it examines that vast chasm between what kids want and what they get. In the "comics about kids" genre, **Patty Cake** is among the best.

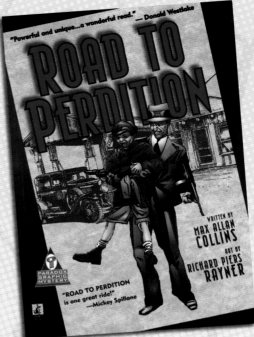

Road to Perdition

Writer: Max Allan Collins
Artist: Richard Piers Rayner
DC/Paradox/Pocket Books (1998 Script © 1998 Max Allan Collins. Art © 1998 Richard Piers Rayner)

This sensational graphic novel is the American counter-part to **Lone Wolf and Cub** with a Depression-era hit-man and his young son seeking revenge on the mob that betrayed them. It was made into a 2002 film starring Tom Hanks and Paul Newman.

Tellos #1

Writer: Todd Dezago
Artists: Mike Wieringo, Nathan Massengill
Image (May 1999 © 1999 Todd Dezago and Mike Wieringo)

An imaginative fantasy series starring a young boy, his half-tiger companion, and a supporting cast that includes a genie, a dragon, a pirate fox, and others. Though only 13 issues were published, it remains a much-loved comic book.

THE NEW MILLENNIUM

CHAPTER EIGHT

The comic-book industry entered the new millennium bruised but not beaten. After all, the heroes in our stories often fought their way back from defeat. Why couldn't the industry do the same?

Marvel came back the strongest, buoyed by the tremendous success of its X-Men and Spider-Man movie franchises and decent returns on a score of other animated features, cartoons, and films. Nor did it neglect the comic books that fed this success: starting a new line of "Ultimate" recreations of its most popular titles; bringing in top comics talent to revitalize its core characters; hiring such high-profile screenwriters as Kevin Smith and J. Michael Straczynski to write *Daredevil, Amazing Spider-Man* and others; and committing to company-wide storylines that would have lasting consequences for the Marvel Universe.

DC had good days in Hollywood, as well. *Smallville*, a TV series that centered on Clark Kent before he donned his familiar tights and cape, has done well for several years, as have cartoons featuring Batman, The Justice League, and The Teen Titans. Most importantly, the Batman movie franchise was successfully relaunched with *Batman Begins* and set records with *The Dark Knight*. On the comics front, DC continued to publish a stunning array of titles for all ages and in nearly every conceivable genre.

Other publishers survived and even flourished. Dark Horse had some of the most valuable licenses in comics: *Star Wars, Aliens, Buffy the Vampire Slayer*. Image began to rival DC for variety, publishing mostly titles owned by its creators. Fantagraphics continued to be the leading publisher of alternative comics while also bringing classic comics collections and informative comics histories to the market. New publishers entered the field, and some of them — Boom! Studios, Devil's Due, and IDW — became strong players in the field.

Some existing publishers continued to add to the growing variety in the field, while others, both old and new, became casualties of the increased competition or their own poor business plans.

Marvel, DC, and most of the major publishers ramped up their trade-paperback and hardcover publishing programs. You could find impressive "graphic novels" sections in most chain and independent bookstores.

The biggest bookstore competition for American comics publishers came from Japan, with hundreds of translated-to-English *manga* series being sold to young and overwhelmingly female readers in convenient paperback formats. However large the "graphic novel" section in most bookstores, the "manga" section was usually two or three times as large by mid-decade.

Hollywood continued to consider the comics industry as its personal research and development department. Hundreds of comics properties were optioned for movies, cartoons, and television in recent years with more announced on a nigh-weekly basis.

One could argue, as I do, that this decade is the *genuine* "Golden Age of Comics." There are lots of great comics in lots of different genres. There are terrific reprints of classic and not-so-classic comics. There are comics coming to America from Britain, Europe, Japan, and around the world. There are books and magazines devoted to the history of comics and the creators of those comics. There are nigh-countless cartoons, movies and TV shows based on comics, including more *anime* from Japan than you could shake a samurai at. There are action figures, high-end sculptures, role-playing games, trading cards, and so many other wondrous comics-related items that not even Scrooge McDuck could build a vault big enough to hold them all. Diamond Comic Distributors' *Previews* catalog generally weighs in at 400 pages every month. I can't think of a better time to be a comics fan.

Welcome to the new millennium …

Faith: A Fable

Writer: Bill Knapp
Artist: Bill Knapp
Carbon-Based Books (January 2000 © 2000 Bill Knapp)

In a small town, a reporter meets a young girl with the seemingly miraculous power to inspire hope in others. Amid relentless media attention, she teaches him about faith … in one's self and in one's choices. A compelling graphic novel.

Eagle: Vol. 1

Writer: Kaiji Kawaguchi
Artist: Kaiji Kawaguchi
Viz (February 2000 © 2000 Kaiji Kawaguchi/Shogakukan, Inc.)

"The Making of an Asian-American President" follows the campaign of Senator Kenneth Yamaoka, a third-generation Japanese-American. Running 22 volumes and more than 2,000 pages, this thrilling epic offers a different perspective on American politics.

Geeksville #1-4

Writer: Rich Koslowski
Artist: Rich Koslowski
Image (May-November 2000 © 1999 3 Finger Prints and Gary Sassaman)

In the hilarious four-issue "Breaking into the Business," clueless fans Keith, Jim, and Allen self-publish their own comic book. What could possibly go wrong? Back-up features include stories by Gary Sassaman and "Tales from the Comic Shop."

Marvels Comics: Daredevil #1

Writer: Tony Isabella
Artist: Eddy Newell
Marvel (July 2000 © 2000 Marvel Characters, Inc.)

One of six comic books supposedly published in the Marvel Universe, this tale of a demon yearning for Heaven is replete with homages to the kid gangs of the 1940s; think Charles Biro's Little Wise Guys and the Simon-Kirby Boys' Ranch.

...this tale of a demon yearning for Heaven is replete with homages to kid gangs of the 1940s.

JLA: Heaven's Ladder

Writer: Mark Waid
Artist: Bryan Hitch
DC (October 2000 © 2000 DC Comics)

In this magnificent oversized (10x13.5-inch) comic book, godlike aliens facing the end of their existence desperately seek an answer to the question of what comes next ... by kidnapping the Earth and several other inhabited worlds!

Shazam! The Power of Hope

Writer: Alex Ross, Paul Dini
Artist: Alex Ross
DC (November 2000 © 2000 DC Comics)

Billy Batson and Captain Marvel are overwhelmed by the enormity of the world's need for them in this ultimately inspirational story. It's one of several oversized specials done to celebrate such iconic DC heroes as Superman, Batman, and Wonder Woman.

Ultimate Spider-Man #1

Writers: Brian Michael Bendis, Bill Jemas
Artists: Mark Bagley, Art Thibert
Marvel (October 2000 © 2000 Marvel Characters, Inc.)

This re-imagining of Peter Parker as a modern-day teenager turns out to be one of the best takes on The Web-Slinger ever. It had all the classic elements of the character, but individual stories would often take wonderfully unexpected turns.

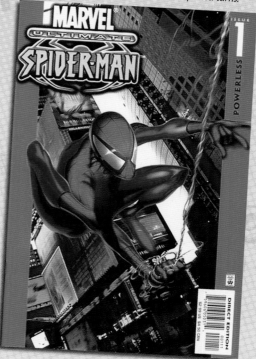

Last Day in Vietnam

Writer: Will Eisner
Artist: Will Eisner
Dark Horse (2000 © 2000 Will Eisner)

Drawn from Eisner's experiences in the military and producing P.S. Magazine for the Army, this anthology focuses on wartime soldiers. Humorous or deadly serious, each of these stories is told with the compelling humanity that is the mark of Eisner's work.

Last Kiss #1

Writer: John Lustig
Artists: various
Shanda Fantasy Arts (February 2001 © 2001 John Lustig)

When Charlton closed shop, it sold the rights to its comics. Lustig bought **First Kiss** *(1957-1965), rewriting and re-lettering those stories into hilarious parodies of the genre. He also does an ongoing comic strip for* **Comics Buyer's Guide** *and the Internet.*

Amelia Rules #1

Writer: Jimmy Gownley
Artist: Jimmy Gownley
Renaissance Press (August 2001 © 2001 Jimmy Gownley)

After her parents' divorce, Amelia adjusts to her life in a new town with the help of friends. Her stories are funny, moving, and true-to-life. **Amelia Rules: Superheroes** *won the 2007 Cybil Award for best graphic novel for readers 12 and under.*

Bizarro Comics

Writers: various
Artists: various
DC (June 2001 © 2001 DC Comics)

Growing from a comic book deemed too subversive for publication in that format, this hardcover anthology features the DC super-heroes as seen by a virtual who's who of the top alternative creators in comics. Me hated it a lot.

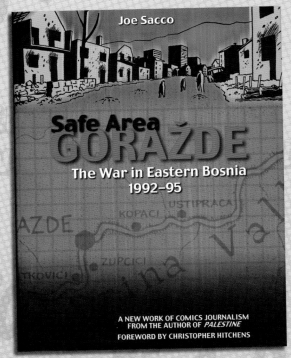

Safe Area Gorazde

Writer: Joe Sacco
Artist: Joe Sacco
Fantagraphics (August 2001 © 2000 Joe Sacco)

In this powerful graphic novel, Sacco covers the Bosnian conflict. Based on his 1994 and 1995 visits to the region and his interviews with Bosnians trapped in the war-torn country, the work is comics journalism at its finest.

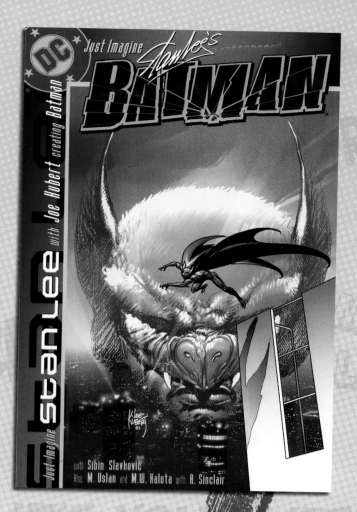

Just Imagine Stan Lee with Joe Kubert Creating Batman

Writer: Stan Lee
Artist: Joe Kubert
DC (September 2001 © 2001 DC Comics)

Marvel's Stan Lee re-imagined DC's heroes in 12 one-shots. Based on a concept by Michael Uslan, the specials were drawn by some of the best artists in comics: John Buscema, Jim Lee, Dave Gibbons, Walter Simonson, John Cassaday, and others. This one, of course, is drawn by Joe Kubert.

> ...the specials were drawn by some of the best artists in comics.

Greyshirt: Indigo Sunset #1

Writer: Rick Veitch
Artist: Rick Veitch
DC/America's Best Comics (December 2001 © 2001 America's Best Comics, LLC.)

Co-created by Alan Moore, this character is partly a take on Will Eisner's Spirit and partly a pastiche of comics and pulp costumed detectives in general. This six-issue series explores Greyshirt's origins and the world in which he operates.

Catwoman #1-4

Writer: Ed Brubaker
Artists: Darwyn Cooke, Mike Allred
DC (January-April, 2002 © 2002 DC Comics)

Catwoman sorts out her place in the world and her relationship with Batman while tracking whoever is killing Gotham City prostitutes. Her actions and her reactions always ring true in one of the best portrayals of the character ever.

The Amazing Spider-Man Vol. 2 #38

Writer: J. Michael Straczynski
Artists: John Romita, Jr., Scott Hanna
Marvel (February 2002 © 2002 Marvel Characters, Inc.)

May Parker has learned her nephew Peter is Spider-Man. What follows in this issue is "The Conversation," a landmark story redefining the characters and their abiding love and respect for one another. This was a Spider-Man I could believe in.

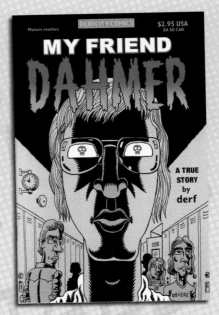

Adventures of Superman #600

Writer: Joe Casey
Artists: Mike Wieringo, Jose Marzan Jr.
DC (March 2002 © 2002 DC Comics)

This anniversary issue, set during the period when Lex Luthor was president, contrasts the respective ideologies of Superman and his foe, gives wonderful moments to the supporting cast, and delivers both an exciting story and a satisfying ending.

Young Jeffrey Dahmer

Writer: Derf
Artist: Derf
SLG Publishing (March 2002 © John Backderf)

Cartoonist John Backderf lived in a farm town south of Cleveland and attended high school with serial-killer-to-be Jeffrey Dahmer. This amazing "I-knew-him-when" comic book recounts the events of those years in a non-sensationalistic, but still chilling, manner.

GTO: Great Teacher Onizuka Vol. 1

Writer: Tohru Fujisawa
Artist: Tohru Fujisawa
TokyoPop (April 2002 © 1997 Tohru Fujisawa. English text © 2002 by Mixx Entertainment, Inc.)

Immature, rough at the edges, Onizuki goes from being a common punk to a high-school teacher who inspires even the most difficult and troubled students. It's funny, heart-warming, rude, and sometimes even unnerving.

Deadline #1-4

Writer: Bill Rosemann
Artist: Guy Davis
Marvel (June-September 2002 © 2002 Marvel Characters, Inc.)

Reporter "Kat" Farrell is involved in a murder case that explores rarely visited corners of the Marvel Universe. The mini-series also features Spider-Man supporting characters Betty Brant, Ben Urich, Robbie Robertson, and J. Jonah Jameson.

Savage Dragon #100

Writer: Erik Larsen
Artists: Erik Larsen
Image (June 2002 © 2002 Erik Larsen)

This 100-page super-spectacular is entirely written and pencilled by Larsen, save for a few pin-ups. Alone among the Image founders, Larsen still does every issue of his own title. He's closing in on his 150th issue and shows no sign of slowing down.

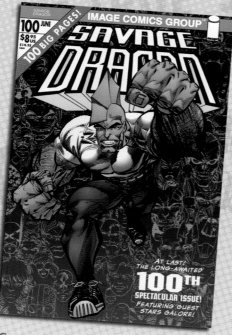

Catwoman: Selina's Big Score

Writer: Darwyn Cooke
Artist: Darwyn Cooke
DC (July 2002 © 2002 DC Comics)

The defining moment in the life of Selina Kyle: the moment in which who she was leads inevitably and tragically to who she is. Comics creators often try to bring a *"crime noir"* feel to their stories, but few have succeeded as well as Cooke.

Fables #1

Writer: Bill Willingham
Artist: Lan Medina, Steve Leialoha
DC/Vertigo (July 2002 © Bill Willingham and DC Comics)

Driven from their homeland by The Adversary, characters from fairy tales live in a secret community in New York City. The ingenious reinterpretations of these classic characters make **Fables** the best fantasy comic-book series since **The Sandman**.

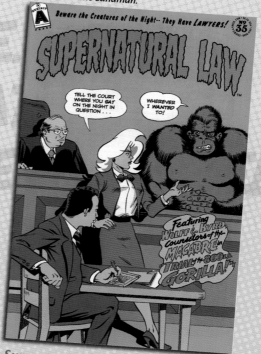

Supernatural Law #35

Writer: Batton Lash
Artist: Batton Lash
Exhibit A Press (July 2002 © 2002 Batton Lash)

"The Trial of the 800-lb. Gorilla" will delight Silver Age comics buffs. Counselors of the macabre Alanna Wolff and Jeff Byrd are the title character's defense attorneys in a funny story that uses many Silver Age themes.

Three Fingers

Writer: Rich Koslowski
Artist: Rich Koslowski
Top Shelf Productions (July 2002 © 2002 Rich Koslowski)

Told documentary-style, this graphic novel is set in a world in which cartoon characters coexist with humans. Koslowski explores the dark side of cartoons and the terrible price people (and cartoons) are willing to pay to attain fame and fortune.

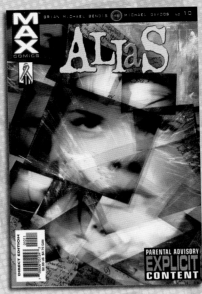

Alias #10

Writer: Brian Michael Bendis
Artist: Michael Gaydos
Marvel (August 2002 © 2002 Marvel Characters, Inc.)

Former super-heroine turned private investigator Jessica Jones is hired by J. Jonah Jameson to learn Spider-Man's civilian identity. Bendis and Gaydos depart from traditional comic-book format in an issue that left a huge grin on my face.

Batman: Gotham Adventures #51

Writer: Jason Hall
Artists: Brad Rader, Terry Austin
DC (August 2002 © 2002 DC Comics)

*A suitable-for-all-ages comic book in the style of the exquisite **Batman: The Animated Series** (1992-1995). Many readers, myself among them, thought this series was superior to the "real" Batman comics of the late 1990s and early 2000s.*

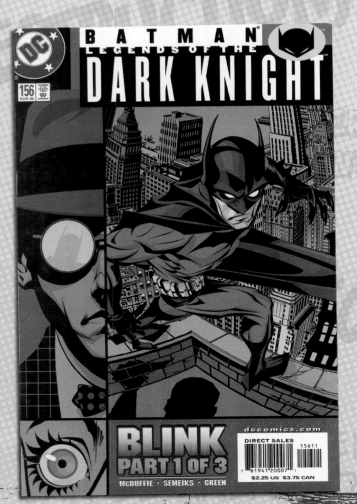

...Batman is competent and sane.

Batman: Legends of the Dark Knight #156-158

Writer: Dwayne McDuffie
Artists: Val Semeiks, Dan Green
DC (August-October 2002 © 2002 DC Comics)

A blind grifter who can see through the eyes of others teams with Batman to stop a serial killer. McDuffie's Batman is competent and sane, eschewing the psychological basket case inflicted on readers whenever someone overthinks the character.

Dexter's Laboratory #30

Writer: Robbie Busch
Artist: Stephen DeStefano
DC (August 2002 © 2002 Cartoon Network)

In the wake of an experiment gone awry, boy genius Dexter prepares to rebuild the world in the aftermath of the impending catastrophe. Channeling Bernard Krigstein and Harvey Kurtzman, this hilarious comic book is based on the cartoon series created by Genndy Tartakovsky.

...Dexter prepares to build the world in the aftermath of the impending catastrophe.

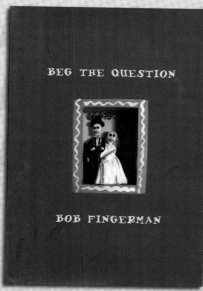

Beg the Question

Writer: Bob Fingerman
Artist: Bob Fingerman
Fantagraphics (October 2002 © Bob Fingerman)

*Revised and expanded from his **Minimum Wage** comic books of the mid-1990s, Fingerman's funny, heartwarming graphic novel about 20-somethings in love in New York City helps makes the case for comics being **the** great American art form.*

Bongo Comics Presents Radioactive Man #6

Writer: Batton Lash
Artists: Dan DeCarlo, Bob Smith
Bongo (October 2002 © 2002 Bongo Entertainment, Inc. The Simpsons © Twentieth Century Fox Film Corporation)

Bart Simpson's favorite super-hero stars in this wonderful homage to the Gold Key comics of the 1960s. This issue is numbered #106 on the cover and dated November 1963 and is one of several issues saluting the comic books of the past.

Iron Wok Jan Volume 1

Writer: Shinji Saijyo
Artist: Shinji Saijyo
ComicsOne (December 2002 Tetsunabe no Jan! 1 © 1995 Shinji Saijyo. English translation 2002 © ComicsOne, Corp.)

A tale of two chefs: Jan Akiyama, grandson of a legendary master, and Kiriko Gobancho, grand-daughter of the owner of the restaurant where they work. It's a delectable mix of characterization, exotic recipes, and good old-fashioned soap-opera intrigue.

Invincible #1

Writer: Robert Kirkman
Artist: Cory Walker
Image (January 2003 © 2003 Robert Kirkman and Cory Walker)

What if Superman had a son? That's where this fresh take on classic super-hero themes starts, but there are shocking surprises to go with the cool new characters, exciting action, and compelling human drama. A great super-hero for the new millennium.

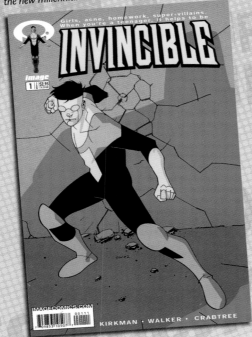

Batgirl Year One #1

Writer: Scott Beatty, Chuck Dixon
Artists: Marcos Martin, Alvaro Lopez
DC (February 2003 © 2003 DC Comics)

First of nine issues. While not all (or many) DC retcons have been creatively successful, this blast from the past seamlessly merges the classic with the contemporary and tells a whopping good story along the way.

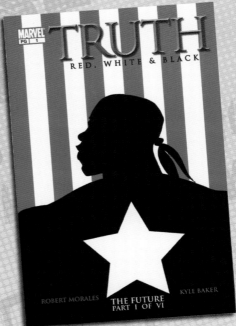

Truth: Red, White, and Black #1

Writer: Robert Morales
Artist: Kyle Baker
Marvel (January 2003 © Marvel Characters, Inc.)

In this controversial seven-issue series, African-American soldiers are subjects in an effort to re-create the super-serum that created Captain America. It echoes the contemptible Tuskegee Experiments conducted by the Public Health Service from 1942 to 1972.

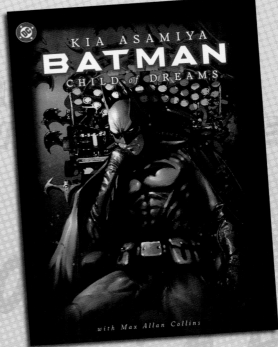

Batman: Child of Dreams

Writers: Kia Asamiya, Max Allan Collins
Artists: Kia Asamiya, Dan Nakrosis
DC (February 2003 © 2003 DC Comics)

If you could be anyone, who would you be? That's the core question asked of virtually every character in this thrilling graphic novel that takes Batman to Tokyo to stop the spread of a deadly new drug that allows users to shapeshift into anyone.

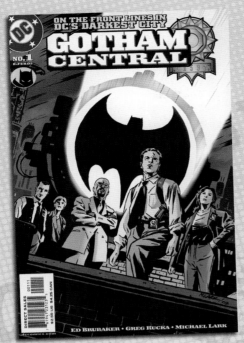

Gotham Central #1

Writers: Ed Brubaker, Greg Rucka
Artist: Michael Lark
DC (Early February 2003 © 2003 DC Comics)

An outstanding police procedural set in Gotham City in and around Batman's activities, but with few appearances by The Dark Knight. It was critically acclaimed but suffered from poor sales. It ran 40 issues before cancellation.

Battle Royale Book 1

Writer: Koushun Takami
Artist: Masayuki Taguchi
Toykopop (May 2003 © 2000 Koushun Takami/Masayuki Taguchi English text © 2003 Tokyopop Inc.)

Reality TV turns monstrous, as 42 high-school students are kidnapped to an island where they must kill or be killed because there can only be one survivor. I think this may be the scariest comic, manga or otherwise, I've ever read.

Usagi Yojimbo #66

Writer: Stan Sakai
Artist: Stan Sakai
Dark Horse (May 2003 © 2003 Stan Sakai)

One of my all-time favorite comics characters stars in this three-issue homage to the giant monsters of Japanese movies, as a fiendish artist uses the blood of children to make the paint that brings his terrifying drawings to life.

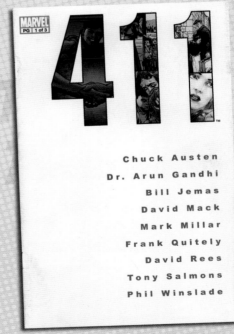

411 #1

Writers: various
Artists: various
Marvel (June 2003 © 2003 Marvel Characters, Inc.)

It took courage for Marvel Publisher Bill Jemas to publish a comic book promoting non-violence just months after the U.S. invasion of Iraq. But, despite its artistic and social merit, the last of 411's three planned issues was never published.

Usagi Yojimbo #67

Writer: Stan Sakai
Artist: Stan Sakai
Dark Horse (June 2003 © 2003 Stan Sakai)

Usagi must battle his way through a gauntlet of monsters to rescue the captive children. Since 1984, Sakai's rabbit ronin has wandered the Japan of the 17th century in great "funny-animal" comic books that are usually more serious than comedic.

Usagi Yojimbo #68

Writer: Stan Sakai
Artist: Stan Sakai
Dark Horse (July 2003 © 2003 Stan Sakai)

The end of the fast-paced thriller proves Sakai needs only his own talent to bring great stories to life. His **Usagi Yojimbo** books have won both the Parents' Choice Award and an American Library Association award.

Blankets

Writer: Craig Thompson
Artist: Craig Thompson
Top Shelf (July 2003 © 2003 Craig Thompson)

An ambitious graphic novel — nearly 600 pages — about family, first love, and surviving family and first love. It tells a human story in epic detail, retaining the heart of the story throughout. It's a genuine page-turner of a comic book.

Palomar: The Heartbreak Soup Stories

Writer: Gilbert Hernandez
Artist: Gilbert Hernandez
Fantagraphics Books (July 2003 © 2003 Fantagraphics Books, Gilbert Hernandez)

Collected from the original **Love and Rockets**, the stories in this 512-page volume focus on a fictional Latin American town, its people, their sorrows, their joys. It's must reading for anyone serious about the comics art form.

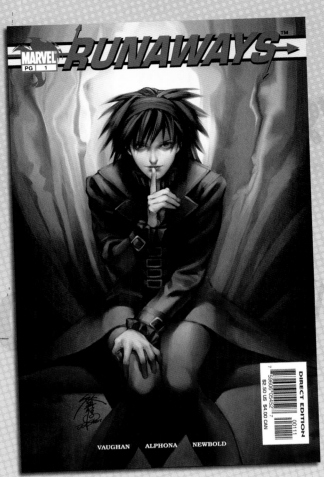

Runaways #1

Writer: Brian K. Vaughan
Artists: Adrian Alphona, Craig Yeung
Marvel (July 2003 © 2003 Marvel Characters, Inc.)

This series has one of the best concepts in comics: "At some point in their lives, all young people think their parents are evil ... but what if they really **are**?" *Hence the running away and the start of a terrific new twist on super-hero comics.*

...all young people think their parents are evil...

Walt Disney's Comics and Stories #635-637

Writer: Don Rosa
Artist: Don Rosa
Gemstone (July-September 2003 © 2003 Disney Enterprises, Inc.)

In this three-issue sequel to Disney's 1944 animated film **The Three Caballeros**, *Donald Duck's nephews attempt to lift their depressed uncle's spirits by reuniting him with his Latin American pals Jose Carioca and Panchito.*

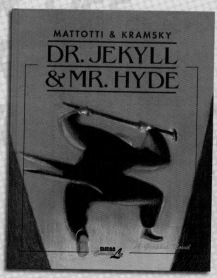

Dr. Jekyll & Mr. Hyde

Writer: Robert Louis Stevenson, Jerry Kramsky
Artist: Lorenzo Mattotti
NBM (September 2003 © 2002 Casterman © 2002 NBM for the English translation)

This near-psychedelic adaptation retains as much of the original prose as possible in its 64 pages. But what sells this version of the story is its dizzying depiction of the darkness that draws — and ultimately destroys — Henry Jekyll.

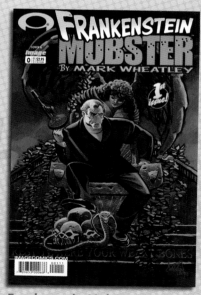

Frankenstein Mobster #0

Writer: Mark Wheatley
Artist: Mark Wheatley
Image (October 2003 © 2003 Mark Wheatley)

This prelude to the story of the late Terry Todd and his hard-as-nails daughter is more than a monsters-and-gangsters thriller. It's a relationship story, it's the story of an oppressed people, and it's a terrific monsters-and-gangsters thriller.

Marvel 1602 #1

Writer: Neil Gaiman
Artists: Andy Kubert
Marvel (November 2003 © 2003 Marvel Characters, Inc.)

Familiar heroes and villains are coming into being centuries before their proper time, putting the universe itself at dire risk. With many surprises, this eight-issue series is brilliantly written and boasts splendid visuals worthy of that brilliance.

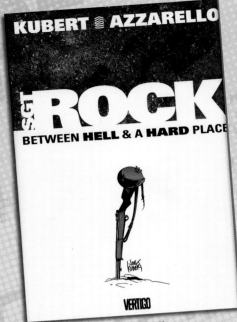

Sgt. Rock: Between Hell and a Hard Place

Writer: Brian Azzarello
Artist: Joe Kubert
DC/Vertigo (November 2003 © 2003 DC Comics)

Azzarello is true to the classic Rock and adds intriguing layers to the "Combat-Happy Joes of Easy Company" in a gritty graphic novel that asks tough questions about morality. The art has all the power of Kubert's previous Rock work — and then some.

Pete Von Sholly's Morbid

Writer: Pete Von Sholly
Artist: Pete Von Sholly
Dark Horse (November 2003 © Pete Von Sholly)

Von Sholly brings "fumetti" into the new millennium with computer-generated effects and a wacky spin born of his love for "B" movies and Lovecraftian horror. This collection squeezes a dozen stories into its 100 pages.

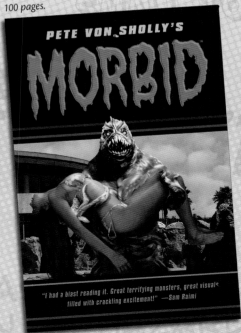

Walt Disney's Uncle Scrooge #324

Writer: Don Rosa
Artist: Don Rosa
Gemstone (November 2003 © 2003 Disney Enterprises, Inc.)

"Gyro's First Invention" reveals the master scientist was hired to save Scrooge's money from falling into the big hole under the money bin shown in "A Christmas for Shacktown." Which makes this story a sort of sequel to that classic tale.

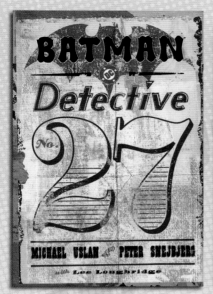

Batman: Detective #27

Writer: Michael Uslan
Artist: Peter Snejbjerg
DC (December 2003 © 2003 DC Comics)

Set in 1939, this Elseworlds story stars a non-Batman Bruce Wayne who must defeat a 75-year-old plan to destroy Gotham. The mixing of historical figures with fictional characters adds an extra layer of delight to the tale.

The Bloody Streets of Paris

Writers: Leo Malet, Jacques Tardi
Artist: Jacques Tardi
ibooks (December 2003 © 1996 and © 2002 Casterman)

A classic detective story set in the shadows of Nazi-held France, Tardi's adaptation of Malet's 1942 novel brought the characters to life while lacing the overall work with an overwhelmingly foreboding atmosphere. A page-turner from start to finish.

Last Exit Before Toll

Writer: Neal Shaffer
Artists: Christopher Mitten, Dawn Pietrusko
Oni Press (2003 © 2003 Neal Shaffer)

He's got a good job and a loving family. But when Charles Pierce's car breaks down and leaves him stranded in a nameless rural town, he finds himself weighing the dissatisfaction of his current life with the possibilities of a new one.

...a stunning look at a culture alien to most Americans.

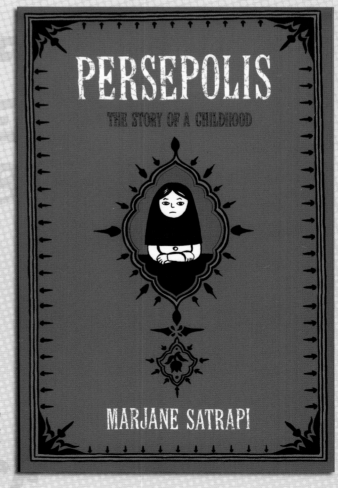

Persepolis

Writer: Marjane Satrapi
Artist: Marjane Satrapi
Pantheon Books (2003 © 2003 L'Association, Paris, France)

Satrapi's internationally acclaimed autobiographical graphic novel relates her childhood in Iran during and after the revolution that drove the Shah from power. It offers a stunning look at a culture alien to most Americans.

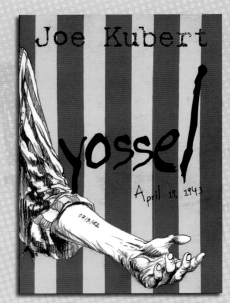

Yossel: April 19, 1943
Writer: Joe Kubert
Artist: Joe Kubert
ibooks (2003 © 2003 Joe Kubert)

In this black-and-white graphic novel, Kubert imagines what would have happened if his parents had remained in Poland and been there during the Holocaust. An almost-overwhelming work, it's one of only two comics that have ever brought tears to my eyes.

Kane Vol. 1: Greetings From New Eden
Writer: Paul Grist
Artist: Paul Grist
Image (January 2004 © 2004 Paul Grist)

Kane is a cop whose job is made more difficult by the corruption in his department. This trade paperback collects the first four issues of a sharp black-and-white mini-series that shows the influences of TV's Hill Street Blues and NYPD Blue.

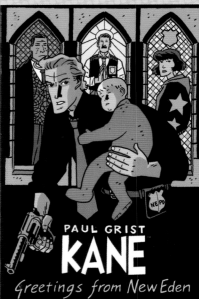

Common Grounds #1
Writer: Troy Hickman
Artists: Dan Jurgens, Michael Avon Oeming
Image/Top Cow (February 2004 © 2004 Top Cow Productions Inc.)

It's a donut shop, but it's also a safe haven for super-heroes and super-villains. It's a social club, confessional, warm-and-gooey therapy for the metahuman soul ... and each story in this six-issue anthology is a small gem of great value.

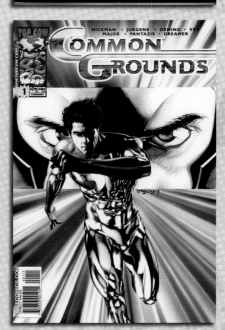

Baraka and Black Magic in Morocco
Writer: Rick Smith
Artist: Rick Smith
Alternative Comics (March 2004 © 2003 Rick Smith)

This comics diary of Smith and his wife's October 2000 travels in Morocco mixes adventure with dread, the former urging them on and the latter reminding them how dangerous the Middle East has always been. It's an exceptional work.

Hard Time #1

Writers: Steve Gerber, Mary Skrenes
Artist: Brian Hurtt
DC/Focus (April 2004 © 2004 Steve Gerber and DC Comics)

Psychically powered teen Ethan is sentenced to 50 years to life for his involvement in a high-school shooting that ended in fatalities. Gerber is at the top of his game with this astonishing coming-of-age-in-the-worst-possible-place story.

> ...astonishing coming-of-age-in-the-worst-possible-place story.

The Pulse #1

Writer: Brian Michael Bendis
Artist: Mark Bagley, Scott Hanna
Marvel (April 2004 © 2004 Marvel Characters, Inc.)

*The title "star" is a weekly section of the **Daily Bugle** newspaper focusing on super-heroes. With a cast including Jessica Jones, Ben Urich, and Luke Cage, the series offers a refreshingly different slant on the Marvel Universe.*

World War 3 Illustrated #35

Writers: various
Artists: various
World War 3 Illustrated (April 2004 © 2004 World War 3 Illustrated Inc., art and stories © 2004 the individual artists)

Founded in 1980 by Seth Tobocman and Peter Kuper, this political comics anthology has a rotating board of contributors and editors, addressing issues of national and global concern. It's challenging reading but always insightful.

Hench

Writer: Adam Beechen
Artist: Manny Bello
AiT/PlanetLar (June 2004 © 2004 Adam Beechen and Manny Bello)

*Misfortunes lead a basically decent man into hiring himself out as a henchman to villains. It's one of those obvious ideas that aren't obvious until someone else comes up with them. Treasures like **Hench** bring new life to the super-hero genre.*

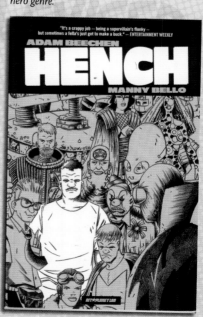

"Brilliant, biting, and witty . . . Hudlin and McGruder have achieved that rarest of things: a political satire that is also an extremely important and moving work of literature."
—HENRY LOUIS GATES, JR.

BIRTH OF A NATION

A COMIC NOVEL

AARON McGRUDER
Creator of *The Boondocks*

REGINALD HUDLIN
Writer/Director of *House Party*

KYLE BAKER
Illustrated by
Author/Illustrator of *Why I Hate Saturn*

Birth of a Nation: A Comic Novel

Writer: Aaron McGruder, Reginald Hudlin
Artist: Kyle Baker
Crown (July 2004 © Aaron McGruder and Reginald Hudlin, illustrations © 2004 Kyle Baker)

Set in East St. Louis, this audacious, brilliant, and hilarious political satire starts with the disenfranchisement of thousands of black voters. When the mayor fails to get justice from the Supreme Court, the city secedes from the United States.

...audacious, brilliant, and hilarious political satire...

Cheeky Angel

Writer: Hiroyuki Nishimori
Artist: Hiroyuki Nishimori
Viz (July 2004 © 1999 Hiroyuki Nishimori/
Shogakukan, Inc. New and adapted art and text ©
2004 Viz, LLC.)

A dishonest genie twists Megumi's wish to be the "manliest of men" by turning him into a girl. This gender-bending series offers great characters and character development, a nice balance of comedy and drama, terrific storytelling, and beautiful art.

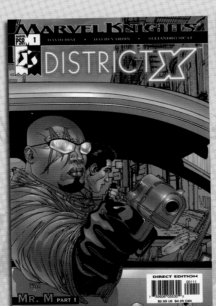

District X #1

Writer: David Hine
Artists: David Yardin, Alejandro "Boy" Sicat
Marvel/Marvel Knights (July 2004 © Marvel
Characters, Inc.)

A police series set in a section of New York City populated by low and no-income people, many of whom are mutants. The situations are realistic for Marvel Universe cops, and the series manages to create a real world within that universe.

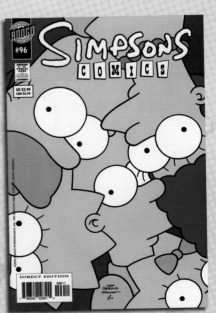

Simpsons Comics #96

Writer: Chuck Dixon
Artists: John Costanza, Phyllis Novin
Bongo (July 2004 © 2004 Bongo Entertainment,
Inc. The Simpsons © Twentieth Century Fox Film
Corporation)

*This long-running series is an ongoing delight. This issue's "A Tale of 2 Pen Pals" — in which Bart and Lisa write to kids in poor countries — is good enough to be an episode of the actual **Simpsons** show and would be one of its best episodes. Ever.*

B. Krigstein Comics

Editor Greg Sadowski
Writers: various
Artist: Bernard Krigstein
Fantagraphics: (July 2004 © 2004 Fantagraphics Books, contents individually copyright 1948-1957 by a variety of copyright holders including William M. Gaines, Agent, Inc.)

This hardcover anthology lovingly presents 34 definitive stories, many restored from the legendary artist's original files. Prepare to be dazzled; then prepare to reread the tales to figure out **how** *Krigstein dazzled you.*

Fade from Grace #1

Writer: Gabriel Benson
Artist: Jeff Amano
Beckett (August 2004 © 2004 Beckett Entertainment, Inc.)

An ordinary guy's love for his wife triggers amazing abilities in him. Feeling responsible to whatever power allowed him to save her, he uses his power to help others. Yes, it's a five-issue super-hero story … and **Moby Dick** *is just a book about a whale.*

Tommysaurus Rex

Writer: Doug TenNapel
Artist: Doug TenNapel
Image (August 2004 © 2004 Doug TenNapel)

A boy and his dinosaur. It'd be too high-concept to be interesting, except that its young protagonist is a fully rounded character who faces crushing sorrows and, in accepting and dealing with them, grows into a capable, compassionate man.

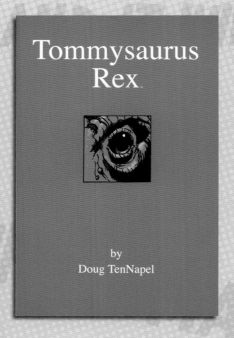

Ultra #1-8

Writers: Joshua and Jonathan Luna
Artists: Joshua and Jonathan Luna
Image (August 2004 © 2004 Luna Brothers)

Heroines, Inc, a super-hero management company, represents Latina Pearl Penalosa. The eight-issue series focuses on her personal life but deals with the super-hero stuff, as well. It's a sharply written story with gorgeous art.

DC Comics Presents: Hawkman

Writers: Cary Bates, Kurt Busiek
Artists: John Byrne, Walt Simonson
DC (September 2004 © 2004 DC Comics)

One of eight memorial tributes to Editor Julius Schwartz. To inspire his writers, the legendary editor would have them write stories around already-designed covers. The cover of this issue is based on that of **Hawkman** #6 (March 1965).

Locas: The Maggie and Hopey Stories

Writer: Jamie Hernandez
Artist: Jamie Hernandez
Fantagraphics Books (October 2004 © 2004 Fantagraphics Books, Jamie Hernandez)

We meet Maggie and Hopey as teen rockers and occasional lovers, watching them age and grow through life's adventures. This 712-page hardcover collects their **Love and Rockets** stories, comics that helped defined the modern art form.

DC Comics Presents: Mystery in Space

Writers: Elliot S! Maggin, Grant Morrison
Artists: J.H. Williams III, Jerry Ordway
DC (September 2004 © 2004 DC Comics

The writers of this memorial one-shot live up to Editor Julius Schwartz's "Be Original" motto, with stories of power-hungry Earthmen coveting Rann's technology. The Alex Ross painting is based on the cover of **Mystery in Space** #82 (March 1963).

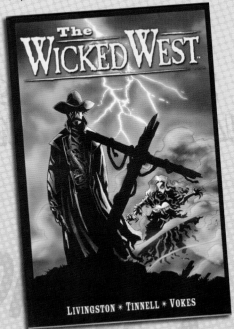

The Wicked West

Writers: Todd Livingston, Robert Tinnell
Artist: Neil Vokes
Image (November 2004 © 2004 Todd Livingston, Robert Tinnell, and Neil Vokes)

This Old West chiller about a man with a past and a town oppressed by vampires would make a wonderful Saturday afternoon movie. It has the heady scent of real buttered popcorn, sticky candy, and Lord-knows-what crunching under your feet. I loved it!

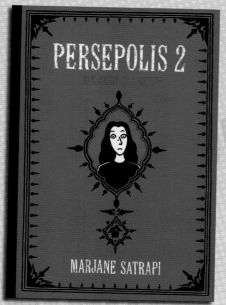

Persepolis 2

Writer: Marjane Satrapi
Artist: Marjane Satrapi
Pantheon Books (2004 © 2002 and © 2003 L'Association, Paris, France; Translation © 2004 Anjali Singh)

This second graphic novel relates Satrapi's high-school years in Vienna and her return to Iran. As much a psychological history as it is an autobiography, it offers further oft-shocking insight into the lives of Iranian women.

Legion of Super-Heroes #1

Writer: Mark Waid
Artists: Barry Kitson, Mick Gray
DC (February 2005 © 2005 DC Comics)

The super-teens from the future have been rebooted and revamped on several occasions, but my favorite is this version: a world in which a youth movement rebels against the constraints of a society that has become hopelessly mired in its ways.

Black Panther #1-6

Writer: Reginald Hudlin
Artists: John Romita Jr., Klaus Janson
Marvel (April-September 2005 © 2005 Marvel Characters, Inc.)

Hudlin revises the history of the Panther and his native Wakanda as an unconquerable king and country who deal with the world on their own terms. The title is as controversial as it is exciting and one of the best comics of the decade.

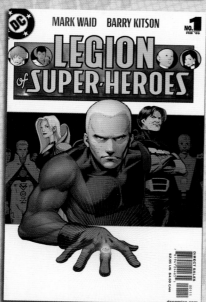

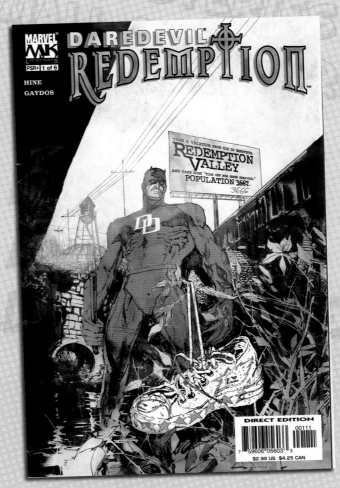

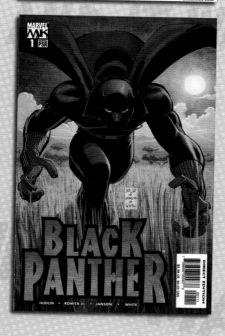

Daredevil: Redemption #1-6

Writer: David Hines
Artist: Michael Gaydos
Marvel (April-August 2005 © 2005 Marvel Characters, Inc.)

A legal thriller and murder mystery that will kick you in the guts. Matt Murdock travels to Alabama to defend an outcast teen accused of a savage murder. The script and art so evoke the human tragedy that it was sometimes painful to read these installments.

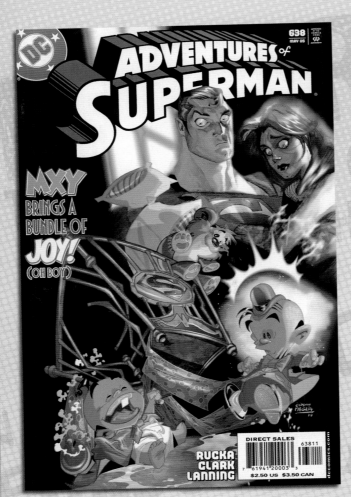

Adventures of Superman #638

Writer: Greg Rucka
Artists: Matthew Clark, Andy Lanning
DC (May 2005 © 2005 DC Comics)

In this heartwarming and magnificently wacky interlude, Mxyzptlk plays stork for Lois and Superman. He brings them a super-baby and skips merrily into the future to show them scenes of what could be their lives to come. A true feel-good comic.

...Mxyzptlk plays stork for Lois and Superman.

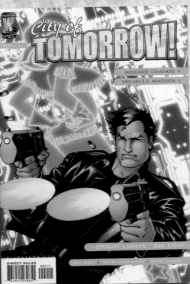

City of Tomorrow #1-6

Writer: Howard Chaykin
Artist: Howard Chaykin
DC/Wildstorm (June-November 2005 © 2005 Howard Chaykin Inc.)

The city is a utopian community served by robots built to re-create a golden age of innocence that never existed. The "tomorrow" is a future America where terrorist attacks have allowed the government to amass and abuse great power. Sound familiar?

Batman: Dark Detective #1-6

Writer: Steve Englehart
Artists: Marshall Rogers, Terry Austin
DC (July-September 2005 © 2005 DC Comics)

The Joker runs for office with the slogan "Vote for me or I'll kill you!" A lost love reenters Bruce Wayne's life as the fiancée of an actual candidate. This six-issue series features the long-awaited reunion of a classic writer-artist team.

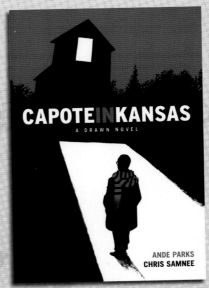

Capote in Kansas

Writer: Ande Parks
Artist: Chris Samnee
Oni Press (July 2005 © 2005 Ande Parks)

Inspired by Capote's *In Cold Blood*, this is a fictionalized account of his research into the 1959 murders of the Clutter family. With art that evokes the 1940s *Crime Does Not Pay* comics, it is one of the best graphic novels of 2005.

Spike: Old Times

Writer: Peter David
Artists: Fernando Goni, Impact Studios
IDW Publishing (August 2005 © 2005 Twentieth Century
Fox Film Corporation © 2005 Idea + Design Works, LLC)

Set after the final season of TV's **Buffy the Vampire Slayer***, this one-shot features a grudge match between vampire-with-a-soul Spike and "justice demon" Halfrek. David's wicked sense of humor works well with these characters.*

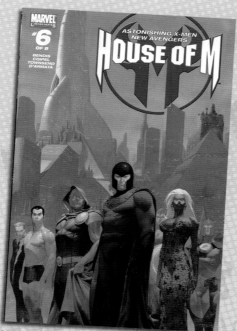

House of M #1-8

Writer: Brian Michael Bendis
Artists: Olivier Coipel, Tim Townsend
Marvel (August-December 2005 © 2005 Marvel
Characters, Inc.)

In this eight-issue series, the mentally unstable Scarlet Witch has altered reality. Mutants now rule the Earth and the ordinary humans around them. Crossing over into other titles, this Marvel Universe-wide event is full of surprises.

The Bakers #1

Writer: Kyle Baker
Artist: Kyle Baker
Kyle Baker (September 2005 © 2005 Kyle Baker)

This mostly pantomime anthology of autobiographical, family-based humor features the epic 32-page "The Mall" and a quartet of equally hilarious shorter tales. All are funny, but "The Mall" should be a big-screen screwball comedy.

7 Days to Fame #1-3

Writer: Buddy Scalera
Artists: Nick Diaz, Dennis Budd
After Hours Press (September-November 2005 © 2006
Buddy Scalera)

For six days, guests of a reality TV show talk about their lives, loves, and disappointments. What they do on the seventh day is what makes this provocative series horrific, riveting, and absolutely unforgettable.

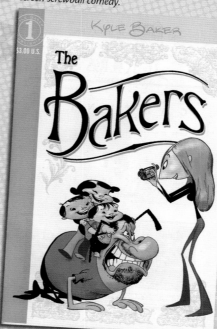

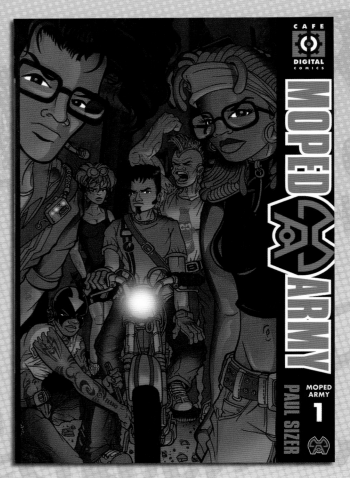

Moped Army

Writer: Paul Sizer
Artist: Paul Sizer
Café Digital Comics (September 2005 © Paul S. Sizer. The Moped Army name used with permission of the Moped Army, Daniel Robert Kastner and Simon King. All other media characters and moped models referenced in this book are © their respective owners.)

"They own the skies. We own the streets." In 2227, a young woman is torn between her above-ground world of shallow privilege and the "below" world where only she can determine her worth. Compelling characters and understated commentary on our own world.

"They own the skies.
We own the streets."

Fell #1

Writer: Warren Ellis
Artist: Ben Templesmith
Image (September 2005 © 2005 Warren Ellis and Ben Templesmith)

A brilliantly stark comic book about a homicide detective transferred to a blighted city "miles from anywhere." An experiment in producing cheaper-but-still-satisfying comics, each issue presented a self-contained 16-page story.

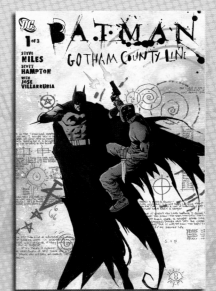

Batman: Gotham County Line #1-3

Writer: Steve Niles
Artist: Scott Hampton
DC (October-December 2005 © 2005 DC Comics)

Asked to help the county sheriff solve a series of gruesome serial murders, Batman finds himself in a horrific "world" that challenges his perceptions of what is real, even concerning his life and how he's chosen to live it. This one's a chiller.

Buja's Diary

Writer: Seyeong O
Artist: Seyeong O
NBM Publishing (October 2005 © 2001 Seyeong O)

From Korea, a collection of 13 emotional, precisely crafted stories by one of that divided nation's greatest artists. O has a gift for effortlessly bringing the reader into his world, though the passage is often heartbreaking.

Death Note

Writer: Tsugumi Ohba
Artists: Takeshi Obata
Viz/Shonen Jump Advanced (October 2005 © 2003
Tsugumi Ohba, Takeshi Obata; English translation
rights arranged by Shueisha Inc.)

A demon's notebook ends up in the hands of a brilliant teenager. If your name is written in it, you die. Whoever holds the notebook can specify when and how. A suspenseful manga on the abuse of power and the fragile nature of humanity.

Ultimate Spider-Man Annual #1

Writer: Brian Michael Bendis
Artist: Mark Brooks, Jaime Mendoza
Marvel (October 2005 © 2005 Marvel Characters, Inc.)

In one of the coolest twists in the Ultimate Universe, Peter Parker goes on a mall date with Kitty Pryde of The X-Men. They even fight a super-villain, albeit a pretty lame one. It's a cute, funny, and downright touching story.

Walt Disney's Donald Duck and Uncle Scrooge

Writers: John Lustig, Carl Barks
Artists: Pat Block, Carl Barks
Gemstone (November 2005 © 2005 Disney
Enterprises, Inc.)

From a concept by Barks, "Somewhere in Nowhere" has Donald trying to prove he can succeed without working for Scrooge. This special also features a classic Barks tale plus Block and Lustig articles on their collaboration with the legendary Barks.

...nostalgic comedy
and super-hero
introspection.

Solo #7

Writer: Michael Allred, Lee Allred
Artist: Michael Allred
DC (December 2005 © 2005 DC Comics)

This title spotlighted different artists in each issue. In this one, Allred uses DC characters Hourman, Teen Titans, and Batman for nostalgic comedy and super-hero introspection, and his "Comic Book Clubhouse" is a delightful salute to the 1960s.

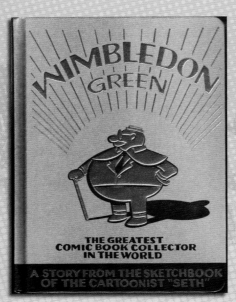

Wimbledon Green: The Greatest Comic Book Collector in the World

Writer: Seth
Artist: Seth
Drawn & Quarterly (December 2005 © 2005 Seth)

Seth uses multiple storytelling formats in an almost scrapbook-like approach to his story of a mysterious comics collector held in awe by friends and enemies alike. It's a quirky but fascinating graphic novel and one cool-looking book.

Banana Sunday #1

Writer: Root Nibot
Artist: Colleen Coover
Oni Press (2005 © 2005 Paul Tobin & Colleen Coover)

Meet Kirby and the three accelerated monkeys who attend high school with her as part of an experiment. She's a believable teen, and the monkeys each have their own distinct personalities. The first of four enormously fun issues.

The Dick Ayers Story: An Illustrated Autobiography #1-3

Writer: Dick Ayers
Artist: Dick Ayers
Mecca Comics Group (2005 © 2005 Dick Ayers)

The legendary artist relates the story of his life and long career in three absorbing graphic novels that offer a first-hand insight into what it was like to work in comics for more than four decades. File these issues under "historical treasures."

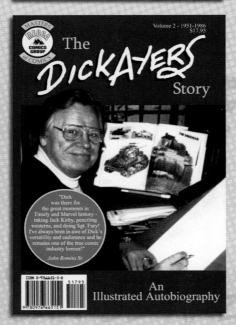

Moonstone Noir: Pat Novak for Hire

Writer: Steven Grant
Artist: Tom Mandrake
Moonstone Books (2005 © 2005 Moonstone Books)

An update of the detective whose radio adventures were broadcast in the 1940s in which an old case comes back to haunt the now-elderly Novak. This one-shot captures the dark humor of its premise and the grim-and-gritty vibe of classic hard-boiled fiction.

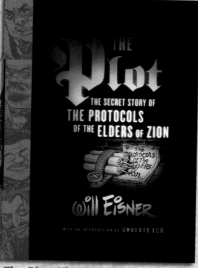

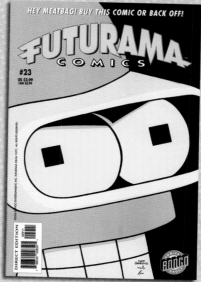

The Plot: The Secret Story of The Protocols of the Elders of Zion

Writer: Will Eisner
Artist: Will Eisner
W.W. Norton (2005 © 2005 The Estate of Will Eisner)

Eisner's final work is a masterful non-fiction graphic novel that challenges one of the most pernicious lies in history and does so on Eisner's terms, making full use of the medium in whose evolution he played such an important role.

Batman: Legends of the Dark Knight #197-199

Writer: Will Pfeifer
Artist: Chris Weston
DC (January-March 2006 © 2006 DC Comics)

A suspenseful story about a criminal who served his entire sentence without escaping from prison and who now seeks revenge on Batman. What makes it more than just another vengeance tale is that the guy isn't even on Batman's radar.

Bongo Comics Presents Futurama Comics #23

Writer: Ian Boothby
Artists: John Delaney, Andrew Pepoy
Bongo (January 2006 © 2006 Bongo Entertainment, Inc. Futurama © Twentieth Century Fox Film Corporation)

Bender, Fry, Leila, and the Planet Express crew lose their jobs to a superior crew from a parallel dimension and become non-persons. Their fight to regain their identities is big fun in the style of the popular TV series.

...Mutants who lost their powers struggle to build new lives.

Generation M #1-5

Writer: Paul Jenkins
Artists: Ramon Bachs, John Lucas
Marvel (January-May 2006 © 2005-2006 Marvel Characters, Inc.)

Mutants who lost their powers struggle to build new lives while a serial killer of ex-mutants stalks them. Reporter Sally Floyd, a non-mutant coping with her own loss, tries to tell their stories with dignity and honesty. An outstanding series.

Jonah Hex #1

Writers: Justin Gray, Jimmy Palmiotti
Artist: Luke Ross
DC (January 2006 © 2006 DC Comics)

DC's classic Western hero returns in an ongoing series featuring mostly complete-in-one-issue tales. The series absolutely nails the look and feel of the character and never fails to deliver a great story. My favorite DC comic book of the new millennium.

Marvel Holiday Special #1

Writers: Shaenon Garrity, Jeff Parker
Artists: Roger Langridge, Reilly Brown
Marvel (January 2006 © 2005 Marvel Characters, Inc.)

The Mole Man's subjects try to bring him cheer by kidnapping Santa Clauses. A robotic Santa tries to kill the heroes at Dr. Strange's party. "Christmas Day in Manhattan" has an almost Dickensian touch. A delightful anthology of heartwarming stories.

Schizo #4

Writer: Ivan Brunetti
Artist: Ivan Brunetti
Fantagraphics (January 2006 © 2006 Ivan Brunetti)

In the brilliant "Whither Shermy?" Brunetti delivers a comic essay on Peanuts, *Charles Schulz, and their relevance to modern readers. The anthology also features Brunetti's funny and sad reflections on his life and romances.*

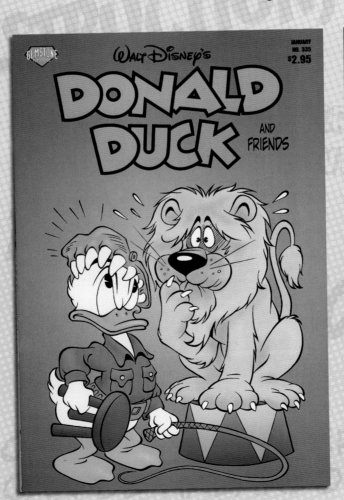

Walt Disney's Donald Duck and Friends #335

Writer: Pat McGreal, Carol McGreal
Artist: Victor Arrigada Rios
Gemstone (January 2006 © 2006 Disney Enterprises, Inc.)

"The Quacking" sends up a classic Stephen King novel with plenty of laughs and wacky suspense. Also: From 1946, "The Master Ice-Fisher" by Carl Barks casts Donald as the worst fisherman you can imagine. Sucks for him, hilarious for us.

...plenty of laughs and wacky suspense.

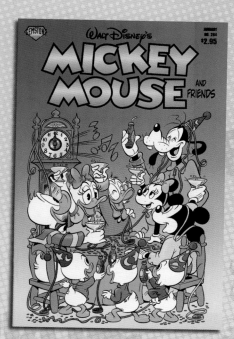

Walt Disney's Mickey Mouse and Friends #284

Writers: Stefan Petrucha, Peter Hardfeldt
Artists: Cesar Ferioli, Peter Hardfeldt
Gemstone (January 2006 © 2006 Disney Enterprises, Inc.)

Mickey and Goofy travel to another dimension and meet sentient fish in dire straits. A terrific story with lots of derring-do, clever concepts, humorous mishaps, and fabulous art. A second story stars Goofy, Donald Duck, and Horace Horsecollar.

X-Factor #1

Writer: Peter David
Artist: Ryan Sook
Marvel (January 2006 © 2006 Marvel Characters, Inc.)

*X-Factor Investigations is a detective agency run by Jamie Madrox with members of earlier teams. The agency's District X location adds a **noir** vibe to the title, which often offers intriguing slants on critical events in the Marvel Universe.*

Mouse Guard #1

Writer: David Petersen
Artist: David Petersen
Archaia Studios Press (February 2006 © 2005 David Peterson)

*In a world much like medieval times but **sans** humans, intelligent mice defend their kind from predators by the skill of their swords and the strength of their courage. An award-winning series from one of the brightest talents of the new millennium.*

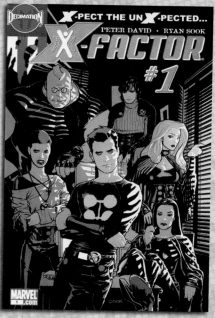

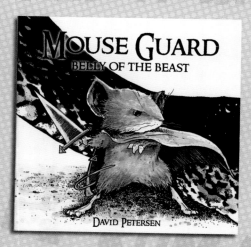

Noaki Urasawa's Monster Volume 1

Writer: Naoki Urasawa
Artist: Naoki Urasawa
Viz Media (February 2006 © 1995 Naoki Urasawa

Tenma sacrificed his career to save a boy later revealed to be an assassin. Blamed for the boy's murders, the doctor is determined to bring an end to the killing while torn between what he must do and his natural instincts as a healer.

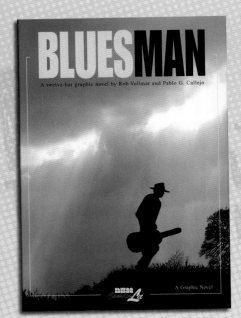

Bluesman #1-3

Writer: Rob Vollmar
Artist: Pablo G. Callejo
ComicsLit (March-September 2006 © Rob Vollmar & Pablo G. Callejo)

The 1920s: In a Deep South juke joint, two traveling bluesmen are offered a recording contract and then caught up in a triple murder. Drawn in a forbidding woodcut-like style, this graphic novel takes readers into an equally forbidding time and place.

Nextwave: Agents of H.A.T.E. #1-6

Writer: Warren Ellis
Artists: Stuart Immonen, Wade von Grawbadger
Marvel (March 2006 © 2006 Marvel Characters, Inc.)

The Highest Anti-Terrorism Effort gathers a team of minor super-heroes to combat UWMDs (Unusual Weapons of Mass Destruction) in a farcical, deliciously snarky series that should only be considered part of Marvel continuity if you want your head to explode.

Plastic Man #20

Writer: Kyle Baker
Artist: Kyle Baker
DC (March 2006 © 2006 DC Comics)

A biting, sarcastic, hilarious assault on the DC Universe and, especially, its grim-and-gritty, soul-killing, violent company-wide crossover events. I don't know how this fits into DC continuity and I don't care.

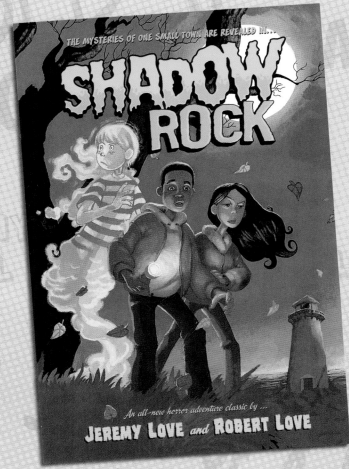

Shadow Rock

Writer: Jeremy Love
Artists: Robert Love, Jeff Wasson
Dark Horse (March 2006 © 2006 Gettosake Entertainment)

A suitable-for-all-ages horror thriller. Following his mom's death, Timothy moves to a New England fishing town, has difficulty adjusting, meets a ghost, and begins to unlock the deadly secrets of Shadow Rock. It's a page-turner.

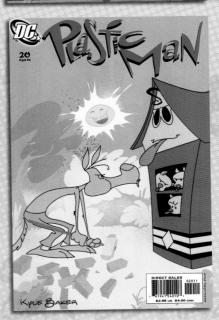

Cancer Made Me a Shallower Person: A Memoir in Comics

Writer: Miriam Engelberg
Artist: Miriam Engelberg
Harper Paperbacks (April 2006 © Miriam Engelberg)

A chronological collection of vignettes that became Engleberg's means of coping with the breast cancer that eventually took her life. Her death doesn't diminish these funny and thoughtful cartoons, nor her courage in creating them.

Ego & Hubris: The Michael Malice Story

Writer: Harvey Pekar
Artist: Gary Dumm
Ballantine Books (April 2006 © 2006 Harvey Pekar, LLC.)

Using Malice's own words, Pekar examines the life and character of a man who has made an art of hatred and vengeance. The result is a fascinating visit with an unlikable character you can't help but liking, if only a little.

Storm #1-6

Writer: Eric Jerome Dickey
Artists: David Yardin, Jay Leisten
Marvel (April-September 2006 © 2006 Marvel Characters, Inc.)

A smoothly told tale of two heroes, a powerful coming-of-age story for Ororo and T'Challa filled with unforgettable moments. A graphic novel of breathtaking beauty perfectly accessible even to readers not familiar with the characters.

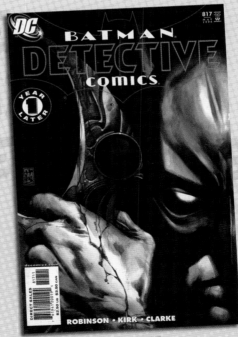

Detective Comics #817

Writer: James Robinson
Artist: Leonard Kirk, Andy Clarke
DC (May 2006 © 2006 DC Comics)

In the opening of the eight-issue "Face the Face," we learn that Harvey Dent, the former Two-Face, has been protecting Gotham in Batman's absence. The story continued through **Batman** #651-654 and **Detective Comics** #818-820.

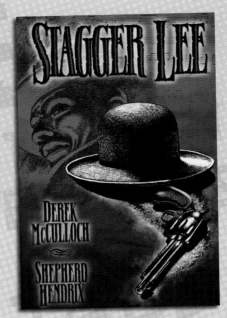

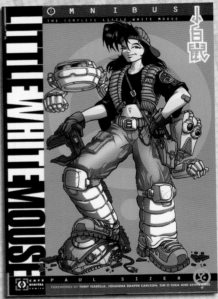

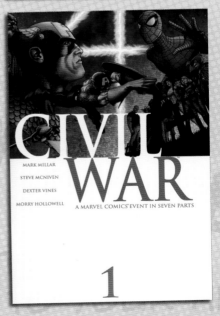

Batman #651

Writer: James Robinson
Artists: Don Kramer, Keith Champagne
DC (May 2006 © 2006 DC Comics)

Several villains have been murdered with the evidence pointing to Dent. While Batman seeks the truth, he must also contend with other villains. Featuring the sanest Dark Knight in years, this was also the best Batman story in years.

Stagger Lee

Writer: Derek McCulloch
Artist: Shepherd Hendrix
Image (May 2006 © 2006 Derek McCulloch and Shepherd Hendrix)

A melodious duet of fact and fiction, the book explores the story behind one of the most famous blues folk songs: a story that inspired hundreds of versions of the song. One of the best and most fascinating graphic novels of the decade.

Little White Mouse Omnibus Edition

Writer: Paul Sizer
Artist: Paul Sizer
Café Digital Studios (June 2006 © 1997-2006 Paul S. Sizer)

Stranded on a automated mining satellite in deep space, 16-year-old Loo must escape before the station's life support shuts down. The complete critically acclaimed series is collected in this edition for the first time.

Civil War #1

Writer: Mark Millar
Artists: Steve McNiven, Dexter Vines
Marvel (July 2006 © 2006 Marvel Characters, Inc.)

The first of a seven-issue series that changed the Marvel Universe. Heroes line up on opposite sides of a government act requiring them to register and then serve the government. It's our real-world concerns about civil liberties brought to comics.

Civil War: Front Line #1

Writer: Paul Jenkins
Artists: Ramon Bachs, Steve Lieber
Marvel (August 2006 © 2006 Marvel Characters, Inc.)

Reporters Sally Field and Ben Urich cover the super-hero civil war from its opposing camps in an anthology that also features stories of related events. The 11-issue series is one of my favorite Marvel Universe titles of all time.

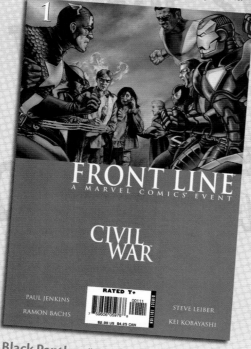

Black Panther #18

Writer: Reginald Hudlin
Artists: Scot Eaton, Kaare Andrews
Marvel (September 2006 © 2006 Marvel Characters, Inc.)

A time of celebration, as T'Challa weds Ororo Monroe, aka Storm of The X-Men in his native Wakanda. Despite their differences, the joyous event is attended by members of both opposing camps in the American super-hero civil war.

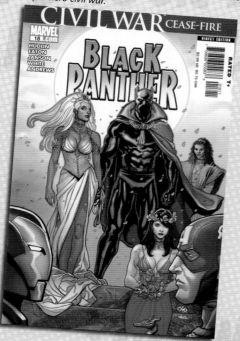

The Drifting Classroom #1

Writer: Kazuo Umezu
Artist: Kazuo Umezu
Viz Media (August 2006 © 1975 Kazuo Umezu/Shogakukan, Inc.)

An earthquake sweeps an elementary school from reality as we know it. To those within, the world has become an unearthly landscape of unending emptiness and life a desperate struggle for survival. One of the scariest manga series ever.

Cancer Vixen: A True Story

Writer: Marisa Acocella Marchetto
Artist: Marisa Acocella Marchetto
Knopf (September 2006 © 2006 Marisa Acocella Marchetto)

Like Miriam Engelberg, Marchetto shapes the fear and pain of breast cancer into a work of artistry, heart, and humor. It's also a love story starring the artist and the fiancé/husband who cherishes her through-out her ordeal.

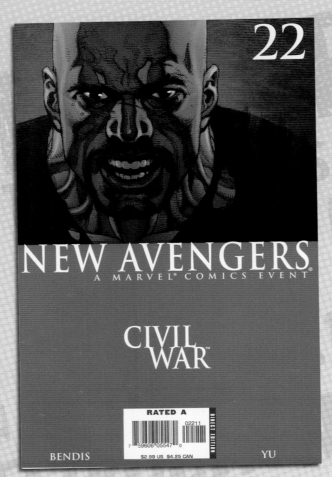

22

New Avengers #22
Writer: Brian Michael Bendis
Artist: Leinil Francis Yu
Marvel (September 2006 © 2006 Marvel Characters, Inc.)

A hero makes his decision to resist the super-human registration act in the finest, most hard-hitting, most impassioned, most important super-hero story of 2006. Bar none, it's also the best Luke Cage story ever written.

...It's the best Luke Cage story ever written.

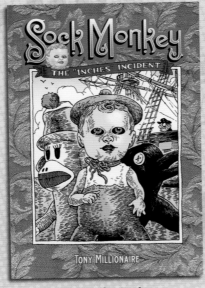

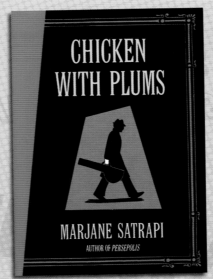

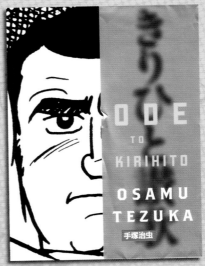

Sock Monkey: The Inches Incident #1
Writer: Tony Millionaire
Artist: Tony Millionaire
Dark Horse (September 2006 © 2006 Tony Millionaire)

My first exposure to this weird, delightful series. There's nothing quite like these comics; they have a certain old-world charm but they also have a childlike sense of wonder and an adult sense of an askew, dark humor.

Chicken with Plums
Writer: Marjane Satrapi
Artist: Marjane Satrapi
Pantheon (October 2006 © 2004 L'Association, Paris; translation © 2006 Anjali Singh)

The sad story of Satrapi's great-uncle Nasser Ali Khan, an Iranian musician who took to his bed on realizing he could not replace his beloved broken tar. He died eight days later. Never has depression been depicted so powerfully in comics.

Ode to Kirihito
Writer: Osamu Tezuka
Artist: Osamu Tezuka
Vertical (October 2006 © Tezuka Productions. Translation © 2006 by Camellia Nieh and Vertical, Inc.)

A doctor searches for the cause and cure of a disease that turns humans into dog-like creatures. Tezuka's 800-page graphic novel is a suspenseful epic of arrogance, brutality, greed, love, loss, and the ultimate triumph of the human spirit.

Christmas Eve, the First Lady of Yuletide Cheer

Writer: George Broderick, Jr.
Artist: George Broderick, Jr.
Cool Yule Productions (Winter 2006 © George Broderick, Jr.)

A Christmas special that retains its abundant charm throughout the years. It tells how three Christmas fairies create a new heroine for the holiday and of Eve's battle with the fiendish Black Peter. Great fun for readers of all ages.

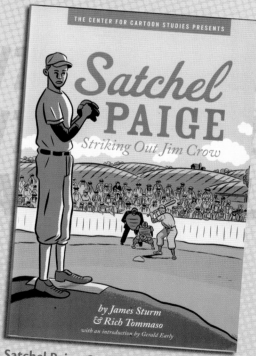

Satchel Paige: Striking out Jim Crow

Writer: James Sturm
Artist: Rich Tommaso
Hyperion/Jump at the Sun (January 2007 © The Center for Cartoon Studies)

Not a biography of "the best and fastest pitcher," but a powerful tale of what he meant to African-Americans in the era of the Negro Leagues. As with the best stories, this one lifts the human spirit. It was never just about baseball.

Cindy and Her Obasan

Writer: George Gladir
Artists: Stan Goldberg, Bob Smith
Rorschach Entertainment (2006 © 2006 George Gladir and Stan Goldberg)

A delightful adventure of a girl and her Japanese fairy godmother. The plucky duo visits Rock and Roll Heaven, tracks Elvis' ghost to Japan, and matches wits with a ranking member of the Yakuza. Hard to find but worth the effort.

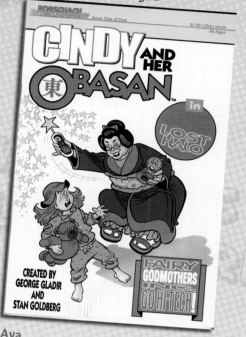

Aya

Writer: Marguerite Abouet
Artist: Clement Oubrerie
Drawn & Quarterly (February 2007 © 2007 Marguerite Abouet & Clement Oubrerie. Preface © 2007 Alisia Grace Chase, PhD)

A sexy, thoughtful comedy set on the Ivory Coast in the 1970s. Aya is a focused young woman who wants to be a doctor. Her friends are all about dancing and romance. Never as crude as American sitcoms, this graphic novel is compelling, funny, and real.

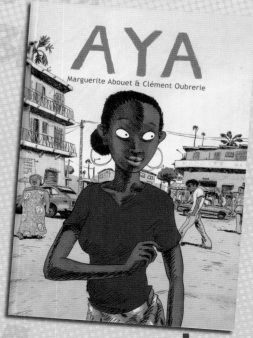

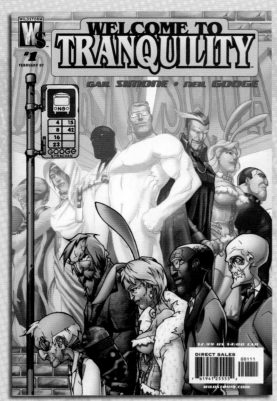

Squadron Supreme: Hyperion vs. Nighthawk #1-4

Writer: Marc Guggenheim
Artist: Paul Gulacy
Marvel (March-June 2007 © Marvel Characters, Inc.)

This has much of what I love in contemporary comics: a real-world tragedy that should demand world attention, conflict between strong protagonists, and as satisfying an end as the terrible complexity of the tragedy can allow.

Welcome to Tranquility #1

Writer: Gail Simone
Artist: Neil Googe
DC/WildStorm (February 2007 © 2007 WildStorm Productions, an imprint of DC Comics)

It's a small town where heroes and villains retire, but not all old scores can be put to rest. One of the best new super-hero series with cool, likable characters, action, human interest, humor, and suspense.

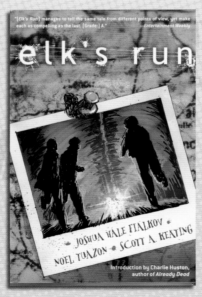

Elk's Run

Writer: Joshua Hale Failkov
Artists: Noel Tuazon, Scott A. Keating
Villard (March 2007 © 2007 Hoarse and Buggy Productions, introduction © 2007 Charlie Huston)

War-scarred veterans looking to create a haven who've watched their dream become a nightmare ... and a group of teens who will change the town forever. A disturbing graphic novel that finishes as strong as it begins.

Alice in Sunderland: An Entertainment

Writer: Bryan Talbot
Artist: Bryan Talbot
Dark Horse (April 2007 © 2007 Bryan Talbot)

Like a music-hall performer, Talbot presents a wondrous history of England, its people, literature, economic development, and society, connected by Lewis Carroll and his works. You should get college credit for reading this enchanting graphic novel.

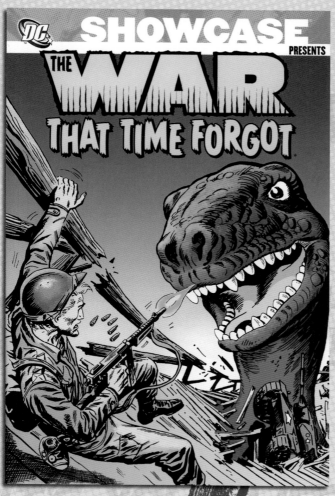

Showcase Presents: The War That Time Forgot #1
Writer: Robert Kanigher
Artists: Ross Andru, Mike Esposito
DC (May 2007 Cover and compilation © 2007 DC Comics. Originally published in single magazine form in *Star Spangled War Stories* #90-128 © 1960, 1961, 1962, 1963, 1964, 1965, 1966)

Kanigher's soldiers-versus-dinosaurs battles are among the goofiest Silver Age of Comics stories of them all and enormous fun in small doses. This bargain-priced, black-and-white collection reprints 37 of them.

...enormous fun in small doses.

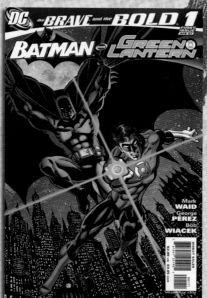

The Brave and the Bold #1
Writer: Mark Waid
Artists: George Pérez, Bob Wiacek
DC (April 2007 © 2007 DC Comics)

The beginning of a truly epic 12-issue story involving dozens of DC heroes in a quest across time and space to keep the omniscient Book of Destiny out of evil. So exciting it made me feel like the comics loving kid I was in 1963.

Miki Falls: Spring
Writer: Mark Crilley
Artist: Mark Crilley
Harper (May 2007 © 2007 Mark Crilley)

What at first glance seems to be a typical "school-girl in love with unattainable guy" manga-style story is actually a modern mythology with a delicious romantic center. A brilliant four-book series by one of comicdom's best storytellers.

The Phantom #17-19
Writer: Mike Bullock
Artist: Silvestre Szilagyi
Moonstone (June-August 2007 © King Features Syndicate, Inc.)

In "Invisible Children," The Ghost Who Walks seeks to rescue some of the thousands of children seized by warlords, indoctrinated, and forced to fight as soldiers in endless wars. It's a meaningful and exciting three-issue story.

Stop Forgetting to Remember: The Autobiography of Walter Kurtz by Peter Kuper

Writer: Peter Kuper
Artist: Peter Kuper
Crown (July 2007 © 2007 Peter Kuper)

In this eclectic graphic novel, Kuper looks at his own life through his fictional alter ego. The emotions, the humor, the political comments ... were Kuper a pitcher, he'd be as much a master of the change-up as he is of comics.

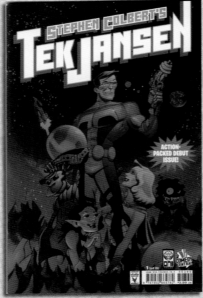

Stephen Colbert's Tek Jansen #1

Writers: John Layman, Tom Peyer
Artist: Scott Chantler
Oni Press (July 2007 © 2007 Comedy Partners)

*Created by the award-winning host of **The Colbert Report** on Comedy Central, this intergalactic hero is a slightly idealized version of Colbert and, as such, irresistible to women of all planets. Tek's animated adventures have appeared on Colbert's show.*

World War Hulk #1-5

Writer: Greg Pak
Artist: John Romita Jr., Klaus Janson
Marvel (August 2007-January 2008 © 2007 Marvel Characters, Inc.)

Banished to outer space by his "friends" and having watched his new world devastated by the rocket that brought him there, The Hulk has returned to Earth to seek vengeance. The most powerful Hulk story of all time.

...A mission to put names to the nameless dead.

Potter's Field #1

Writer: Mark Waid
Artist: Paul Azaceta
Boom! Studios (September 2007 © 2007 Mark Waid)

The mission of the mysterious "John Doe" is to put names to the nameless dead in New York City's potter's field. It's a fascinating twist on the detective hero with a premise so rich with possibilities that I long for an ongoing series.

Sentences: The Life of M.F. Grimm

Writer: Percy Carey
Artist: Ronald Wimberly
DC/Vertigo (September 2007 © 2007 Percy Carey and DC Comics)

The autobiography of Carey, who was both a perpetrator and a victim of violence on his road to Hip-Hop success. His writing is honest, powerful and lyrical on occasion. It's the best book to come out of DC's "mature readers" imprint in 2007.

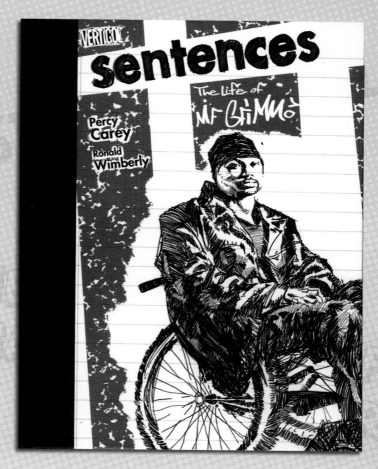

...both a perpetrator and a victim of violence...

Super-Villain Team-Up: Modok's 11 #1-5

Writer: Fred Van Lante
Artists: Francis Portela, Terry Pallot
Marvel (September 2007-January 2008 © 2007 Marvel Characters, Inc.)

Modok seeks a prize that will bring him wealth and safety from his former masters. He recruits down-on-their-luck villains and semi-heroes to carry out his caper. Filled with twists and turns, this series delivers solid entertainment.

Thor #1-6

Writer: J. Michael Straczynski
Artists: Olivier Coipel, Mark Morales
Marvel (September 2007-February 2008 © 2007 Marvel Characters, Inc.)

*Thor returns in a series contrasting the lives of gods and humans and reveling in both. Example: Asgard now floats near a small town in Oklahoma. Always surprising, often lyrical, and never less than spectacular, it's the best **Thor** since Walter Simonson's run.*

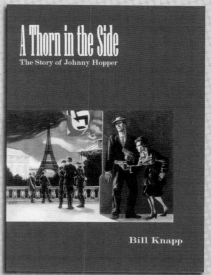

A Thorn in the Side: The Story of Johnny Hopper

Writer: Bill Knapp
Artist: Bill Knapp
Carbon-Based Books (September 2007 © 2007 Bill Knapp)

The British-born Hopper was living in France when the Germans came, opposing them from the start. This graphic novel is a brutally stark, yet ultimately life-affirming, true tale of courage, resolve, loss, and triumph. An amazing story told with passion and skill.

The Last Fantastic Four Story

Writer: Stan Lee
Artists: John Romita Jr., Scott Hanna
Marvel (October 2007 © 2007 Marvel Characters, Inc.

The human race has been judged and con-demned by a cosmic tribunal. As the Four fight a hopeless fight, we see them at their finest and their most human. It's a story that lives up to its title with an ending wholly and wonderfully satisfying.

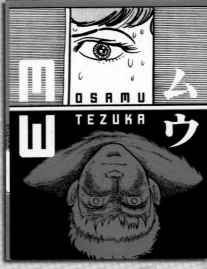

MW

Writer: Osamu Tezuka
Artist: Osamu Tezuka
Vertical, Inc. (October 2007 © Tezuka Productions. Translation © 2006 by Camellia Nieh and Vertical, Inc.)

Two people survive a toxic gas disaster on a remote island. One tries to atone for his crimes by becoming a priest. The other, once an innocent boy, becomes a psychopathic killer. Running nearly 600 pages, this is one big scary hunk of manga.

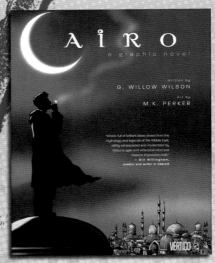

Cairo

Writer: G. Willow Wilson
Artist: M.K. Parker
DC/Vertigo (November 2007 © 2007 G. Willow Wilson and M.K. Parker)

*Filled with intriguing, often contrary, characters, exotic locales, and deadly menaces of and beyond this world, this graphic novel is an exciting comics debut from a respected journalist whose credits include **The New York Times** and Egypt's **Cairo Magazine**.*

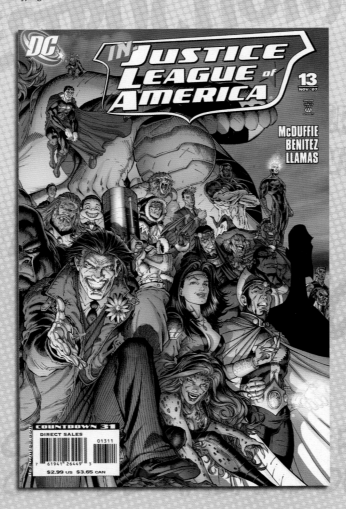

Justice League of America #13-15

Writer: Dwayne McDuffie
Artists: Joe Benitez, Victor Llamas
DC (November 2007-January 2008 © 2007 DC Comics)

A scary-smart Luthor and his Injustice League take down The JLA, but the heroes aren't slouches, either. McDuffie is one of comics' best writers and, in this thriller, he choreographs dozens of combatants with his uncommon dexterity.

...Luthor and his Injustice League take down The JLA.

Action Comics #858-863
Writer: Geoff Johns
Artists: Gary Frank, Jon Sibal
DC (Late December 2007-May 2008 © 2007, 2008 DC Comics)
This six-issue serial combines elements of the classic Legion with fresh ideas that reestablish Superman's inspirational role in the group. Johns also wrote an episode of TV's **Smallville** introducing The Legion to that series.

Holly Jolly Christmas Comics
Writer: George Broderick Jr.
Artist: George Broderick Jr.
Cool Yule Productions (Winter 2007 © 2007 George Broderick, Jr.)

It's 52 pages of festive fun with a tiny dollop of good-natured sarcasm added to its seasonal cheer. It has comics, puzzle pages, craft pages, and black-and-white pictures for coloring. I think my pal George might be an elf.

Rob Hanes Adventures #10
Writer: Randy Reynaldo
Artist: Randy Reynaldo
WCG (2007 © 2007 Randy Reynaldo)

Hanes goes undercover as a baseball player to investigate steroid scandals on a minor-league team. Reynaldo's work is classically inspired, distinctive, and an example of the way solid storytelling can trump comics published by bigger outfits.

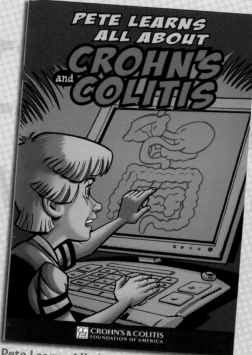

Pete Learns All about Crohn's and Colitis
Writer: Hilarie Staton
Artist: Joe Staton
Crohn's and Colitis Foundation of America (2007 © Crohn's and Colitis Foundation of America)

An informational comic may seem an odd choice for inclusion in this book, but I was impressed by how well the comics presented the kid-friendly, kid-sensitive material. Besides, this is my book and I can include it if I want to.

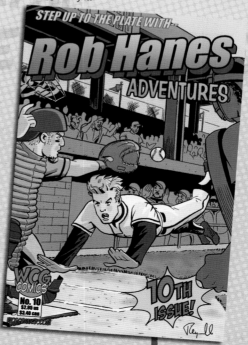

Veronica #187

Writers: Dan Parent, George Gladir
Artists: Dan Parent, Jim Amash
Archie (April 2008 © 2008 Archie Comic Publications, Inc.)

Upset by how she's portrayed, Veronica refuses to appear in her own comic book. Then the Riverdale High kids get competitive about finding the most unusual way to invite their dates to the prom. It's one of the best Archie comics of 2008.

...Veronica refuses to appear in her own comic book.

Wonder Woman #14

Writer: Gail Simone
Artists: Terry and Rachel Dodson
DC (January 2008 © 2008 DC Comics)

Simone starts her run with Diana confronting and winning over young warriors from Gorilla City. While the tempers of their ape elders cool, they crash at Diana's apartment. Teenage gorillas. How can I **not** love this comic book?

Hulk vs. Fin Fang Foom

Writer: Peter David
Artists: Jorge Lucas, Robert Campanella
Marvel (February 2008 © 2007 Marvel Characters, Inc.)

An homage to the 1960s Marvel monsters and The Hulk of a few years after that. David's angry, slow Hulk who reviles the "puny humans" is on the money, and his nods to **The Thing from Another World** — the science-fiction movie of 1951 — are cool.

Archie #584

Writers: Angelo DeCesare, Craig Boldman
Artists: Stan Goldberg, Bob Smith
Archie (June 2008 © 2008 Archie Comic Publications, Inc.)

The Archie comics have continued into the new millennium, combining up-to-date technology with traditional themes. The lead tale in this issue is about ring tones, while others build to their "punchlines" in the classic manner.

Showcase Presents: Enemy Ace #1

Writers: Robert Kanigher, Joe Kubert
Artists: Joe Kubert, others
DC (February 2008 © 2008 DC Comics)

From 1965 to 1982, the collected adventures of German pilot Hans Von Hammer in the killer skies of World War I. Gripping stories with intense art by Kubert, Neal Adams, Howard Chaykin, Russ Heath, John Severin, and Frank Thorne.

All-Star Superman #10

Writer: Grant Morrison
Artist: Frank Quitely
DC (March 2008 © 2008 DC Comics)

A Silver Age story that makes use of the artistic and technological advances since the 1960s. The issue packs more character bits and story into 22 pages than most comics do in a year. Comic books this good are to be treasured.

Ultimate Spider-Man #117

Writer: Brian Michael Bendis
Artists: Stuart Immonen, Wade von Grawbadger
Marvel (February 2008 © 2007 Marvel Characters, Inc.)

The finale of the six-issue "Death of a Goblin" has everything you could ask for from a super-hero comic. It's got exciting action, great characters bits, terrific art, and an epilogue set in a high-school classroom that had me close to tears.

Fairy Tail #1

Writer: Hiro Mashima
Artist: Hiro Mashima
Random House/Del Rey Manga (March 2008 © 2006 Hiro Mashima; English translation © 2008 Hiro Mashima)

Girl wizard Lucy joins Fairy Tail, a guild noted for its rebellious attitude. She teams with a fire-wizard prone to motion sickness and a talking cat that grows temporary wings. Their cases are serious but filled with humor. I love these characters.

Astro City: Beautie #1

Writer: Kurt Busiek
Artist: Brent E. Anderson
DC/Wildstorm (April 2008 © 2008 Juke Box Productions)

Beautie is an amazing android based on a popular doll who doesn't know her origins but who uses her powers to help people. The one-shot is brilliant, funny, sad, and uplifting. Just one exceedingly beautiful comic book.

Love and Capes #7

Writer: Thom Zahler
Artist: Thom Zahler
Maerkle Press (May 2008 Cover and story © 2008 Thomas F. Zahler)

This marks a major development in the romance of Abby and Mark, the most powerful hero on Earth. Heartwarming moments, clever dialogue, likeable characters and inviting art. Which is what you expect from one of the best comics published today.

The Nearly Complete Essential Hembeck Archives Omnibus

Writer: Fred Hembeck
Artist: Fred Hembeck
Image (June 2008 © 2008 Fred Hembeck)

Comicdom's revered court jester collects more than three decades of his hilarious comic strips, personal commissions, and more in this 900-page volume. That's 900 hilarious pages, so let's not quibble over the "nearly complete," okay?

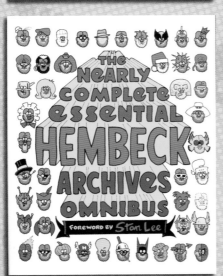

Nat Turner

Writer: Kyle Baker
Artist: Kyle Baker
Abrams (June 2008 © 2008 Kyle Baker)

*This story of the man who led the 1831 slave rebellion in Virginia is told **sans** words save Turner's own, but the art is so strikingly alive it draws the reader into that world. A shocking, important, brilliant graphic novels.*

True Story, Swear to God Archives Vol. 1

Writer: Tom Beland
Artist: Tom Beland
Image (June 2008 © 2008 Tom Beland)

A cartoonist meets the love of his life at a Disney World bus stop in one of the best romance comics of all time. This tome reprints Beland's entire self-published run of his funny, heart-warming, and six-time Eisner Award-nominated series.

...one of the best romance comics of all time.

American Splendor Vol. 2 #2

Writer: Harvey Pekar
Artists: various
DC/Vertigo (July 2008 © 2008 Harvey Pekar)

Pekar being Pekar, always a treat for me. Some of his life stories make me laugh, some of them make me nod my head in recognition of some tiny truth he reveals. But I never put down one of his comics without wishing there were more pages of it.

Comic Book Comics #2

Writer: Fred Van Lente
Artist: Ryan Dunlavey
Evil Twin Comics (July 2008 © 2008 Fred Van Lente and Ryan Dunlavey)

This issue covers the American comic book from its infancy to the 1950s backlash against crime and horror. Van Lente and Dunlavey are respectful to creators in presenting their behind-the-scenes tales of the industry — and funny, to boot.

Dear Dracula

Writer: Joshua Williamson
Artist: Vincente "Vinny" Navarrete
Image/Shadowline (September 2008 © 2008 Joshua Williamson and Vincente Navarrete)

Sam wants to be a real vampire for Halloween and so writes a letter to Dracula. I've never used "heart-warming" to describe a Dracula story, but it fits this one perfectly. A terrific comic book that looks like a hardcover children's book.

"Wonderful!" —Alan Moore
Fame Fortune Conspiracies
La Muse
Adi Tantimedh
Hugo Petrus
—3—

La Muse

Writer: Adi Tantimedh
Artist: Hugo Petrus
Big Head Press (November 2008 © 2008 Adi Tantimedh and Hugo Petrus)

A political activist foils a terrorist attack, revealing godlike powers that she decides to use to save the world. Her way. A sexy, smart graphic novel that surprises and delights at every turn, it was originally published online.

...A political activist foils a terrorist attack.

Bruce the Little Blue Spruce

Writer: Kristen Koerner Simon
Artists: Jim Valentino with Avery Butterworth
Image/Shadowline (December 2008 © 2008 Kristen Koerner Simon)

The poignant, beautifully drawn tale of the only blue spruce in a forest full of green Christmas trees and his yearning to be part of Christmas for some special family. Like Dear Dracula, it's a comic book that looks like a hardcover children's book.

...A poignant, beautifully drawn tale.

Illustrations by Jim Valentino with Avery Butterworth.

THE NOW AND FUTURE FAQ

AFTERWORD

With sincere apologies to the thousand lawyers who have been driven off cliffs in buses, eaten by sharks, swallowed by earthquakes, or painfully disposed of in other jokes …

What do you call a book about a thousand comic books?

The answer is, of course: **A good start.**

Way back in the foreword of this book, I opined the most difficult thing about writing this book was being limited to just a thousand comics. One thousand issues and 60,000 words later, I feel just as strongly about that.

Now that you've read — or at least skimmed your way to — these closing thoughts, you might have a few questions about this book. Ah, who am I kidding? We're all comics fans here. I already know what your most frequently asked questions will be and I'm going to save us a lot of time by answering them now.

How could you leave out [fill in name of your favorite comic book that didn't make it into this book]?

My aim was never to include the best 1,000 comic books — or even the most important 1,000 comic books. I wanted to write about 1,000 great comic books that showed the quality and variety of the comics art form in this country.

I couldn't include everything and, believe me, just like you, I'll be asking myself how I could possible leave out *[fill in name of a favorite comic book that didn't make it into this book]*.

Sometimes a comic book was left out because there wasn't a decent cover scan to be found. Sometimes a comic book was left out because I couldn't say anything meaningful about it in the relatively small space available to me. Sometimes a comic book was left out because I just plain forgot about it. Sometimes a comic book was left out because I didn't like it. I'm looking at you, *Batman: The Killing Joke*. But it doesn't mean that's the end of it. You will have your chance to have your say.

(That's a teaser, by the way.)

The next most frequently asked question will be:

How could you include [fill in name of a despised comic book that did make it into this book]?

This is an easy one. Any comic book included in this book is here because I like it, because I thought it should be in this book, or because someone whose opinions I respect suggested it should be in this book. If you disagree with my choices, well, you'll have your chance to have your say.

(That's another teaser for you.)

The third and fourth most frequently asked questions:

Where can I learn more about the comic books in this book and how I can read them?

Between such magazines as **Comics Buyer's Guide**, **Alter Ego**, and **The Comics Journal** … such books as **Kirby: King of Comics** by Mark Evanier; **Man of Rock: A Biography of Joe Kubert** by Bill Schelly; and **Men of Tomorrow: Geeks, Gangsters, and the Birth of the Comic Book** by Gerard Jones … and more websites than you could surf, if you were chained to the computer for years on end, there's an Uncle Scrooge-like wealth of information out there. Or …

You can visit me at the new website I've launched with my friend and long-time associate Justin Chung of World Famous Comics:

www.1000ComicBooksYouMustRead.com

A main feature of that website will be a message board where you can ask questions of your fellow comics fans and me, complain about my comic-book choices for this book, and suggest comic books to be included in the next book.

Which brings us to our fifth and final question:

Will there be a next book?

That pretty much depends on how many copies of this book you buy.

For what it's worth, I'll be starting on that next book as soon as I finish proofreading this one. Of course, if you don't buy enough copies of this book to justify the publishing of a next book, then you'll have to come over to my house to read that next book. Bring a nice gift.

In the meantime …

Thanks for picking up this book and allowing me to share my love of comic books with you. After reading comics for virtually my entire life and having worked in comics for the past 37 years, I still get a thrill out of discovering a new great comic book, comics writer, or comics artist. If this book instills a fraction of that thrill in you, I'm excited for you and happy for me.

That's what this book is all about. Sharing the love. Sharing the thrill. Sharing the great American art form.

See you at the comics shop.

—*Tony Isabella*

POSTSCRIPT

The challenge for anyone who loves to read comic books has always been obtaining them in the first place. As Tony indicates in this book, the challenge of locating individual issues led to the formation of today's network of specialty shops and services devoted to filling the holes in collectors' "wants" lists. Even people who have devoted their lives to building complete files of favorite characters, titles, topics, publishers, or creators usually have found one or two items eluding their grasp.

This book is designed to set you on your own quest: identifying some of the most striking publications in the context of what comics have offered over the years. Luckily for you, many of the issues chosen are now available in reprint form, thanks to today's publishers' reprint programs. For others, you may have to search more deeply. Here's a sampling of the websites we use to locate these treasures of the past. (And, hey, consider starting with the comics shops nearest to where you live. They may have some reprints in stock right now. You can find many via the Comic Shop Locator Service www.comicshoplocator.com or by looking under "Comics" or "Book Dealers — Used and Rare" in your Yellow Pages.)

Basic Information:
There are many websites at which you'll find more information about comic books new and old. These are four among many.
• 1000 Comic Books You Must Read:
  www.1000ComicBooksYouMustRead.com
• CBGXtra.com: www.cbgxtra.com
• Collect.com: www.collect.com
• Tony Isabella: www.worldfamouscomics.com/tony

Interactive Sales:
Often, comic books are sold collector-to-collector or via auction houses in which negotiations do not necessarily begin with a fixed price.
• Atomic Avenue: www.atomicavenue.com
• ComicConnect: www.comicconnect.com
• ComicLink: www.comiclink.com
• Craig's List: www.craigslist.com
• eBay: www.ebay.com
• Heritage Comics Auctions: http://comics.ha.com
• Neat Stuff Collectibles: www.neatstuff.com

Publishers:
Many current comic-book publishers can be found most easily by searching under the company's name. (Of course, publishers active in 1940 are not necessarily still publishing today.) These are among today's major comics specialty publishers.
• Dark Horse Comics: www.darkhorse.com
• DC Comics: www.dccomics.com
• IDW Publishing: www.idwpublishing.com
• Image Comics: www.imagecomics.com
• Marvel Comics: www.marvel.com

Comic-Book Stores Online:
Many other stores carry new and back-issue comics. These are a few of the long-time stores with an online presence.
• A&S Comics and Cards: www.ascomics.com
• Atomic Comics: www.atomiccomics.com
• Bedrock City: www.bedrockcity.com
• Classics Central.com: www.classicscentral.com
  [specializing in Classic Comics and Classics Illustrated]
• ComicsForSale.com: www.comicsforsale.com
• East Coast Comics: www.eastcoastcomics.com
• Gary Dolgoff Comics: www.garydolgoffcomics.com
• G-Mart Comic Book Store: www.g-mart.com
• Graham Crackers Comics: www.grahamcrackers.com
• Greg White: www.gregwhitecomics.com
• Harley Yee: www.harleyyee.com
• House of Comics: www.houseofcomics.com
• Impulse Creations: www.impulsecreations.net
• Metropolis Comics and Collectibles:
  www.metropoliscomics.com
• Mile High Comics: www.milehighcomics.com
• The Nostalgia Zone: www.nostalgiazone.com
• Terry's Comics: www.terryscomics.com
• Things from Another World: www.tfaw.com
• Torpedo Comics: www.torpedocomics.com
• Westfield Comics: www.westfieldcomics.com

Back issues are also available at hundreds of comics conventions held across the country each year. In addition to the listings in each issue of Comics Buyer's Guide and its semi-annual "Convention Planner Supplement" as well as online at www.cbgxtra.com, listings also appear at www.comicbookconventions.com.

—Brent Frankenhoff & Maggie Thompson